The *Green* Lifestyle Handbook

The *Green* Lifestyle Handbook

Jeremy Rifkin, *Editor*

An Owl Book
Henry Holt & Company / New York

Published by Henry Holt and Company, Inc.,
115 West 18th Street, New York, New York 10011.
Published in Canada by Fitzhenry & Whiteside Limited,
195 Allstate Parkway, Markham, Ontario L3R 4T8.

Library of Congress Cataloging-in-Publication Data
The Green lifestyle handbook:
Edited by Jeremy Rifkin and staff of the
Greenhouse Crisis Foundation—1st ed.
p.   cm.
ISBN 0–8050–1369–5 (An Owl Book: pbk.)
1. Environmental protection—Citizen participation.
I. Rifkin, Jeremy.
II. Greenhouse Crisis Foundation.

TD170.2.G74 1990   89–26944
363.7′05—dc20   CIP

Henry Holt books are available at special discounts
for bulk purchases for sales promotions, premiums,
fund-raising, or educational use. Special editions or
book excerpts can also be created to specification.

For details contact:
Special Sales Director
Henry Holt and Company, Inc.
115 West 18th Street
New York, New York 10011

First Edition

Designer: Kirk B. Smith
Printed in the United States of America
on recycled, acid-free paper. ∞
1 3 5 7 9 10 8 6 4 2

Contributing Authors

Thomas Berry
Donald E. Davis
Larry Dossey, MD
Dr. Michael Fox
Carol Grunewald
Wes Jackson
Gene Karpinski
Andrew C. Kimbrell
Frances Moore Lappé
Cindy Mitlo
David Morris
John O'Connor
Jeremy Rifkin
Maria Rodale
Robert Rodale
Edward Lee Rogers
R. Neil Sampson
Rep. Claudine Schneider
Kirk B. Smith
Martin Teitel
Jay Walljasper

Editorial Staff

Jeremy Rifkin, *Editor*

Andrew C. Kimbrell
and Kirk B. Smith
General Editors

❖

Tips researched & compiled by staff of
The Greenhouse Crisis Foundation

Kathy Vessa, *Project Manager*

Anna Awimbo   Kitty Houghton
Carolyn C. Bennett   Mark Huntley
Beulah W. Bethea   Clara Elizabeth Mack
Deidre Buehll   Irma A. Mason
Caroline Curry   Helen E. Mathis
Tania Dickerson   Todd O. Sinkins
Jennifer S. Edmonson   Troy Thielmann
Jennifer Grant   Regina Thompson
Elizabeth Haynes

Table of Contents

Introduction by Jeremy Rifkin, xi

Overview, xix

I. Back to Basics

II. Lifestyles

III. Cultivating Solutions

IV. Getting Organized

V. Appendices

Introduction

The Global Environmental Crisis
by Jeremy Rifkin

Our generation faces the first truly global environmental crisis in recorded history. While our ancestors experienced traumatic environmental threats, they were limited to specific geographic regions.

Even then, the consequences were often far reaching. The great hydraulic civilizations of Mesopotamia and Sumer, the Roman Empire, and the principalities of medieval Europe all suffered human-made environmental catastrophes that undermined and occasionally devastated these cultures. Still, from a larger anthropological perspective, even the disintegration and collapse of once great civilizations appear parochial matters in our ecological history.

Now as we near the second millennium A.D., a new environmental threat is emerging, so enormous in scope that we find it difficult even to fathom. We have no equivalent past experience from which to mount an appropriate response.

Only in the past few years has the public been introduced to the greenhouse effect, ozone depletion, acid rain, and mass species extinction. This new genre of environmental threats is global in scale and could affect the very viability of life on earth. Through our industrial way of life, our species has affected the biochemistry of our entire planet. If we measured human accomplishments in terms of sheer impact, global warming, ozone depletion, acid rain, and species extinction may well be considered the greatest accomplishments of the human race.

Some scientists now predict a four to nine degree Fahrenheit rise in the earth's surface temperature over the next fifty years as we continue to spew carbon dioxide(CO_2), methane, chlorofluorocarbons (CFCs), and nitrous oxides into the atmosphere, blocking solar heat from escaping the planet. Just as every living species lives within a narrow temperature band, so does the earth. The planet is a living organism—an extremely complex, self-regulating system of interrelated biochemical processes. The earth's temperature has not varied more than about four degrees Fahrenheit since the last ice age 18,000 years ago. Now, scientists project a change in temperature in less than one human generation that may well exceed an entire geological epoch in world history. The implications are far reaching and potentially catastrophic. Thermal heat expansion may result in a three to five foot rise in sea water, imperiling coastal regions and the very existence of low lying countries. Radically fluctuating weather patterns could turn the midwest farm belt and other agricultural regions into giant deserts. Cities like New York and Chicago may be transformed into tropical climates in a few decades. Mighty lakes and rivers like the Mississippi could turn into giant mud flats. A new generation of super hurricanes could wreak havoc on our great port cities.

While the greenhouse gases accumulate in the earth's atmosphere, man-made products containing CFCs are tearing an ever wider hole in the delicate ozone layer that forms a protective shield around the planet, blocking deadly ultra-violet radiation from reaching the earth's surface. The EPA estimates that up to 170 million human beings may develop cancer in the coming decades from exposure to deadly ultra-violet radiation. The ultra-violet radiation also undermines the immune systems of living creatures, making them vulnerable to a broad range of traditional and novel bacterial and viral diseases.

At the same time, fossil fuel burning plants are spewing out ever greater amounts of sulphur dioxide and nitrogen oxide, contaminating the rain water over much of the planet. Acid rain has seriously damaged over 14 percent of the forest cover on the European continent and polluted thousands of streams, rivers, and lakes in North America, killing marine life in unprecedented numbers.

As the earth's atmosphere continues to deteriorate, the flora and fauna of the planet are being destroyed at a breathtaking pace. Millions of acres of tropical rain forest in Central and South America, Africa, and Asia are being razed to provide lumber and paper products and range land for cattle. Thousands of rare plant and animal species—many of them potentially beneficial to mankind—are being destroyed in the process. Scientists now estimate that we destroy a species every sixty minutes. Between now and the end of the century we may exterminate upwards of 15 percent of all the remaining plant and animal species on earth. The environmental and economic consequences of this mass genocide of the earth's biotic community are beyond calculation.

Global warming, ozone depletion, acid rain, and species extinction are not simply by-products of poor management decisions or callous government policies. Today's global environmental crisis is the inevitable result of a unique way of thinking about humanity's relationship to nature first introduced into Western civilization at the dawn of the modern age several hundred years ago. To understand the roots of the present environmental debacle, we need to examine the philosophy of man and nature that gave rise to it.

In 1620 A.D., Francis Bacon, the founding father of modern science, wrote a small tract entitled *Novum Organum*. In this tome, he challenged both the traditional wisdom of Socratic science, with its emphasis on the why of things, and the thinking of the medieval Church, which emphasized faith and reason. Bacon's approach to science and earthly phenomena was more utilitarian and Promethean. He was far more interested in how over why, and expediency over revelation. Bacon redefined the human mission in strictly materialistic terms. Relying on what he called the "scientific method," Bacon claimed that we could detach ourselves from the environment and, acting as disinterested observers, manipulate the workings of nature to advance human ends.

Bacon viewed the environment as an exploitable medium. He stripped nature of any sacred value, reducing all earthly phenomena to quantifiable standards that could be easily manipulated to serve human economic interests. "The goal of all scientific study," said Bacon, "is to enlarge the bounds of human empire, to the effecting of all things possible." Bacon's philosophy and method of science provided Western civilization with both a vision and a vehicle to advance the short-term material interests of human beings on a scale never before imaginable.

Bacon declared that "knowledge is power." Successive generations of scholars relied on the new Baconian dictum to reframe their respective disciplines. Adam Smith argued that material self-interest is the essential motivating factor behind human activity. Smith cast aside the communal spirit of the Medieval commons with a daring, if slightly incredulous, suggestion. Turning the traditional wisdom upside down, Smith argued that each individual maximizes the "common good" by exercising his or her own selfish material interest. According to Smith:

> Every individual is continuously exerting himself to find out the most advantageous employment of whatever capital he can command. It is his own advantage, indeed, and not that of society, which he has in view. But the study of his own advantage naturally, or rather necessarily, leads him to prefer that employment which is most advantageous to society.

While Bacon turned nature into an exploitable medium, Smith provided Western man with a socially redeeming rationale for selfish exploitation of the earth's treasures. The political philosopher John Locke then elevated the new self-centered materialism onto a metaphysical plane, arguing that the new era of utilitarian greed placed humanity on an irreversible sojourn toward an earthly cornucopia. "Material progress" became the banner of a new secular regime as Locke and his contemporaries championed the virtues of an earthly Eden over the vision of an otherworldly paradise extolled by the Church.

Locke's idea of progress deserves a closer examination, as it established a sense of missionary zeal that impassioned the spirit of modernity. Locke looked upon nature as a vast unproductive wasteland. The environment took on value only when human labor and technology transformed it into useful products. The faster nature could be transformed into a store of material goods, the more secure society would become and the more progress civilization would achieve. According to Locke, "land that is left wholly to nature . . . is called, as indeed it is, waste. . . . On the other hand, he who appropriates land to himself by his labor, does not lessen but increase the common stock of mankind." The scientific method, material self-interest, and unlimited progress provided a new blueprint for reorienting man's relationship to his fellow human beings and the environment.

The new way of thinking about people, nature, and history helped usher in a fundamental change in the temporal values of Western civilization. The cyclical rhythms of an agricultural and pastoral tradition gave way to the restless and relentless drive for industrial efficiency, a temporal concept that became possible with the invention of the steam engine and the development of mass production, interchangeable parts, and division of labor. Maximizing material output in minimum time, while exerting minimum energy, labor, and capital in the process, challenged the seasonal time orientation that had locked human activity to the rhythms of the planet over eons of history. At the end of the nineteenth century, Frederick Taylor espoused an inclusive philosophy of efficiency in his principles of scientific management. Economic historian Daniel Bell says of Taylor:

> If any social upheaval can ever be attributed to one man, the logic of efficiency as a mode of life is due to Taylor . . . with scientific management, as formulated by Taylor in 1895, we pass far beyond the old rough computation

of the division of labor and move into the division of time itself.

Efficiency rose from relative obscurity to become the dominant temporal value of contemporary society. With its ascension, Western man and woman completed their metamorphosis into a new world view. We now regard each other and the world largely in instrumental terms. Humanity has increasingly separated itself from nature and from a distance has learned how to exercise greater power over the environment. Armed with the scientific method, Western civilization transformed the "unproductive resources" of the earth into "valuable wealth" to advance its own material aspirations. In the process, civilization became the beneficiary of an increasingly expansive largesse. By removing social time from its sacred and seasonal moorings and reorienting it to the exclusive task of increasing material output in less time, humanity became locked into an evermore efficient process of consuming the earth's endowment, all in the name of progress.

Today, we Americans have the highest *standard of consumption* in the world. Our material success, however, has been purchased at the expense of the rest of the planet. While the American population is little more than 6 percent of the world's population, we consume over 30 percent of the earth's resources. Americans use twice as much energy per capita as other industrial nations with comparable standards of living, and we are the major contributors to both global warming and ozone depletion, being responsible for 25 percent of CO_2 emissions and 27 percent of CFC emissions.

Through our profligate way of life, we have squandered the earth's environment, stripped the forest to feed our insatiable demands for lumber and paper products, overgrazed rangelands to feed our meat addiction, and poisoned the air with the exhaust fumes of over 120 million automobiles to meet our demands for ever greater personal mobility. We boast that we are the first consumer society in history and even tout a consumer movement, apparently unaware of the irony implicit in the word. The term "consumer" dates back to the fourteenth century and, in both its English and French form, has meant "to devour," "to lay waste," "to destroy," and "to exhaust."

Only in the past several decades of the twentieth century has the word been elevated to its present lofty status. Today, the consumer is someone who participates in the good life and enjoys the material benefits of the Age of Progress. We have attempted to mask the consequences of the consumer society, refusing to acknowledge the relationship that exists between over consumption and the depletion and pollution of the earth around us.

Americans have embraced the modern world view with abandon. We have conquered and subdued nature, harnessed its riches to advance our material self-interests, and reveled in the belief that we are securing an ever more progressive vision. Our missionary zeal, however, has been tempered of late by a growing awareness of the global environmental crisis that has ensued from our unrestrained passion for consumption.

As environmental destruction begins to impact the biosphere, we are coming to realize that the environment is not merely a factor or externality. Nor is it simply an issue to be weighed and quantified. The environment is the primordial context; it is the place where we live, work, and sustain the processes of life. Once we begin to view the environment as the essential grounding of our being, we begin to see that our modern world view is Janus-faced. The underlying principles of modern science, technology, and economic development become suspect.

To begin with, the founding assumption of Baconian science, that exercising unrestrained power over nature provides the basis for increasing individual and collective security, has proven to be illusory at best. While we have been quite adept at developing scientific and technical means to subdue nature, it is becoming increasingly difficult to defend the proposition that we have become more secure in the process. We shouldn't be surprised that, in our attempt to make nature conform to our own short-term selfish interests, the world has become a less secure place in which to live. Our personal relationships are instructive in this regard and can help us understand the inherent failings in Baconian science. In personal relationships, if we attempt to exercise control and

dominion over our loved ones, constantly manipulating them from a distance, viewing them in purely instrumental and utilitarian terms, always attempting to make them conform to our selfish whims and caprices, the relationship inevitably becomes less secure and is eventually weakened or destroyed.

Environmental relationships are similar to personal relationships. By attempting to subdue nature, by refusing to accept it on its own terms, by manipulating it to serve expedient short-term material ends, we have made our long-term relationship with the environment less secure and now face the prospect of a wholesale depreciation of the life-supporting processes of the planet.

A new, more sophisticated vision of science is now called for if we are to reheal our relationship to the earth. The new, post-modern view of science is based on empathy with the environment as opposed to subjugation over it. The new approach to science is based on respecting the delicate and complex evolutionary wisdom of the natural world and working with it as a participant rather than as a usurper and detached observer. We extend ourselves to the environment as we do to our loved ones, meeting nature as a partner, accepting and respecting the natural world on its own terms. When we engage nature on an intimate level, the relationship grows and deepens and becomes more secure.

For example, consider the case of two types of architects, one extolling the virtues of Baconian science, the other espousing the possibilities of a new empathetic approach to understanding and interacting with the natural world. The traditional architect may wish to construct a giant skyscraper, a powerful monument isolated from its surroundings, serving as a testimonial to the exercise of dominance and power. The new architect may choose to construct a passive-solar home, a building so elegant in design, so integrated with the natural surroundings that it is difficult to distinguish where its contours end and the rhythms of nature begin. The solar building is designed to work in tandem with the circadian reference of the sun, winds, currents, and seasonal variations of nature. For the old architect, knowledge is expressed in terms of raw power and the exercise of control over the environment. For the new architect, knowledge is based on an empathetic union with the rest of creation. In the first instance, architectural security is found in hermetically sealed isolation from the environment. In the second, architectural security is found in re-participation in the larger communities of nature in which the solar structure is embedded.

Is the new solar architect any less scientific than the architect who builds skyscrapers? In fact, one could argue that the new empathetic science is far more sophisticated and intellectually challenging than traditional Baconian science. After all, it's far easier to divide, reduce, isolate, and dissect, and far more difficult to join, engage, integrate, and coalesce. The great challenge that lies before the next generation is to expand the bounds of human inquiry, to create a new approach to scientific pursuit that is inclusive and respectful of the myriad layers and vast network of relationships that animate the natural world of which we are an intimate part.

A new approach to science is going to force a rethinking of the nature and role of technology. We have come to think of technology as a neutral force, which can be used for good or evil purposes. Rarely, if ever, do we entertain the thought of rejecting a new technology if it has some redeeming utilitarian value.

To a great extent, modern society assumes a strict laissez faire attitude to new technological innovations. The technological motto of modern man is "if it can be done, it will be done." By granting a carte blanche to virtually any and all new technologies, we have eschewed our responsibility to participate in societal changes that intimately affect both the character of our culture and our daily lives in society.

Major technological innovations often have a greater impact on the personal and public life of a nation than any other phenomena, yet we rarely subject them to public deliberation. The parliaments of the world did not debate the environmental, economic, political, cultural, and ethical implications of the petro-chemical revolution, the electronic revolution, or the television and computer revolutions. Yet, these technologies have profoundly affected virtually every aspect of our lives.

For too long, we have allowed ourselves to be passive spectators, letting the marketplace be the exclusive arbiter in the process of introducing new technologies into our lives. The technological decision-making process needs to be extended beyond the narrow confines of a small scientific elite and the self-interest of multinational corporations to include substantial input and involvement by an informed and knowledgeable public. By extending the concept of participatory democracy directly into the deliberations over new technologies, we assume our responsibilities as active participants in the decisions that affect the future course of our society, civilization, and, ultimately, the planet.

Once we redefine our relationship to our tools, we realize that new technologies are rarely neutral. On the contrary, all technologies reflect the value the society places on the exercise of power. We inflate our physical being and extend it into the environment through our tools. For example, the computer is an extension of our mind, the rifle of our throwing arm, the automobile of our legs and feet. Technology amplifies our species and gives us greater power.

With this in mind, we need to continually ask ourselves how much power is appropriate. Are some new technologies so inherently powerful that, in the mere act of utilizing them, we exercise inordinate power over the environment, power that is potentially out of scale with our appropriate relationship to the rest of the natural world? Certainly nuclear power plants represent a form of power that is inappropriate and that poses a threat to the sustainability of the earth's ecosystems. Genetic engineering may be another such technology. On occasion then, we have to be prepared to reject a new technological innovation if it is found to be so inherently powerful that it threatens to destabilize long established ecological relationships that make up the larger environmental community.

Rethinking science and technology goes hand-in-hand with reevaluating our ideas about the nature of economic progress. We have long held the misguided belief that greater consumption somehow means "progress" when, in fact, it means depleting the earth's resources faster than the earth can recycle the pollution or replenish the stock that future generations will need to sustain their existence. Locke's aphorism that nature is little more than unproductive waste until transformed by human ingenuity into a valuable store of wealth needs to be reversed. Nature is imbued with intrinsic value as well as utilitarian value. We merely transform that value into temporary products and utilities. Eventually, the material store of wealth we consume is discarded back into the environment as waste and pollution, some of it irreversibly lost in the form of entropy, the remainder recycled back into the environment for potential use at some future time.

By this new way of thinking about economics, gross national product (GNP) is not merely a measure of the wealth a society generates in goods and services over a year. Rather, it is a measure of the temporary value of the products and services we consume at the expense of the environmental resources we have used up and the waste and pollution we have created in the process. We also need to realize that even the goods and utilities we include in the yearly GNP figures eventually end up in the waste stream.

Although we call our era the Age of Growth, nothing could be farther from the truth. In actuality, we borrow things from the environment for our temporary use. All of the tools, monuments, and accoutrements of civilization are merely borrowed resources that we have transformed for our use for a moment of time, only to find their way back to nature in a more degraded state somewhere in the near or distant future. Borrowing conjures up the notion of indebtedness and mutuality. It is a word steeped in responsibility. Growth, however, is an amoral concept, devoid of ethical intent. As we begin to think of economic activity in terms of borrowing rather than growing, our sense of indebtedness to the natural world and future generations becomes more poignant and apparent.

If borrowing is a more appropriate way of defining the relationship between economic activity and the environment, then what becomes of our ideas about progress and efficiency?

We have narrowly defined progress as "ever expanding" material output and used the standards of efficiency as a tool to achieve that objective. Now that we are experiencing the worldwide depletion of our planetary environment in the name of "ever expanding material output," we need to recast our image of progress in wholly new terms. The post-modern view of progress is squarely centered in environmental reality and rests on our sense of responsibility to the broad sweep of history and to the entire geography of the planet. Progress, in the new scheme of things, is defined as human initiatives in science, technology, economic activity, and ethics that enhance the well-being of the community, sustain the environment, protect future generations, and respect the rights of all other living creatures.

As we reevaluate our ideas of economic progress, we will need to examine the role of efficiency in a post-modern world. While greater efficiency in our use of energy will be important, we will need to reconsider our obsessive need to extend efficiency standards to every aspect of our lives. Efficiency is often practiced at the expense of sustainability. For example, the green revolution has often been praised as the most efficient form of agriculture ever practiced, yet it can hardly be denied that it is also the least sustainable. American building design is often heralded as being the most efficient in history, yet few American cities and suburbs are likely to last as long as many European cities and towns built hundreds of years ago. These earlier architectural forms were invested with far greater time, labor, energy, and capital and for that very reason have proven more sustainable.

Our society places a premium on the short run and quick gains, often at the expense of the future. We prize expediency over sustainability and therefore put an inordinate emphasis on efficiency. Ironically, we would never think of treating anyone we deeply care for in a purely efficient manner. The very idea of relating to someone close to us on the basis of maximizing our output in the minimum time, expending the minimum labor, energy, and capital in the process, would appear ridiculous. Yet, in our public life, at the work place, and in the community, we rely almost exclusively on efficiency as the dominant temporal standard. As anyone knows that has ever had to labor within this kind of temporal setting, a hyper-efficient environment is rarely a playful, joyful, empathetic, or caring environment because everything becomes instrumental to expanding output in shorter time segments.

If we would not think of treating those we care for in purely efficient terms, then perhaps we should reconsider our relationship to nature in other than simply efficient terms. This is not to suggest that efficiency is inherently bad, but only that it ought to play a smaller role in the affairs of civilization. In his "Nicomachean Ethics," Aristotle cautioned his contemporaries always to find the proper balance between extreme forms of behavior. Efficiency has its place, but it needs to be balanced by the competing temporal standards of sustainability if we are to properly adjust our short-term needs to the long-term needs of the planet.

In the final analysis, our attitude toward nature will hinge on our view of other living creatures. Unfortunately, many public officials, and even environmentalists, continue to think of the rest of the plant and animal kingdom exclusively as resources to be managed rationally. While living creatures certainly have utility, they also have intrinsic value. That is, they have an inherent right to exist and experience the fullness of their being just as we humans do.

It is unlikely that we would be facing the threat of global warming, ozone depletion, acid rain, and species extinction if we lived in empathetic partnership with nature, acknowledged our indebtedness to the environment from which all wealth is borrowed, and held a deep and abiding respect for the intrinsic value of all living creatures.

In science, technology, economics, as well as in the time values and future visions of our civilization, a new ecological world view is beginning to take form. Accompanying this transformation in the consciousness of the culture is a newly emerging environmental politics. The traditional politics of the modern world was fought along a right/left, conservative/liberal, capitalist/socialist spectrum. The new politics of the post-modern era will be joined along a new spectrum, with the re-sacralization of all of life on one pole and strict utilitarianism on the other. Increasingly, a new ecologically oriented world view will challenge the instrumental world view of the past, forcing society to balance its own self-serving material interests against our responsibility to the rest of the living kingdom.

In the new ecological scheme of things, American education shifts its emphasis from churning out successive generations of "productive," consumer oriented citizens to nurturing successive generations of more self-reliant, earth-caring human beings. The politics of expediency would then be tempered with the new politics of empathy as our children begin to view themselves as an integral part of the larger biotic community on earth.

As the shadow of the cold war fades, humanity is beginning to turn its attention to a new threat to individual and national security that transcends traditional military rivalries. The global environmental crisis threatens the security of every human being on the planet and is impervious to national boundaries. We are on the cusp of a new global environmental movement. While it is community-centered, its perspective and allegiance is planetary. The theme of the new ecological movement is "Think Globally, Act Locally."

The new movement is as concerned with changing personal lifestyles and world views as with changing the political and economic priorities. Many Americans are incorporating part of the new ecological vision into their personal lives, providing the framework for a deep cultural transformation away from the rank consumerism of the 1980s toward a green lifestyle in the 1990s. The green lifestyle is the cultural embodiment of the new ecological thinking. Empathy, partnership, sustainability, indebtedness, and re-sacralization capture the spirit of the new green way of living. Changing our relationship to the earth is seen as both a personal and a societal mission.

By living an ecological lifestyle, we set a prophetic example for the rest of the community and provide a new vision for a post-modern world. Equally important, by adopting a green lifestyle, we establish a cultural framework that promotes and reinforces a new approach to science, technology, economics, and politics. Transforming ourselves, recasting our world view, remaking our institutions, and restoring the earth are all viewed as part of the same process.

In the pages that follow, the authors examine the many ways that our current American lifestyle contributes to the global environmental crisis. They also suggest hundreds of steps that all of us can take in our personal lives to address the issue of planetary stewardship at home, at the marketplace, in the office, on the road, in our communities, at our places of worship, and in our leisure pursuits. *The Green Lifestyle Handbook* offers an alternative way of living and acting in the world that sets the stage for a new ecological world view in the coming years.

The term ecology comes from the Greek word *oikos*, and means "the household." Ecological responsibility, then, begins at home and expands to fill the entire planet. All of the contributors to *The Green Lifestyle Handbook* are committed to a new ecological world view. They hope that their experiences will prove helpful to the rest of us as we begin our sojourn into the green decade.

The **Green** *Lifestyle Handbook*

- Burning fossil fuel to provide electricity to power the average light bulb results in the emission of 500 pounds of CO_2 into the environment.

- Up to 4 percent of the solid waste stream in the United States is made up of disposable diapers.

- The refrigerant in auto airconditioners is now the single leading cause of ozone depletion.

- The average United States citizen uses 200 pounds of plastic per year, about 60 percent for packaging; only 3 percent is recycled.

- For each quarter-pound hamburger made from Central American beef, fifty-five square feet of tropical rainforest are destroyed for grazing land. When the cleared trees are burned, 500 pounds of CO2 is emitted into the atmosphere. We import approximately 135 million pounds of Central American beef each year.

- American offices throw away enough paper each year to build a wall twelve feet high stretching from Los Angeles to New York City.

For most people, the environmental crisis is a frightening yet distant concern. Media reports on global warming, acid rain, and ozone depletion are often couched in difficult to understand scientific terminology. This may lead to the view that the best way to deal with these problems is through international conferences of scientific experts. Not so.

Each of us in our daily lives makes choices that cumulatively have a significant impact on the environment. How we heat our homes and wash our clothes, the cars we drive, the products we buy, the companies we invest in, the paper we use in the office—all these decisions directly affect the planet. Clearly, the job of healing the planet shouldn't be left just to distant experts; instead, it is our responsibility in each of our daily actions.

This book is designed to help the reader better understand the relationship of her/his choices on the earth, and to recommend a variety of strategies, steps, precautions, and products that will help create a sustainable "Green" lifestyle.

Back to Basics

In the first section, "Back to Basics," we describe the impacts on the environment of some of our most basic lifestyle choices, including our use of energy and products at home, in the office, and in our automobiles.

In the opening chapter, "Home ECOnomics," Kirk B. Smith describes the enormous impact that our use of home energy has on the planet. In the information that follows, the reader will find a chart of many of the most efficient home appliances by brand, as well as many helpful steps that can be taken throughout the home to help heal the earth.

In chapter 2, "Environmental House Cleaning," Andrew C. Kimbrell writes about the growing problem of hazardous and toxic household products. The essay is complemented by an information and advice section in which Kimbrell gives a detailed description of which products to avoid, how to dispose of household toxics safely, and how to create safe alternatives to these products.

In chapter 3, "Shopping As If the Earth Matters," Gene Karpinski focuses on the supermarket, pointing out that every dollar spent is a vote for or against the environment. He helps us understand how the products we purchase play a major role in the growing environmental crisis. This section contains helpful pointers on how to choose sustainable products.

In chapter 4, "Steering towards Ecological Disaster," Andrew C. Kimbrell takes on America's favorite icon, the automobile. Kimbrell describes how the automobile is linked to an astonishing number of the earth's problems, from global warming to city smog. The section ends with tips on how we can limit the destructiveness of the auto. Additionally, the section includes a listing of the most and least fuel efficient automobiles.

In "Taking Charge of the Work Environment," Kirk B. Smith describes how energy conservation and environmental consciousness can be brought into the office. From electricity use to recycling paper, the office can be a key element in adopting a green lifestyle. Smith describes an alarming number of toxic hazards that now threaten the office worker. The section contains advice on how to create an environmentally sound work place.

In chapter 6, "A Materials Policy from the Ground Up," David Morris describes the importance of recycling. Morris surveys the current solid waste crisis and makes it clear that recycling is no longer a choice but rather a necessity. In the how-to part of the chapter, Morris provides information that helps us to begin recycling. This section contains a complete list of state recycling numbers.

Lifestyles

Most of us learn ethics by example. Seeing a friend give to charity or work in a soup kitchen is more likely to stir us to action than reading an essay on compassion.

It's no different with environmental ethics. In a wide range of lifestyle choices—in diet, financial investment, recreation and leisure, personal health, and religion—we are helping or hurting the environment. And our actions act as an example to others. This "Lifestyle" section describes ways to make a positive contribution to resolving the environmental crisis in various lifestyle areas. The information and advice in this section empowers the reader to bring environmental ethics into a wide variety of life choices. By following the recommended steps, we can help the environment and also become examples to our family, friends, and neighbors as stewards of nature.

In chapter 7, "Choose to Eat Low on the Food Chain," Francis Moore Lappé describes how our eating habits affect the environment. This section reveals some surprising facts. For example, few of us realize that producing a one pound steak uses as much water as a household uses in a month. Lappé shows us throughout how to better align our diet choices with the needs of the planet.

In the next chapter, "Personal Investments: Casting a Vote for Social Responsibility," Cindy Mitlo points out how the choices each of us makes about spending, saving, and investing our money can have an influence—positive or negative—on the environment. She provides the reader with several strategies on how to invest in the environment. The section also provides a listing of socially responsible investment houses and counselors.

In chapter 9, "In Praise of Idleness," Jay Walljasper observes that with all our time-saving gadgets, we still have less and less time for ourselves and our families. Moreover, he shows how our patterns of behavior are not just overtaxing us but also the planet. Walljapser advises us to take more leisure time and to use it with the planet in mind.

In chapter 10, Dr. Michael W. Fox explores the philosophy and practice of "Cruelty-Free Living." For many years, those involved with animal welfare and rights have been concerned with the suffering of animals. At the same time, environmentalists have been addressing the urgent issue of species preservation. Increasingly, both groups realize that, whether on the level of individual animals or animal species, our fate is intertwined with that of the rest of the biotic community. The essay is followed by substantial information on animal cruelty-free products and corporations, which will help the reader make choices towards a more humane and sustainable future.

In chapter 11, "Personal Health and the Environment," Dr. Larry Dossey describes how our affinity with the earth can transform us into "green" clinicians. He urges us to identify our personal health with that of Mother Earth and understand the relationship between our illnesses and those of the planet. He also provides several steps each of us can take to enhance our personal health and that of the environment.

In chapter 12, "The Role of Religion," Thomas Berry describes a new environmental awakening in the world's religions. Berry provides new insight into the relationship between religious practice and environmental ethics. He also supplies suggestions on how we can become involved at our place of worship in the stewardship movement.

Cultivating Solutions

Many environmentalists, for all their concern about the natural world, have been reluctant to advocate getting their hands dirty to save it. Author Wendell Berry has described this problem in environmental consciousness as the "nature under glass" approach. Environmental concern, according to this view, is either vacation-oriented or crisis-oriented—we want to protect the wilderness and avoid global threats to the earth.

There is another approach. To save the earth, we must start working with it. Gardening, tree planting, and sustainable farming are important parts to the solution of many of our most pressing environmental ills. Tree planting and gardening are also environmental strategies that are available to millions of Americans. This section will help the novice and those already involved in these areas to better understand the relationship of their activity to the environment.

In chapter 13, "Organic Gardening for a Healthier Planet," Robert and Maria Rodale describe the extraordinary potential of gardening to regenerate the earth and ourselves. The Rodales remind us that organic gardening principles not only help

sustain the environment and the planet, but also provide useful metaphors for organizing the human community. The essay is followed by extensive information on gardening, including where and how to purchase organic gardening products.

In chapter 14, "The Tree of Life," Neil Sampson helps us better understand why the tree, long a symbol of life, is now an important element in the solution to global warming and other environmental problems. Because trees absorb CO_2 and other air pollutants, tree planting, whether in the city, suburb, or country, is an environmental step that almost all of us can take. Sampson also provides information and advice on how to get started in tree planting.

In chapter 15, "Wrong Assumptions and the Patterns They Impose," Wes Jackson challenges the basic assumptions of modern agricultural production. Jackson argues that many current farming methods are destroying topsoil and water quality and are causing wide ranging environmental havoc. Jackson then describes how sustainable agriculture can be a stable source of food production and a vital part of healing the earth.

In "Saving for the Future," Martin Teitel explains the vital importance of maintaining genetic diversity in our plants and animals. Teitel describes several steps each gardener can take to help in the struggle to preserve the world's germplasm.

Getting Organized

One of the most effective ways to deal with environmental problems is through collective action. Often, organizing ourselves and our communities can help bring sufficient pressure on recalcitrant corporations or local, state, and federal legislators to help change policies that harm the environment.

In this section, the contributing authors explore the various tools citizen groups can use to affect corporate and government policy. Demonstrating, boycotting, lobbying, and taking polluters and government agencies to court have all been shown to be successful in helping to save the environment. This section provides a blueprint for successful community action.

In chapter 17, "Grass Roots Organizing," John O'Connor examines the key role grass roots organizing plays in environmental action. Moreover, he provides a practical step-by-step guide for activists interested in mobilizing public support at the neighborhood and community levels. This chapter includes information that will be helpful to every activist, including a model good neighbor agreement with corporations, a list of America's twenty worst polluters, and a list of the ten worst Superfund sites.

In "Boycott: The Activist Consumer's Weapon of Choice," Carol Grunewald covers one of the most effective tools that organizers have—the boycott. Grunewald describes the wide range of coalitions now coming together to make boycott power a principle mode of social change for the 1990s. This section also includes a current listing of all environment and animal-cruelty related boycotts. Source material is also included so the reader can stay up-to-date on boycotts around the country.

In chapter 19, "Exercising Citizenship for a Healthy Body Politic," Rep. Claudine Schneider writes of the vital role that citizen organizing plays in passing local, state, and federal legislation. From local decisions on treeplanting to federal legislation on global warming, citizen pressure can be the key to passing environmental legislation. Rep. Schneider also gives valuable tips on how best to lobby legislators.

In "The Environment, the Law, and You," Andrew C. Kimbrell and Edward Lee Rogers show the reader how to use the courts as part of an overall organizing strategy. The authors gives background information and tips on a wide range of legal actions—from gaining information under the Freedom of Information Act to filing suit against toxic polluters who have injured you, your family, or the environment.

In the final chapter "A Bibliography for Community Organizers," Donald E. Davis provides a comprehensive guide to books, periodicals, and organizations for those interested in community organizing.

Section One/Chapter 1

Home ECOnomics
by Kirk B. Smith

Unless we change direction, we are likely to end up where we are headed.
— Chinese proverb

Every year, homes and apartments in the United States consume quadrillions of British thermal units (Btus) of energy produced by fossil fuel burning energy plants. These power plants produce a number of air pollutants, including carbon dioxide (CO_2) and sulphur dioxide (SO_2). Consequently, our homes contribute significantly to the greenhouse effect, ozone depletion, and acid rain. Our homes also discard billions of tons of trash and other wastes, which contribute to the solid waste crisis and cause air and water pollution.

With only 5 percent of the world's population, the United States consumes fully one-third of the total energy produced from fossil fuel combustion each year. In 1987 alone, the United States consumed seventy-six quadrillion Btus of energy—more than Canada, France, Italy, Japan, the Netherlands, the United Kingdom, and West Germany *combined*. A large portion of this energy powers and heats our homes. Worldwide, homes and apartments use one-sixth of the total energy output. That's more energy than all the Middle Eastern oil nations produce in an average year. Today, United States homes and apartments account for the largest share of CO_2 released into the atmosphere by all industrial, commercial, and residential sources worldwide—a total of 770 million tons of CO_2 annually.

The United States Department of Energy estimates that the average American home guzzles the energy equivalent of 1,253 gallons of oil at a cost of $1,123 each year. Space and water heating together account for 57 percent of this, while lighting, refrigeration, air conditioning, and cooking take up most of the remainder. Electric lighting alone burns up to 25 percent of the average home energy budget. The electricity used over the lifetime of a single incandescent bulb costs five to ten times the original purchase price of the bulb itself. Even

Today, United States homes and apartments account for the largest share of CO_2 released into the atmosphere by all industrial, commercial, and residential sources worldwide.

more discouraging is that, when electricity is generated in a typical power plant, about two-thirds of the energy used (from coal, uranium, etc.) is lost in wasted heat. Only about one-third of the energy is converted to usable power. Transmission and distribution take another 10 percent.

In generating electricity for the average American household over a year's time, a fossil-fuel-fired power plant spews 4.5 tons of CO_2 into the atmosphere. Heating a single home with oil for a year emits 6.5 tons of CO_2. This means that the combined use of energy for lighting and heating the average home in many parts of the country releases well over *10 tons* of CO_2 into the atmosphere every year.

CO_2 is not the only greenhouse gas generated in home-related processes. Burning fossil fuels also releases nitrous oxides, which account for 10 percent of the greenhouse effect. Nitrous oxides, along with sulfer dioxide (SO_2) and other compounds emitted by coal-fired power plants, also cause acid rain.

Lighting accounts for 25 percent of United States electricity use. Substituting a fluorescent light for a traditional bulb can keep a half-ton of CO_2 out of the atmosphere over the useful life of a bulb.

Additionally, the foam insulation in a kitchen refrigerator, when it is disposed of, releases up to three pounds of chlorofluorocarbons (CFCs). CFCs, which also attack the earth's ozone layer, hold thousands of times more heat in the atmosphere than CO_2 molecules and remain in the atmosphere for over 100 years.

Furthermore, as garbage rots in the local landfill, it emits tons of methane gas into the atmosphere. Methane accounts for about 18 percent of the greenhouse effect. Household wastes contribute to a host of other environmental ills. Each year, the average United States household discards 1,800 plastic items, 13,000 individual paper items, 500 aluminum cans, and 500 glass bottles, along with tons of organic wastes, gallons of hazardous chemical wastes, and even a small but significant amount of radioactive material. For each of these items we throw "away," there is an ecological price to pay.

About 90 percent of the solid waste leaving the average home ends up in landfills, and most United States landfills are filling up rapidly. According to David Morris and Neil Seldman of the Institute for Local Self Reliance, over half of our cities nationwide will have run out of landfill space by next year. Furthermore, as landfills expand and deepen, they pose ever greater threats to human beings and to countless animal and plant species.

Landfills not only lay waste—literally—to large tracts of land (depriving many species of crucial habitat), they also threaten groundwater. As discarded toxic and other materials break down and seep into the soil, they pose a potential threat to every link in the food chain. Sub-riverine and other aquatic ecosystems have been poisoned by detergents and many common household products. The effects of groundwater contamination resulting from the decay of organic and other wastes have forced hundreds of communities nationwide to stop drinking their own well water.

The usual alternative to landfills is incineration. But incineration is hardly an environmental panacea. Apart from being costly to build and maintain, incinerators spew tons of particulates and toxic gases into the atmosphere.

What can we do? Perhaps the greatest strength of the American nation has been its ability to deal with immediate crises. Although the environmental crisis is the most pervasive and potentially harmful crisis the *world* has ever faced, it is not too late to avert disaster. We can start in our homes by moderating our insatiable appetite for trivial conveniences that waste energy and pollute the planet. In practical terms, that means adopting a sustainable lifestyle for the 1990s and the millennium to come—by conserving energy and creating less household waste.

As much energy leaks through American windows each year as flows through the Alaskan pipeline.

Tips

* **If you're purchasing a home, check its energy efficiency.** To find out how energy-efficient the home is, get an energy audit and examine past utility bills. Contact your utility company and ask them to conduct an energy audit of your home.

* **Buy energy-efficient appliances.** When shopping for appliances, look for the Energy-Guides label, required by law on each appliance. The Energy-Guide information is useful in determining the efficiency and cost of running the appliance. If there is not an Energy-Guide label available for the appliance, do not buy it.

    For further information on appliance efficiency, contact the following organizations: **Association of Home Appliance Manufacturers**, 20 North Wacker Drive, Chicago, IL 60606. **Gas Appliance Manufacturers Association**, 1901 North Fort Meyer Drive, Arlington, VA 22209. (*The Directory of Certified Furnace and Boiler Efficiency Ratings* is also available through this association.) **Air Conditioning and Refrigeration Institute**, 1815 North Fort Meyer Drive, Arlington, VA 22209.

    Here are a few recommended publications providing information on efficient appliances and household products: *Saving Energy and Money with Home Appliances* and *The Most Energy-Efficient Appliances*, both available from the American Council for an Energy-Efficient Economy (ACEEE), 1001 Connecticut Avenue, Suite 535, Washington, DC 20036; (202) 429–8837. *Tips for Energy Savers*, United States Department of Energy, Editorial Services, Office of Public Affairs, Washington, DC 20585; (202) 586–5000.

Heating and Cooling

It is estimated that 50–70 percent of energy use in the average American home is devoted to heating and cooling. If every household lowered its average heating temperature 4° F for a twenty-four hour period, we'd save the energy equivalent of 380,000 barrels of oil per day. Likewise, if we raised the average air conditioning temperature 4° F, we could save the energy equivalent of 130,000 barrels of oil daily. Also, when we reduce our home heating temperature below 68.6° F, each degree saves 3 percent on heating costs. When we turn up our home air conditioners to above 78° F, each degree saves 5 percent in cooling costs. Reducing air conditioning also reduces the emission of CFCs.

One person's annual home electricity causes 4.5 tons of CO_2 to be spewed into the atmosphere.

- **Obtain home energy conservation information.** Your regional Government Printing Office (GPO) and local environmental organizations can provide information on home energy conservation. The pamphlets these agencies and organizations provide often suggest energy management ideas that can help you save each month on your utilities bill.

  Here are some organizations and publications that can help maximize energy efficiency in the home: *Resource Efficient Housing Guide*, **Rocky Mountain Institutes**, 1739 Snowmass Creek Road, Snowmass, CO 81654; (303) 927–3851. *Energy Unbound*, by Hunter and Amory Lovins, **Sierra Club Books**, 730 Polk Street, San Francisco, CA 94109; (415) 776–2211. *Tips for an Energy-Efficient Apartment*, **United States Department of Energy**, Office of Conservation and Renewable Energy, Building Energy Research and Development, Washington, DC 20585; (202) 586–5000. The Environmental Science Department of the **Massachusetts Audobon Society**, with the help of the **American Council for an Energy-Efficient Economy**, has written eight booklets dealing with insulation, weatherizing, wood, coal, oil, and gas heating systems, solar ideas, and home improvement financing. These booklets come as a set of eight. To order, write Public Information Office, Massachusetts Audubon Society, Lincoln, MA 01773. **Seventh Generation** has compiled a catalog of energy-efficient appliances, biodegradable household products, and natural personal products. Send for the Seventh Generation Catalog, 126 Interval Road, Burlington, VT 05401; (802) 862–2999. For alternative energy sources, see *The Wind Power Book*, by Jack Park, Cheshire Books, Palo Alto, CA. This book discusses the advantages of wind power, how it works, and how to create your own wind power set-up.

  For information on every aspect of energy conservation and energy alternatives, the United States government offers a toll-free number to the **Conservation and Renewable Energy Inquiry and Referral Service (CAREIRS)**. CAREIRS puts out pamphlets and fact sheets on almost every home energy topic. CARIERS can also put you in touch with someone to help you with your question if they cannot answer it themselves. **CAREIS**, PO Box 8900, Silver Spring, MD 20907; (800) 523–2929, (800) 462–4983 in Pennsylvania, (800) 233–3071 in Alaska and Hawaii. **National Appropriate Technology Assistance Service**, United States Department of Energy, PO Box 2525, Butte, MT 59702–2525; (800) 428–2525, (800) 428–1718 in Montana.

- **Insulate your home.** Inadequate insulation is one of the leading causes of energy waste in most American homes. An estimated 20–30 percent of the load on heating and cooling systems could be reduced by adequate insulation.

- **Caulk and weatherstrip your doors and windows.** Air leakage causes significant home energy waste. It is estimated that if every gas-heated home were properly weatherstripped and caulked, enough natural gas would be saved to heat four million homes. Weatherstripping and caulking can save the average home up to 10 percent annually on energy costs. Caulking and weatherstripping is a relatively simple do-it-yourself job. The cost for materials for an average-sized house is about $25.

- **Install storm windows.** Storm windows create a space of dead air through which air drafts must pass. This "pocket" acts as an effective insulator. Adding storm windows, preferably with low E glass, benefits you in many ways, by increasing your comfort and reducing heating bills, condensation, maintenance, and noise. Remember, as much energy leaks through American windows every year as flows through the Alaskan pipeline.

- **Avoid the use of air conditioners** and opt for alternatives such as ceiling or attic fans, which cost only a few cents per day to operate. The refrigerant in air conditioners is a leading cause of ozone-destroying CFC emissions. If using an air conditioner, make sure that the Freon used in the refrigerant is recycled when the unit is repaired or thrown away. Always fix a leak in the air conditioner immediately to prevent the release of CFCs into the air.

- **If you do purchase an air conditioner, look for an energy efficiency ratio as well as a seasonal energy efficiency ratio of at least eight.** Do not buy an air conditioner that does not have these ratings. To maximize the efficiency of your air conditioner, make sure to keep it free of dust and to check the refrigerant regularly.

- **Close off unused areas in your home.** This reduces the area that requires heating and cooling. Also, shut off the heater or air conditioner in these areas and block off vents.

- **Unless you have a fire going, keep your fireplace damper closed.** According to government tests, an open damper can let up to 8 percent of your home's heating escape through the chimney.

- **Opt for a woodburning stove instead of a fireplace.** Woodstove inserts may be placed in the fireplace opening and result in up to a 40 percent increase in fuel efficiency. *The ASHRAE Book of Fundamentals*, from the American Society of Heating, Refrigerating, and Air Conditioning Engineers, can provide you with energy efficiency ratings of wood heaters. *Wood Heat*, by John Vivian (Emmaus, PA: Rodale Press, 1976) is a good general reference about the most efficient way to use wood heat.

- **Test your furnace or boiler for efficiency regularly.** If its efficiency level is not above 70 percent, it is not operating to maximum capacity, and replacing it might save more money than keeping it.

- **Use a clock thermostat for heating and air conditioning units.** This device saves energy by automatically adjusting the temperature in your home.

- **Wear warmer clothing in cooler temperatures.** It is the simplest way to retain your body heat. Also wear light clothing in warmer temperatures to minimize air conditioning use.

Heating one home with oil for a year causes 6.5 tons of CO_2 to be dumped into the environment.

Wood Heating Values

**Highest heat value
(27 or more Btus per cord):**

Black Birch
Hickory
Live Oak
Locust
Northern Red Oak
Rock Elm
Sugar Maple
White Oak

**Low heat value
(13–19 million Btus per cord)**

Alder
Aspen
Balsam Fir
Basswood
Cedar
Cottonwood
Hemlock
Northern White Cedar
Red Fir, Spruce
Sugar Pine
White Pine

- **Keep windows near the thermostat tightly closed.** An open window could keep your furnace working overtime. Of course, when heating or air conditioning your home or office, keep all windows closed whenever possible.

- **Put an insulating water heating jacket on your hot water heater and turn down the temperature to 110–120° F.** These "jackets" are generally available at your local hardware store and also may be provided free of charge by many stores selling water heaters.

Lighting

Lighting accounts for 25 percent of United States electricity use. If we're going to reduce emission of greenhouse gases, saving lighting energy in the home is crucial.

- **Use compact fluorescent lighting instead of incandescent bulbs.** Making this simple switch can keep a half-ton of CO_2 out of the atmosphere over the useful life of one bulb. Fluorescent bulbs are made by Sylvania, Phillips, and Panasonic. Consumers may also order fluorescent bulbs from the Seventh Generation Catalog, a catalog of environmentally sound products for the home from fluorescent lighting to water-conserving showerheads (see address above).

  Information on which fluorescent lighting is best for each intended use is available through the Rocky Mountain Institute (see address above). "Lighting the Way toward More Efficient Lighting," from the Institute's *Home Energy Guide*, provides basic information on different types of fluorescent lighting, as well as how to determine which lighting is best for each use.

- **Turn off lights in any room you aren't using.** This simple step can prevent a significant amount of home electricity waste.

- **Reduce overall lighting.** Replace existing bulbs with lesser-wattage bulbs (when fluorescent bulbs are unsuitable) and remove one bulb from multi-bulb fixtures. (Remember to replace the bulb with a non-working bulb for safety.) Use outdoor lights only when necessary. Remember to turn off outdoor lights during the day.

- **Use curtains to keep out unwanted heat or cold.** Curtains can keep out unwanted summer sun and heat and can help reduce heat loss in winter.

Saving Energy in the Kitchen

- Whenever possible, **use cold water rather than hot water for your kitchen tasks.** Using cold water for rinsing dishes, food disposal, and other kitchen tasks will save the energy it takes to heat water.

- **Run your dishwasher, which uses up to 14 gallons of hot water per load, only when it is full, and use energy-saver modes when available.**

- **Avoid keeping your refrigerator or freezer too cold.** The government-recommended temperature for the fresh food compartment of refrigerators is 38° F. For the freezer it's 5° F.

- **Use mugs or glasses instead of paper cups, and cloth instead of paper towels and napkins.**

Saving Energy in the Laundry

You can save energy in the laundry room by limiting hot water use and reducing use of automatic washers and dryers.

- **Fill your washers, but don't overload.** As with dishwashers, combining loads saves on electricity and hot water use.

- **Presoak dirty laundry and don't use excessive amounts of detergent.** Too many suds makes your washing machine work harder and consume more energy.

- **Run a full load in the dryer, but air-dry your laundry when possible.** If you must use a dryer, make sure it is full to maximize energy use. However, when weather and circumstances permit, use air drying.

- **Keep the lint screen in your dryer clean.** A clogged lint screen stops the flow of air in the dryer and makes the machine consume more energy.

Bathroom Energy Savings

- **Take showers of five minutes or less instead of baths.** It takes about 30 gallons of water to fill the average bath tub. But a five-minute shower with a three-gallon-a-minute flow uses only about 15 gallons. Over the course of a year, this could save thousands of gallons of hot water.

- **Install a flow control device in the showerhead.** This do-it-yourself device limits the flow of water in your shower, which translates into energy and money savings. An inexpensive washer that restricts the flow of water in the showerhead can be purchased at plumbing and hardware stores. A specially designed showerhead for reduced water flow is available through the Seventh Generation Catalog (see address above).

Saving Water

The greenhouse effect, ozone depletion, and acid rain will further deplete our already dwindling water resources. Droughts are expected in many areas of the world as temperatures increase. Water conservation measures will become increasingly important in order to offset the coming greenhouse crisis.

In the United States, we depend on our groundwater resources. Over half of our population drinks groundwater. Yet we waste water in many ways, often through excessive use in our homes.

Our eating habits are also wasting water. Over half the water used in the United States is consumed by livestock; 2,500 gallons of water are needed to produce one pound of meat. By comparison, only 25 gallons of water are needed to produce one pound of wheat.

The need for water conservation is heightened by increasing water pollution. Industrial and agricultural pollutants, landfill seepage, and chemical wastes

It has been shown that up to 50 percent of the water wasted in the home is attributed to taps that run unnecessarily.

from mining and petroleum production steadily accumulate in the water cycle. Once contaminated, groundwater is difficult and prohibitively expensive to purify. Aquifers, our underground water supplies, are decreasing worldwide.

The following steps can help conserve precious water resources.

* **Turn off the water in your sinks, baths, and showers when you're not using them.** It has been shown that up to 50 percent of the water wasted in the home is attributed to taps that run unnecessarily. Paying attention to faucet use can significantly save water.

* **Investigate companies that pollute your water supply and report them to appropriate authorities, elected officials, and the media.** It is important to encourage public action on water waste and contamination. If necessary, organize boycotts against offending companies.

* If you live in an area without certified well or spring water, **filter your tap water.** Drinking filtered water is healthier and also conserves water by avoiding tap waste. The National Safety Associates (NSA) has a cost efficient system that operates for three cents a gallon and is easily installed. It is a bacteriostatic granular activated carbon (GAC) filter that removes chlorine, organic chemicals, odor, and bad taste. A maintenance free system, it is monitored and registered by the EPA. Avoid distilled water, which tends to leach nutrients from the body. For further information, contact Environmental Systems, Inc., 444 Pine Street, Boulder, CO 80302; (303) 444–2020.

* **Have a low-flush or air-assisted toilet installed.** Installing these toilets can save 60–90 percent of water used in toilet operation. Eljer makes a low-flush toilet, called the "Ultra I," which only uses 1.4 gallons of water per flush. The Eljer Ultra I is available in many plumbing supply shops across the country. For a list of local distributors look in the *Yellow Pages.*

* **Water lawns and gardens only when necessary and only at night.** This limits evaporation and enables you to use less water.

* **Repair all leaks and drips as soon as they occur.** Fixtures that leak or drip cause substantial water loss. A moderate drip from a leaky faucet wastes 2 gallons or more per hour.

* **Purchase water-efficient appliances.** Choose appliances that offer maximum water efficiency. See either the Rocky Mountain Institute Guide or the Seventh Generation Catalog for various water efficient appliances (see above).

Reducing Solid Waste in the Home

* **Separate paper, glass, aluminum, and plastic items and deposit them at your recycling center.** (See chapter on Recycling for information on how to turn your trash into a valuable natural resource.)

* **Start your own compost heap in your back yard.** Build a cage of chicken wire and metal posts and fill it with vegetable peelings, egg shells, grass clippings, leaves, etc. Within a year, you will have the best fertilizer available—just in time to start your organic garden (see chapter 13). Meat, dairy, and grain leftovers will attract flies, so dispose of them separately.

To make one pat of butter takes 100 gallons of water.

- **If you can use it, don't throw it away.** Make your own pet and bird feeders, kitchen containers, and household gadgets from things you would otherwise throw out. Instead of using plastic bags, line your garbage can with paper grocery bags or old newspapers. Be creative in using all kinds of containers. Used cans make good nail-holders, for example, and plastic 35mm film cans make great travel containers for toiletries, etc.

- **Designate places in your kitchen for paper bags, plastic bags, glass jars, containers, and other things you can reuse.**

- **Substitute reusable sponges or cotton rags, napkins, and handkerchiefs for disposable paper towels, napkins, and tissues.**

- **Use egg cartons or milk cartons as containers for seedlings or as materials for arts and crafts projects.**

- **Use cloth coffee filters instead of disposable paper ones.**

- **Keep a coffee mug or folding cup at work and in your car to avoid using foam or other disposable cups.**

- **Save and reuse envelopes, boxes, and packing materials that you receive in the mail.** It is especially important to reuse styrofoam "peanuts" or other plastic or foam packing, which is made from petroleum and which destroys the ozone layer.

- **Don't accept junk mail.** The average American adult is on over fifty mailing lists. This results in a lot of wasted paper and little else. To have your name removed from the major mailing list networks, send a written request to The Direct Marketing Association, 6 East 43rd Street, New York, NY 10017. In the meantime, write "return to sender" on your junk mail and put it back in the box.

- **Use old newspaper and other paper to pad items you package for mailing or moving.**

- **Make desk and telephone table note pads from scrap paper.** All it takes is a few staples.

- **Share, borrow, or rent items you don't use often,** such as tools, lawn mowers, camping equipment, charcoal grills, etc. Share magazine and newspaper subscriptions with friends, family, and co-workers. When you're finished, give them to a library, senior citizen center, or other organization. (Glossy magazines are often unrecyclable.)

- **Donate unwanted items to community groups.** For example, give excess lumber and paint to a theater group or donate old tires for a playground.

- If you tire of clothing that hasn't worn out, **a clothes swap is a fun way to reduce waste.** Invite friends over for a party with their no-longer-exciting clothes as the ticket for admission. Trade around to avoid buying new apparel when all you really need is something different.

- **If you can fix it, don't buy a new one.** Resoling a pair of shoes or boots, for example, can save you one half to nine tenths of the purchase price of a new pair.

- **Use and support alternative energy sources.** Information on alternative energy conservation is available from: **Alternative Sources of Energy**, 107 South Central Avenue, Milaca, NM

Don't accept junk mail. The average American adult is on over fifty mailing lists. This results in a lot of wasted paper and little else.

56353; (612) 983–6892. **Environmental Action Resource Service**, PO Box 8, Laveta, CO 81055. *Practical Homeowner*, Rodale Press, 33 East Minor Street, Emmaus, PA 18090; (215) 967–5171) *Real Goods Alternative Energy Sourcebook*, Real Goods Trading Company, 3041 Guideville Road, Ukiah, CA 95482; (707) 468–9214. *State of the World Report*, Worldwatch Institute, 1776 Massachusetts Avenue, NW, Washington, DC 20036; (202) 452–1999. **Synergy**, PO Box 4790, Grand Central Station, New York, NY 10017; (212) 865–9595. *The Energy Saver's Handbook for Town and City People*, by the Scientific Staff of the Massachusetts Audubon Society (Emmaus, PA: Rodale Press, 1982). *The Energy Wise Home Buyer: A Guide to Selecting an Energy-Efficient Home*, by Technology+Economics, Inc., United States Department of Housing and Urban Development (Washington: Government Printing Office, 1979). *All through the House: A Guide to Home Weatherization*, by Thomas Blandy and Denis Lamoreux (New York: McGraw-Hill, 1980; contains a self-audit). *The Residential Energy Audit Manual*, by the United States Department of Energy with Oak Ridge National Laboratory and the University of Massachusetts Cooperative Extension Service (Atlanta: Fairmont Press, 1980). *A Comparison of Products for Reducing Heat Gain through Windows*, the United States Department of Energy. Publication 8.15 (Washington, DC: Government Printing Office, 1981). Available from Lawrence Berkeley Laboratory, University of California, Berkeley, CA 94720. *Thermal Shutters and Shades: Over 100 Schemes for Reducing Heat Loss Through Windows*, by William A. Shurcliff (Andover, MA: Brick House, 1980). *Movable Insulation*, by William T. Langdon (Emmaus, PA: Rodale Press, 1980). *Solar Retrofit: Adding Solar to Your Home*, by Daniel K. Reif (Andover, MA: Brick House, 1981). *Solarizing Your Present Home: Practical Solar Heating Systems You Can Build*, edited by Joe Carter (Emmaus, PA: Rodale Press, 1981). *The Homeowner's Handbook of Solar Water Heating Systems*, by Bill Keisling (Emmaus, PA: Rodale Press, 1983).

Environmental House Cleaning
by Andrew C. Kimbrell

The environmental crisis is often thought of as a distant threat. Water pollution and air pollution seem the responsibility of corporations and farms far removed from our homes. Yet, while industry and agriculture are our major sources of pollution, the American home is also a significant contributor to the destruction of the environment.

The home's responsibility for toxic pollution centers on a large variety of household products containing chemicals that, when discarded, significantly contaminate water and air. The average American home uses approximately 25 gallons of hazardous chemicals per year. The major sources of these household hazards include automotive products (such as antifreeze, batteries, gas, and oil), household cleaners (oven, floor, toilet, and drain cleaners), grease and rust solvents, paints and related home improvement products, lawn and garden products (fertilizers, herbicides, and pesticides), and miscellaneous products (arts and crafts supplies, nail-polish removers, and shoe polish).

Tens of millions of gallons of these dangerous household chemicals pollute American water systems and groundwater supplies. It has been estimated that in a city of one million people, about 31 tons of toilet bowl cleaner and 130.75 tons of liquid household cleaners are discharged into city drains each month. Moreover, according to the Environmental Protection Agency (EPA), each year about 180 million gallons of motor oil—the equivalent of sixteen Exxon Valdez spills—is sent to landfills or poured down drains. Additionally, household toxic wastes account for 7 to 20 percent of all toxic pollutants in municipal sewage treatment plants.

Water pollution caused by household products can affect human health. According to the Sierra Club Legal Defense Fund, "Household chemicals poured down the drain can pose an immediate health threat, especially if the end of the drain is a septic system and the homeowner relies on local groundwater for

> The average home today contains more chemicals than were found in a typical chemistry lab at the turn of the century.
>
> — *Debra Lynn Dadd*

It has been estimated that in a city of one million people, about 31 tons of toilet bowl cleaner and 130.75 tons of liquid household cleaners are discharged into city drains each month.

drinking supplies." These household chemicals also destroy fish and other aquatic life when they end up in rivers and streams.

Hazardous household wastes disposed of at landfills also contribute to groundwater pollution. Household chemicals buildup at these landfills and leach into groundwater supplies. This is one reason that municipal landfills usually make up about 20 percent of the EPA's Superfund cleanup sites.

These household toxics not only pollute the water but also the air—both inside the home and in the environment. Incinerator operators regularly report a high concentration of toxic chemical in ash due to disposal of household hazardous wastes. Indoor air pollution, in part due to household toxics, is also becoming an acute environmental and human health problem.

Many household products also pose a serious and direct threat to human health. Household products can have several hazardous properties. Hazardous products include those that are (1) flammable—can be set on fire or ignited at any temperature; (2) toxic—can cause physical injury upon inhalation, ingestion, or absorption—long term toxic effects can include cancer, genetic damage, and fetal damage; (3) explosive—can explode when exposed to heat, shock or pressure; (4) caustic, corrosive—can burn living tissue on contact; (5) irritant—can cause skin, mucous membrane, and eye irritation, inflammation, and soreness.

According to the National Research Council, fifteen percent of the population is hypersensitive to chemicals found in common household products. This sensitivity can result in a wide variety of acute and chronic health effects. Acute responses include poisoning from swallowing household poisons, burns from various caustic and acidic household products, and irritations from cleansers to unprotected eyes and hands. Chronic effects can include kidney and liver damage caused by ingesting household chemicals, brain damage due to lead poisoning, and various cancers and birth defects due to exposure to household carcinogens and mutagens. Seemingly innocuous activities such as drinking a cup of chemically decaffeinated coffee, polishing shoes, cleaning the oven, using arts and crafts supplies, shampooing, or driving a car may put us in contact with chemicals that cause these acute or chronic health impacts.

Children are especially susceptible to household hazards. As pointed out by consumer consultant Debra Lynn Dadd in her book, *The Non-Toxic Home*, children's size, biology, and physiology make them more vulnerable to indoor pollutants than adults. Children breathe in more hazardous substances—their respiratory rates are ten times faster than adults, and since household pollutants are heavier than air, they concentrate more at child height than at adult height.

Additionally, given equal chemical intake, chemical exposure to body weight is far greater for children, given their smaller size, than for adults. Household hazards poisonings are also a major problem with children. Each year between five million to ten million household poisonings are reported—the vast majority of poisoning victims are children who have ingested household chemicals. Many of these cases are fatal.

What You Can Do

Proper handling and disposal of household toxics is crucial in avoiding the environmental and human health impacts of these pollutants. Each user of a household product is responsible for carefully following directions on household product labels and for safe disposal of these hazardous wastes. Warnings, including keeping products away from children and wearing protective gloves or masks, should be scrupulously followed. Disposal directions should be followed. Service stations and reclamation centers will accept some hazardous waste, like used motor oil. Other wastes can be poured down the drain if sufficiently diluted by water. Still other, more hazardous, wastes should be disposed of only through community hazardous waste collection or through licensed contractors. (See information section below for details on handling and disposal of various products and chemicals.)

Hazardous solid waste can be legally dumped at municipal solid waste facilities. However, as noted, the buildup of these wastes can cause serious water and air pollution. Local and national organizations and certain chemical companies may provide household hazardous waste disposal programs that you can utilize. For example, both the League of Women Voters and Dow chemical have initiated disposal programs in some areas.

American households have between 50 and 100 pounds of hazardous material that should only be disposed of through recycling or professional hazardous waste collection. Unfortunately, many of these hazardous wastes end up being poured down drains or dumped in trash cans. In 1989, for example, approximately 628 communities across the country had programs of some sort to collect household hazardous wastes. Several of these programs ended up collecting tens of thousands of gallons of toxics. However, in most cases only 1 to 5 percent of residents in the community cooperated. This indicates that over 95 percent of all extremely hazardous household wastes are disposed of improperly.

Arsenic Poisoning

When residents in a small town in Chile began showing a high incidence of lung and heart disease, as well as malignant skin cancers investigators discovered that the culprit was arsenic. The towns water supply had been contaminated with .8 mg of arsenic per liter.

Across the globe in Taiwan, residents also reported a high incidence of skin cancer, as well as "Blackfoot" disease, a condition which blocks circulation to fingers and toes eventually leading to gangrene. Once again the cause was arsenic contamination of water supplies.

Arsenic is used in the production of wood preservatives, glass and semi-conductors. Six million pounds of arsenic each year are emitted by coal burning power plants, and 75 million pounds are used in manufacturing.

One way out of the disposal and recycling problem is to avoid using hazardous household products. Often, for various cleaners and miscellaneous household products, environmentally sound and less dangerous alternatives exist. (See information section below for listing of safe alternatives.) However, for many products including many automotive products and solvents no adequate alternatives exist and safe disposal is necessary.

While it is unrealistic to expect a total environmental house-cleaning overnight, it is important to take the first steps in eliminating household hazards as soon as possible. We can all begin to protect ourselves and the environment from household toxic pollution. Here's how.

As much as 25 percent of all toxic waste originates in individual households.

Tips

- **Read the label.** Make sure it is the product you want to buy and that you are not uncomfortable with the ingredients. The Federal Hazardous Substances Act of 1960 establishes labeling requirements for consumer products containing hazardous substances. By definition of the law, a hazardous substance is one that is toxic, corrosive, caustic, flammable, explosive, hypersensitizing, generative of pressure, radioactive, or otherwise potentially injurious. (See appendix for how to read a label.)

- **Buy the least hazardous product. Watch for signal words.** With pesticides, "DANGER" means highly toxic, "WARNING" means moderately toxic, and "CAUTION" means slightly toxic. With household products, "POISON" means highly toxic, "DANGER" means extremely flammable or corrosive or highly toxic, "WARNING" or "CAUTION" means less toxic. Note that "nontoxic" is an advertising word and has no federal regulatory definition.

- **Avoid aerosol products.** Aerosol disperses the substance in tiny droplets that can be inhaled or absorbed through the skin. Also, aerosol cans can explode when heated.

- **Use the proper safety equipment when working with hazardous chemicals.**

- **Substitute safer products.** Look for the extensive suggestions in "Safer Alternatives" below.

- **Be wary of products that fail to list their ingredients.**

- **Leave products in their original container with the label that clearly identifies the contents.** Never put hazardous products in food or beverage containers.

- **Do not mix products unless directed to do so by label directions.** This can cause explosive or poisonous chemical reactions. Even different brands of the same product can contain incompatible ingredients.

- **Use only what is needed for a job.** Twice as much doesn't mean twice the results. Follow label directions.

- **If pregnant, avoid toxic chemical exposure as much as possible.** Many toxic products have not been tested for their effects on unborn children.

- **Avoid wearing soft contact lenses when working with solvents and pesticides.** They can absorb vapors from the air and hold the chemical near your eyes.

- **Use products in well-ventilated areas to avoid inhaling fumes.** Work outdoors whenever possible. When working indoors, open windows and use an exhaust fan, making sure air is exiting outside rather than being recirculated indoors. Take plenty of fresh-air breaks. If you feel dizzy or nauseous, take a break and go outside.

- **Do not eat, drink, or smoke while using hazardous products.** Traces of hazardous chemicals can be carried from hand to mouth. Smoking can start a fire if the product is flammable.

- **Clean up after using hazardous products. Carefully seal products.** Properly refasten all childproof caps.

- **Store hazardous products safely.** Keep products out of reach of children and animals. Store all hazardous products on high shelves or in locked cabinets, away from food items.

- **Make certain all hazardous products are clearly labeled before storing them.**

- **Make sure lids and caps are tightly sealed and childproof.**

- **Make sure containers are kept dry to prevent corrosion.** If a product container is beginning to corrode, place it in a plastic bucket with a lid, and clearly label the outside container with contents and appropriate warnings.

- **Store volatile chemicals or products that warn of vapors or fumes in well-ventilated area, out of reach of children and pets.**

- **Store rags used with flammable products (furniture stripper, paint remover, gasoline, etc.) in a sealed, marked container.**

- **Keep products away from heat, sparks, flames, or sources of ignition.** This is especially important with flammable products.

- **Store gasoline only in safety approved containers, away from all sources of heat, flame, or sparks, in a well-ventilated area.**

- **Know where flammable materials are located and know how to extinguish them.** Keep a working fire extinguisher in your home.

Each year over 100 million square feet of timber surfaces are treated with wood preservatives.

Hazardous Products

AUTOMOTIVE PRODUCTS

Antifreeze.   Ethylene glycol, the active ingredient in antifreeze, is toxic. Ingestion can cause severe depression, respiratory or cardiac failure, and brain or kidney damage.

- Household pets are especially prone to poisoning as a result of drinking from sweet tasting puddles of antifreeze left after car repair work; it is important to store antifreeze away from children and pets.

- When heated, antifreeze produces toxic fumes; storage areas should be especially well-ventilated.

- Antifreeze should be disposed of at wastewater plants where treatment with bacterial organisms will break down the ethylene glycol.

- Do not pour antifreeze directly on the ground or into storm drains.

Batteries.   Used in automobiles as well as boats and farm machinery, wet cell batteries are toxic and contain corrosive sulfuric acid and lead. Avoid skin contact and inhalation of fumes.

- Heavy gloves are an important safety measure—if contact with clothes or skin is sustained, wash thoroughly and apply baking soda to affected area. If swallowed, avoid using sodium bicarbonate in hopes of diluting the acids, this will only exacerbate the reaction.

- Batteries must be stored away from heat sources and out of reach of children.

- Used batteries are easily recyclable. Consult your local "Yellow Pages" for battery recyclers.

Brake Fluids.   Glycol ethers are flammable toxics found in brake fluid. Kidney failure, extreme depression, and other nervous system disorders may result from ingestion or inhalation.

- Once brake fluids have been used, they, like transmission fluids, contain solvents, lead and other heavy metals that must be disposed of appropriately with authorized hazardous waste collectors.

- Brake fluids must be stored away from heat sources and out of childrens' reach, as they are highly flammable. The original metal container for the brake fluid should itself be stored inside a dependable, labelled, plastic container until a community hazardous waste program is organized.

Car Wax.   Most car waxes contain naphtha, a flammable irritant. Avoid ingestion, skin contact, or inhalation of fumes. Cumulative exposure to car wax may lead to increased skin sensitivity, particularly to light. To prevent skin irritation, wear heavy gloves when applying car wax.

- Seal car wax containers securely and store out of childrens' reach. If stored for too long, hardening will occur. Hardened wax may be disposed of in regular landfill.

Gasoline.   A highly flammable toxin, gasoline contains tetraethyl lead in its leaded form and benzene and ethylene dichloride in its unleaded form. Avoid skin contact, ingestion, and inhalation of fumes. Repeated exposure to gasoline fumes may cause brain damage.

- Gasoline should be stored away from flames or heat sources and should be kept out of childrens' reach or use. A number of commonly accepted practices of gasoline are extremely dangerous—mouth siphoning, car storage for emergency use, use as a camp fuel and use as a paint cleaner should be avoided. When storing gasoline, leave room in the container for the gasoline to expand.

- Gasoline that has been contaminated cannot be burned and must therefore be stored carefully in a dependable container and disposed of at a specialized reclamation center. It is imperative that contaminated or dirty oil never be mixed with waste oil or used as a solvent or cleaner.

- Note: these same guidelines apply to the handling of diesel fuel.

Motor Oil, Used.   Mineral oil and hydrocarbons such as benzene, lead, zinc, copper, magnesium along with other heavy metals are the main flammable toxins in used motor oil. Skin contact, ingestion, and inhalation of used motor oil should be avoided at all costs; heavy gloves are an important safety measure.

- Careless disposal of even small quantities of used oil can cause significant groundwater contamination and other environmental problems. As with other used automobile fluids, motor oil should be stored away from heat sources and out of reach of children in a sturdy, labelled plastic container.

- Many service stations accept used motor oil for recycling. Specialized reclamation centers highway departments are other disposal alternatives.

Transmission Fluids.   Containing hydrocarbons and mineral oils, transmission fluids are flammable and toxic.

- Used transmission fluids contain lead and other toxic heavy metals that, if not disposed of properly, can harm wildlife.

- Take used fluid to a service station or reclamation center for recycling.

Windshield Wiper Fluid.   Containing detergent and methanol, wiper fluid is toxic. Skin contact, ingestion or inhalation should be avoided. Absorption of methanol can effect normal thought patterns. Heavy gloves are an important safety measure. Storage should of course be out of childrens' reach.

- If wiper fluid is not entirely used up, it should be disposed of by a licensed hazardous waste collector.

- Do not pour wiper fluid into a household septic system, as it will destroy beneficial bacteria that break down organic wastes.

HOUSEHOLD CLEANERS

Abrasive Cleaners or Powders.   Most scouring powders are corrosive, toxic irritants, containing trisodiumphosphate, ammonia, and ethanol.

- Use up product as intended and rinse container thoroughly before disposing.
- An alternative scouring method is to rub the soiled surface with a 1/2 lemon dipped in borax.

Ammonia-Based Cleaners.   Containing ammonia, ethanol, and other hazardous ingredients, these cleaners are corrosive, toxic irritants. Avoid contact with skin. Use and store ammonia products only in well-ventilated areas. Never mix ammonia-based products with bleach, as the two will produce a poisonous gas when combined.

- Thoroughly rinse empty containers with water (rinse water should be reused or diluted with large quantities of water) and dispose of container in trash.
- An excellent, safe, alternative cleaner for most household surfaces is a mixture of vinegar, salt, and water. Baking soda and water make a good tub and tile cleaner for the bathroom.

Bleach Cleaners.   Containing sodium or potassium hydroxide, hydrogen peroxide, sodium or calcium hypochlorite, these cleaners are corrosive toxins. Never mix bleach with ammonia, as a poisonous gas will be produced. Wear heavy gloves when working with bleach products. Store in well-ventilated area.

- Thoroughly rinse empty containers with water (rinse water should be reused or diluted with large quantities of water) and disposed of in trash.
- Alternatives include borax, dry oxygen bleaches and sodium hexametaphosphate. For laundry, use 1/2 cup sodium hexametaphosphate per five gallons of water.

Disinfectants.   Household disinfectants may contain the following hazardous ingredients: diethylene or methylene glycol, sodium hypochlorite, phenols, ammonia, cationic detergents, cresol, lye, phenol, and pine oil. Most disinfectants are corrosive and toxic. Use and store disinfectants in well-ventilated areas.

- Use up product as intended. Rinse container before disposing.

- Alternatives: soap and hot water will kill many bacteria; 1/2 cup borax mixed with 1 gallon of hot water; isopropyl alcohol (use in well-ventilated area).

Drain Cleaners. Containing sodium or potassium hydroxide, sodium hypochlorite, hydrochloric acid, and petroleum distillates, most drain cleaners are extremely corrosive and toxic.

- Use up product as intended. Do not dispose of unused portion; save for collection by licenced hazardous waste handler.

- Alternatives: use plunger; flush with boiling water; pour baking soda and vinegar down drain. DO NOT use plunger or other methods after pouring commercial drain cleaners into the drain, as splashback, toxic fumes, or explosion may result.

Floor and Furniture Polishes. Hazardous ingredients may include ammonia, diethylene glycol, petroleum distillates, nitrobenzene, naphtha, and phenol. Most commercial polishes are both flammable and toxic.

- Save unused product for hazardous waste collector.

- A safe alternative is 1 part lemon juice and 2 parts olive or vegetable oil.

Metal Cleaners and Polishes. A variety of metal cleaning products contain corrosive and toxic ingredients such as acidified thiourea and sulfuric acid.

- Save unused product for hazardous waste collection.

- Alternatives: for aluminum, brass, bronze, chrome, copper, pewter, and stainless steel, use vinegar or a combination of vinegar and salt. For gold, use toothpaste. For silver, soak in boiling water with baking soda, salt, and strips of aluminum foil.

Oven Cleaners. Most commercial oven cleaners contain potassium or sodium hydroxide, and ammonia, and are thus corrosive and toxic.

- Disposal: Use up product as intended.

- A safe alternative is baking soda and water rubbed in with very fine steel wool.

Rug Cleaners. Hazardous ingredients may include naphthalene, perchloroethylene, oxalic acid, and diethylene glycol. Such cleaning fluids are corrosive, toxic, and irritant. Use only in well-ventilated areas.

- Disposal: Save unused product for collection by hazardous waste handler.

- Instead of using toxic liquids and powders, sprinkle cornstarch on rug, wait one hour, and vacuum thoroughly.

Toilet Bowl Cleaners.   Corrosive, toxic, and irritant, such cleaners may contain muriatic (hydrochloric) or oxalic acid, paradichlorobenzene, and calcium hypochlorite.

- Disposal: Store unused product for licenced hazardous waste collector.

- As an alternative, use baking soda or a mild detergent.

MISCELLANEOUS PRODUCTS

Aerosol Spray Products.   A wide variety of household cleaning and personal care products come in aerosol cans. Inhalation of aerosol particles can cause headache, nausea, shortness of breath, throat irritations, liver damage, heart problems, and even death.

- Make sure aerosol cans are completely empty before throwing them away—they may otherwise explode en route to the landfill, possibly injuring sanitation workers.

- Aerosol products are generally more expensive ounce for ounce. Buy pumps and solids instead, or make your own safe alternatives at home.

Air Fresheners.   These products contain flammable and irritant chemicals that coat the mucous membranes in the nasal passages to interfere with the natural sense of smell.

- An open dish of vinegar will remove many odors.

Ant and Roach Killers.   Most of these products are toxic, containing organo-phosphates, carbamates, and pyrethrins.

- Disposal: Save unused product for hazardous waste collection.

- Alternatives: To deter ant infestation, wash kitchen surfaces with vinegar solution; also, sprinkle bone meal, chili powder, lemon juice, or powdered charcoal in and around suspected points of entry. To kill roaches, spread a mixture of baking soda and powdered sugar in infested areas.

Flea and Tick Repellents.   Most pet flea collars and sprays contain carbamates, pyrethrins, and organo-phosphates.

- Disposal: Use up product as intended; rinse containers thoroughly before disposal.

- Alternatives include herbal ointment, herbal collar, citronella preparation, or powdered brewer's yeast in pet's food.

Glues and Adhesives.   Rubber cement, epoxy, model glue, instant glues, and plastic adhesives all contain toxic solvents. These substances are flammable and irritant.

- Disposal: Use up product as intended. Dried residues may be thrown in the trash.

- As an alternative to solvent-suspended glues, use white or yellow wood glue whenever possible.

House Plant Insecticides.   Toxic ingredients may include methoprene, malathion, tetramethrin, and carbaryl.

- Store unused product for hazardous waste collection.

- As an alternative to commercial insecticides, spray used dishwater or other soap and water solution on leaves, then rinse.

Mothballs.   Mothballs that contain naphthalene and paradichlorobenzene are toxic.

- Store unused mothballs for hazardous waste collection.

- Alternatives include cedar chips, newspaper, lavender, and flower petals.

Nail Polish and Nail Polish Remover.   The primary ingredient in nail polish is a formaldehyde resin, that can cause bleeding and discoloration under the nail. Nail polishes also contain toxic solvents—phenol, tolulene, and xylene. Nail polish remover contains primarily the solvent acetone, a toxic and irritant. Use these products only in a well-ventilated area.

- Store liquid leftovers for hazardous waste collection.

Photographic Chemicals.   Developers and other photographic products contain hazardous ingredients such as silver, acetic acid, hydroquinone, sodium sulfite, ferrocyanide. These products are corrosive, toxic, and irritant.

- Save unused product for hazardous waste collection.

Pool Chemicals.   Products containing chlorine, muriatic acid, sodium hypochlorite, algicides, and petroleum distillates are toxic and corrosive.

- Give away leftovers or save for hazardous waste collection.

- Alternatives include ozone or ultraviolet lighting systems.

Shoe Polish. Shoe polishes that contain trichloroethylene, methyl chloride, or nitrobenzene should be avoided. Inhalation of fumes from these chemicals may cause vomiting and shortness of breath. For someone with alcohol in his/her bloodstream, absorption of these chemicals through the skin can be fatal. Do not buy shoe polish products that lack ingredient labels.

- Store unused product for hazardous waste collection.

- Alternatives include olive oil, walnut oil, beeswax, or lemon juice. Remove stains from leather with vinegar.

PAINTS AND FINISHING PRODUCTS

Enamel or Oil Based Paints. Flammable and toxic ingredients include ethylene, aliphatic hydrocarbons, mineral spirits, and various pigments.

- Give away or save unused product for professional hazardous waste collection.

- Alternatively, use latex or water-based paints.

Furniture Strippers. Hazardous ingredients include acetone, methyl ketone, alcohols, xylene, tolulene, methylene chloride. Most commercial furniture strippers are flammable and toxic.

- Unused product should be stored for hazardous waste collection.

- Alternatives include sandpaper, electric sander, or heat gun.

Latex or Water-Based Paints. Non-flammable and less toxic than oil-based paints, latex and water-based paint products nevertheless contain toxic ingredients such as resins, glycol ethers, esters, pigments, and phenyl mercuric acetate.

- Air dry leftover paint and discard container.

- Possible alternatives include limestone-based white wash or casein-based paint.

Rust Paints. Rust paints, that are flammable and toxic, contain methylene chloride, petroleum distillates, and tolulene.

- Give away or store unused paint for hazardous waste collection.

Stains and Finishes. Flammable and toxic, these products contain mineral spirits, glycol ethers, ketones, halogenated hydrocarbons, and naphtha.

- Store leftovers for hazardous waste collection.

• Alternatives include latex paint or natural pigment finishes.

Thinners and Turpentine.   Flammable and toxic, these products contain n-butyl alcohol, acetone, methyl isobutyl ketone, petroleum distillates.

• Strain used liquid through fine steel mesh; reuse liquid and save concentrated contaminants for hazardous waste collection.

• To avoid using solvent-based thinners, use water-based paints, that require only water as a thinner.

Wood Preservatives.   These flammable and toxic products contain hazardous ingredients such as chlorinated phenols, copper or zinc napthenate, creosote, and magnesium fluorosilicate.

• Store leftover product for hazardous waste collection.

Shopping As If the Earth Matters
by Gene Karpinsky

The world is too much with us: late and soon,
Getting and spending, we lay waste our powers . . .
— William Wordsworth

In our energy-intensive, "consumer" society, the way we shop is a major factor in the environmental crisis. Food, clothing, toiletries, household necessities, appliances, luxury items—all of these things have an environmental past, present, and future. A box of individually wrapped cupcakes doesn't just appear on a shelf in your grocer's stockroom. Nor do the paper box and individual plastic wrappers neatly disappear when tossed into the trash can. From the oilfield and the farmer's field to the market, and finally to the landfill, energy is wasted and pollutants are generated at every stage in the production of any product.

Raw materials—grain, cotton, wood, petroleum, iron ore, bauxite, silicon, and hundreds of other materials—are either grown on mechanized, chemical-intensive "farms" or extracted from the earth by oil-guzzling machines. The result is irreversible topsoil erosion, deforestation, water pollution, and the release of billions of tons of carbon dioxide into the atmosphere. For example, topsoil losses worldwide currently amount to about twenty-five billion tons per year, roughly the amount covering the wheat lands of Australia. Because of careless plowing practices, American farmers lose as much as six tons of soil for every ton of grain harvested. To make up for the lost nutrients and natural soil defenses, they must rely more and more on chemical fertilizers and pesticides. According to one estimate, about half of the fertilizer spread on United States farmland each year simply replaces soil nutrients lost through erosion.

Furthermore, oil spills have devastated marine ecosystems, spoiled seacoasts on six continents, and threatened the livelihoods of thousands of people. Further inland, according to a recent federal government study, 372 million barrels of toxic oil-drilling wastes (often containing arsenic, lead, mer-

Packaging accounts for 50 percent of all paper produced in the United States, 90 percent of all glass, and 11 percent of aluminum.

cury, and other carcinogens) are dumped each year into unlined pits across the country. This practice causes significant harm to farmland, crops, and livestock.

After raw materials are drawn from the earth, they must be processed or manufactured into useful forms. It takes a surprising amount of energy to transform a barrel of oil, sand, and copper into a television set—or a stalk of sugar cane and an ear of wheat into a Deluxe Moon Pie. Manufacturing processes require vast quantities of electricity and water, and they often create tons of toxic by-products that end up in the atmosphere and groundwater. Even the so-called "clean industries," like computer manufacturing, generate many environmentally damaging by-products (CFC–113, for instance, which depletes the ozone layer).

In addition, transporting, packaging, and marketing consumer products require substantial energy inputs. In the United States, finished articles are transported from factory to store almost exclusively by inefficient diesel, and gasoline-powered trucks, which emit carbon monoxide, nitrogen oxides, hydrocarbons, sulfur oxides, and a variety of particulates. Combustion engines also produce ground-level ozone (which does not float up to the stratosphere); this is a component of smog, which irritates respiratory systems, strains eyes, and causes headaches and other ailments. The Environmental Protection Agency estimates that ozone pollution reduces crop yields by as much as 30 percent in some areas. Furthermore, marketing—including warehouse storage, advertising, administrative support, and retail sales—uses massive amounts of electricity and heating oil.

Americans throw away 2.5 million plastic bottles every hour.

Much of the packaging found in any grocery or discount store is made for convenience (although anyone who has ever tried to extract a couple of "D" cell batteries from a "blister pack" knows how convenient some packages really are). Even more, commercial packaging is designed solely to attract the customer and conceal the size and appearance of the product. One way or another, most of it is unnecessary, and all of it represents a past energy drain and a future buildup of solid waste. Packaging accounts for 50 percent of all paper produced in the United States, 90 percent of all glass, and 11 percent of aluminum. It also accounts for 50 percent of the volume and 30 percent of the weight of the municipal waste stream. Ten cents out of every dollar spent for groceries in the United States pays for packaging (more than the farmers earn from the same dollar). A single aluminum can—containing twelve ounces of soda—requires six ounces of gasoline to manufacture and transport.

Americans throw away 2.5 million plastic bottles every hour. In a year's time, the average United States citizen uses 200 pounds of plastic, about 60 percent of it for packaging. To produce these plastics, the United States in 1987 used almost one billion barrels of oil—enough to meet the nation's demand for imported oil for five months—and millions of tons of ozone-depleting chlorofluorocarbons (CFCs). Currently, only about 3 percent of the plastic waste stream is recycled. Most of it ends up in landfills, although some of it is burned in incinerators, thus emitting dioxins, furans, and hydrochloric acid.

Still more disconcerting is that 45,000 tons of plastics are dumped into the world's oceans every year, with devastating ecological consequences. Up to one million seabirds and one hundred thousand marine mammals are killed each year by plastic trash such as fishing gear, six-pack yokes, sandwich bags, and styrofoam cups. Besides damaging life offshore, plastics also wash up on beaches, marring the landscape and interfering with natural ecosystems. Plastics, in one form or another, including cups, bags, and soda bottles, make up eight of the twelve most prevalent types of debris that wash ashore on American beaches. In Texas, volunteers have picked up over three thousand pounds of such debris per mile of coastline.

In the home, a variety of hazardous household products pose an *immediate* threat to our health. According to the Missouri Household Waste Project, there are almost twenty-seven thousand different hazardous materials in consumer products sold in the United States. Last year alone, the Regional Poison Center of Missouri had over fifteen thousand calls concerning harmful exposure to adhesives, batteries, deodorizers, cleaning compounds, gasoline, moth repellents, paints, art and craft supplies, pesticides, and many other common household items. Certainly the risks of many consumer products far outweigh their convenience.

Every American likes a bargain. A car, new clothes every year, eating out three times a week, a home with all the modern conveniences, all at an affordable price—this is the dream millions of Americans have lived for. But has it really been a bargain? Unfortunately, when all the environmental costs are tallied, it looks like the American Dream may turn out to be an ecological nightmare. However, by taking immediate and substantive action, we *can* change our wasteful ways and halt the fouling of the earth. For each of us, this effort should include shopping with the good of the whole earth in mind. In the grocery store, at the shopping center, in restaurants, or anywhere else we spend money, we can use the power of the "dollar-ballot" to make a difference in the global environmental crisis.

The Bottom Line on Diapers

About four out of every five parents use disposable diapers on their babies. Each year Americans use eighteen billion disposable diapers. On average, a baby will use 10,000 diapers before toilet training. Plastic diapers make up about 4 percent of our solid waste—enough diapers to fill a garbage barge every six hours.

A disposable diaper takes an estimated 500 years to decompose in a landfill. A cotton diaper (after multiple uses) decomposes in six months. For every dollar spent on disposable diapers about twelve cents will be spent on disposal. Disposing of these diapers at landfills is estimated to cost $100 million per year. In addition to the solid waste nightmare, the untreated sewage that comes to landfills in these diapers often contains dangerous bacteria and viruses. These pathogens can contaminate groundwater and pose a health threat to sanitation workers and to the public.

Plastic diapers are also less comfortable for babies. Studies have demonstrated that babies wearing plastic diapers get diaper rash five times more often than those who wear cotton. Moreover, due to chemicals in certain disposables, babies can get severe rashes from plastic diapers.

Tips

Up to one million seabirds and one hundred thousand marine mammals are killed each year by plastic trash such as fishing gear, six-pack yokes, sandwich bags, and styrofoam cups.

- **Avoid excessive packaging.** Paper, plastic, glass, and aluminum containers and wrappers account for the vast majority of the solid waste stream in the United States. Many plastic packaging materials are mildly toxic, and some of the coloring materials on paper packages are dangerous as well. All packages use up energy in being manufactured.

- **Buy recycled and recyclable packaging wherever possible.** Look for the recycling symbol on packages, indicating that the package is recycled or made from recyclable materials.

- **Don't use plastic bags.** Insist on paper at the check-out. Better yet, reuse paper bags or bring your own tote bag. Avoiding plastics and reducing paper can remove 10–20 percent from your household garbage and reduce carbon dioxide (CO_2) emissions significantly.

- **Substitute cellulose bags for plastic.** Cellulose bags are made from wood pulp and are clear, like plastic, though not quite as strong.

- **Choose paper containers over plastic.** The United States produces 1.6 billion pounds of plastic soda, milk, and water bottles each year, enough to fill a line of dump trucks stretching from New York City to Cleveland, Ohio. Although the plastic gallon milk jug is a little cheaper than two paper, half-gallon containers, it will not break down quickly or safely in a landfill.

- **Don't buy "shatterproof" plastic bottles and jars.** Glass is nontoxic and much easier to recycle.

- **Buy returnables whenever possible.** Many states and localities now have recycling laws that require a deposit on aluminum cans, glass bottles, and even plastic bottles. Buy only containers that can be recycled in your area.

- **Buy in bulk.** Larger packages generally have less packaging per ounce of product. A ten pound sack of rice and a few stock seasonings create a lot less trash than twenty boxes of Rice-A-Roni. Home freezing takes less energy than driving to and from the supermarket.

- **Don't use styrofoam.** Some foam plastics may be manufactured using CFCs, and none of them break down safely when disposed of.

- **Avoid products containing CFCs.** Despite government action, some CFC products are still on the market, including aerosol dust removers, plastic confetti makers, and various cleaning sprays for electronic equipment like sewing machines, VCRs, and boat horns. Check the labels for these CFC gases: CFC 11 (Trichlorofluoromethane); CFC 12 (Dichlorodifluoromethane); CFC 113 (Trichlorotrifluoroethane); CFC 114 (Dichlorotetrafluoroethane); CFC 115 (Monochloropentafluoroethane); Halon 1211 (Bromochlorodifluoroethane); Halon 1301 (Bromotrifluoroethane); Halon 2402 (Dibromotetrafluoroethane).

- **Don't buy Halon fire extinguishers.** These fire extinguishers contain ozone-depleting Halon gases. Purchase traditional types of fire extinguishers instead.

- **Avoid buying foods out of season.** The production and transport of out-of-season products requires excessive energy consumption. These products are often contaminated with preservatives, pesticides, and herbicides primarily to increase shelf-life and to enhance appearance. Ask your grocer which food items are in season.

- **Encourage your market to stock locally grown, pesticide-free produce.** Tapping local food sources reduces the energy consumed and air pollution generated in the transportation and refrigeration of centrally processed foods.

- **Get to know your store and its manager.** Locate the health food aisles and the preservative-free foods. Learn the buying season of your supermarket, so you can plan your fresh food purchases ahead of time. Your supermarket manager will respond to persistent consumer requests for environmentally sound products.

- **Read labels on food.** Buy foods that have not been heavily processed and do not contain artificial additives or preservatives.

- **When shopping for clothes, choose comfortable cotton and wool fabrics over petroleum-based synthetics.**

- **Don't buy motorized or electric tools or appliances when hand-operated ones will do the job.** Just because the work will be easier for you, does not mean it is more energy-efficient. The likely fact is, the more automated the tool, the more energy it will use.

- **Buy things that will last.** These days, clothing and other necessary items are not always made to last. Look for quality materials and workmanship. Avoid "bargains" that will disintegrate after three washings.

- **Combine shopping trips.** Keep a list of what you need to purchase. Make fewer trips to the supermarket and make the most of those trips. Quick, one item pick-ups, or repeated trips to the market waste time and energy.

- **Avoid impulse buying.** Read labels and research the different brands of products you plan to buy. *Consumer Reports* is a reliable resource when you are deciding which products to buy.

- **Avoid toxic and otherwise dangerous products.** (See chapter two for information on hazardous household products.)

- **Use cotton diapers instead of plastic.** A disposable diaper takes an estimated 500 years to decompose in a landfill. A cotton diaper, after years of service diapering one or more children (and then being used as a rag) will decompose within six months. In most areas, using cotton diapers is also less expensive than using disposables, whether you wash them yourself or use a diaper service. For more information on diaper alternatives, write to The National Association of Diaper Services, 2017 Walnut Street, Philadelphia, PA 19103; (215) 569–3650.

  Biobottoms Inc. can provide you with information as to where the cloth diaper service closest to you can be found. Biobottoms Inc., PO Box 6009, Petaluma, CA 94953; (707) 778–7945. The Biobottoms Catalog features cotton diapers and biodegradable disposable diapers.

- **Give a gift certificate for a diaper service or a few dozen cotton diapers to a friend as a new baby gift.**

There are about twenty-seven thousand different hazardous materials in consumer products sold in the United States.

- **Instead of plastic, try wooden or metal toys, wicker laundry baskets, ceramic or wooden bowls, cotton shower curtains, and so on.**

- **Buy a live Christmas tree** that you can plant outside after the holidays.

- **Shop at farmers' markets or cooperatives.** Shopping at co-ops and local farmers' markets can be beneficial. Produce is fresh, packaging is minimal, and your travel time is usually reduced. Co-op America may be helpful in locating cooperatives in your area: Co-op America, 2100 M Street NW, Suite 310, Washington, DC 20063. Part of the National Association of Cooperatives, Co-op America puts out a quarterly publication that features an organizational directory of all of its members both categorically and by state. The types of cooperatives found in the directory range from advertising to wood products.

The United States produces 1.6 billion pounds of plastic soda, milk, and water bottles each year, enough to fill a line of dump trucks stretching from New York City to Cleveland, Ohio.

Shopping Sources

These publications and catalogues help you buy with good conscience by listing goods that do not harm animals or the environment:

- **Co-op America Alternative Catalogue**, Catalogue Services Dept., 126 Intervale Road, Burlington, VT 05401; (802) 658–5507.

- **EccoBella**, 6 Provost Square, Suite 602, Caldwell, NJ 07006; (201) 226–5799. (Biodegradable plastics, etc.)

- **National Boycott Newsletter**, 6506 28th Avenue, Seattle, WA 98115; (206) 523–0421.

- **Seventh Generation Catalogue**, 126 Intervale Road, Burlington, VT 05401; (802) 862–2999.

- **Shopping for a Better World Catalogue**, Council on Economic Priorities, 30 Irving Place, New York, NY 10003; (800) U–CAN–HELP, (212) 420–1133 in New York.

- **Americans for Safe Food/Center for Science in the Public Interest**, 1501 16th Street, NW, Washington, DC 20036; (202) 332–9110. National coalition of consumer, environmental, and farm organizations publishes a list of eighty-five mail-order suppliers of organic foods.

- **Healthy Harvest II: A Directory of Sustainable Agriculture and Horticulture Organizations**, Potomac Valley Press, 1424 16th Street, NW, Suite 105, Washington, DC 20036. Lists organizations, publications, and retailers working to make our food supply safer and our agricultural methods more environmentally sound.

- **Shopper's Guide to Natural Foods: A Consumer's Guide to Buying and Preparing Foods for Good Health**, Avery Publishing Group, Inc., Garden City Park, NY 11040. A guide of the "healthiest" food in the supermarket or natural food store.

Organic Food Sources

- **Cascadian Farm**, 5375 Highway 20, Rockport, WA 98283; (206) 853–8175.

- **Country Life Natural Foods**, Oak Haven, Pullman, MI 49450; (616) 236–5011. Offers nuts, dried fruits, wheat germ, rice, bran, seeds, beans, pasta, honey, and such meat substitutes as oatburgers and vegeburgers. Discounts on quantity purchases of single items.

- **Deer Valley Farm**, RD 1, Guilford, NY 13780; (607) 764–8556. Offers grains, seeds, and fresh fruits and vegetables, baked goods, beef, cheese, eggs, fertilizers, food supplements, and apprenticeships.

- **Diamond K Enterprises**, RR 1, PO Box 30, St. Charles, MN 55972; (507) 932–4308. Offers grains grown in the Midwest without chemical fertilizers, herbicides, or insecticides.

- **Dutch Mill Cheese Shop**, Route 2, Box 203–D, Cambridge City, IN 47327; (317) 478–5847. Offers twelve varieties of cheese made by the Amish community. Cheeses are made without additives, preservatives, or chemicals.

- **Frontier Cooperative Herbs**, Box 299, Norway, IA 52318; (319) 227–7991. Offers numerous teas, coffees, spices, potpourri, cookware, and body-care products.

- **Garden Spot Distributors**, 438 White Oak Road, New Holland, PA 17557; PA, (800) 292–9631 in Pennsylvania, (800) 445–5100 in the Northeastern United States. Offers baked goods, grains and cereals, granola, dried fruit, flours, fruit and nut mix, beans, and seeds.

- **Gold Mine Natural Food Company**, 1947 30th Street, San Diego, CA 92101; (800) 647–2929, (800) 647–2927 in California. Offers brown rice, soy sauce, miso, seaweed, dried tofu, shiitake mushrooms, and teas as well as cookware and body-care products.

- **Harvest Health, Inc.**, 1944 Eastern Avenue, SE, Grand Rapids, MI 49507; (616) 245–6268. Offers herbs, spices, teas, oils, extracts, perfume oils, many types of potpourri, and more than 600 titles on health and nutrition.

- **Jaffe Brothers**, PO Box 636, Valley Center, CA 92082–0636; (619) 749–1133. Offers foods grown without chemicals or preservatives.

- **Living Farms**, PO Box 50, Tracy, MN 56175; (507) 629–4431. Offers grains and beans (including alfalfa, pinto beans, and wheat) raised with crop rotation and natural farming techniques without herbicides.

- **Mountain Ark Trading Company**, 120 S East Avenue, Fayetteville, AR 72701; (800) 643–8909, in Arkansas (501) 442–7191. Offers macrobiotic foods, including seaweed, nuts, seeds, brown rice, bulgar wheat, couscous, cereals, flours, beans, seasonings, and vegetarian burgers. Discounts on some bulk orders.

- **Neshaminy Valley Natural Foods Distributor, Ltd.**, 5 Louise Drive, Ivyland, PA 18974; (215) 443–5545.

- **New American Food Company**, 2833 Duke Homestead Road, Durham, NC 27705; (919) 479–1654. Offers collection of natural foods and beauty-care products.

- **Nu-World Amaranth, Inc.**, PO Box 2202, Naperville, IL 60540; (312) 369–6819. Amaranth, a food staple of the Aztecs, is a small seed grain that is high in protein and total dietary fiber and contains no gluten.

Every year some 45,000 tons of plastic waste are dumped into the world's oceans.

- **Ozark Cooperative Warehouse**, PO Box 30, Fayetteville, AR 72702; (501) 521–COOP. Wholesale natural-foods cooperative selling soy foods, wheat germ, bulgur wheat, vegetarian burgers, pastas, nuts, and seeds.

- **Purity Foods, Inc.**, 4211 Okemos Road, Suite 21, Okemos, MI 48864; (517) 349–7941. Offers several types of soybeans, amaranth, black turtle beans, lentils, rice, wheat, organic soup mix, and hazelnuts.

- **Rising Sun**, Box 627, I–80 & Route 150, Milesburg, PA 16853; (814) 355–9850. Offers organic produce and meat as well as dried fruits and nuts. Also sells or rents a videotape (on VHS format) demonstrating organic farming techniques.

- **Timber Crest Farms**, 4791 Dry Creek Road, Healdsburg, CA 95448; (707) 433–8251. Has organic dried fruits and nuts for thirty years.

- **Walnut Acres**, Penns Creek, PA 17862; (717) 837–0601. Offers cheeses, rice, seeds, flours, nuts, pasta, dried fruits, granola, and peanut butter.

Steering towards Ecological Disaster
by Andrew C. Kimbrell

If someone were to tell you he had seen strings of noxious gasses drifting among buildings of a city, black smoke blotting out the sun, great holes in the major streets, filled with men in hard hats, planes circling overhead, unable to land, and thousands of people choking the streets, pushing and shoving in a desperate effort to get out of the city . . . you would be hard pressed to know whether he was talking about a city at war or a city at rush hour.

— Former Secretary of Transportation Alan Boyd

In 1891, the first American gasoline-powered automobile motored down the streets of Ohio City, Ohio. This first United States car, a product of several years of labor by John William Lambert, was destroyed later that year in a fire, but not before Lambert sent out a sales brochure—beginning the long tradition of auto advertising in the United States. The going price for a Lambert was $550. He received several inquiries but made no sales.

Over the past century, Americans have used over 700 million automobiles. The automobile has dominated our culture, seized our psyches, and become our ultimate "love machine." The American dream of two cars in every garage has largely been realized. There are over 125 million privately owned cars and trucks in the United States. About 36 percent of American households have one car, 35 percent have two cars, and almost 18 percent have three or more cars. American drivers log well over a trillion miles per year and individually average about forty-five eight-hour days per year behind the wheel.

In the United States the car remains, overwhelmingly, the transportation of choice. About 80 percent of all trips are made in cars—compared to 13 percent by air and 7 percent by all other forms of transport. Since 1976, we have seen a 30 percent increase in the volume of United States car travel (Japan has experienced an over 45 percent increase in the same time period), while the amount

> "Can you imagine growing up and finding the first rabbit you encounter is a Volkswagen?"
> — *Charles Varon*

of travel by public transport both in the United States and around the world has hardly changed.

More recently, automania has been sweeping the globe. In 1950, the United States owned 75 percent of the world's 50 million autos. Now, we own only about 35 percent of the 400 million cars on the world's roads.

And more cars are on the way. Current automobile production is at 38 million cars a year and is expected to rise to 60 million by the year 2000. The industrializing nations of Asia report the greatest growth.

These statistics are not difficult to understand. Compared to public transportation, the car offers endless convenience. Unlike mass transport systems, the car generally goes where we want to go, when we want to go there. There's no waiting, and we're guaranteed a seat. We have complete privacy and can glide down the highway in air-conditioned comfort surrounded by stereophonic sound.

Automobile accidents have slain far more Americans than all the wars of the twentieth century combined.

The allure of the car involves more than convenience. Few can resist the emotional addiction and attraction of the auto. Kenneth Boulding aptly describes the automobile as a "suit of armor with two hundred horses inside, big enough to make love in." The automobile driver becomes the mobile knight among a world of slow peasant-like pedestrians. As Boulding notes, "Once having tasted the delights of a society in which almost every one can be a knight, it is hard to go back to being a peasant."

Auto companies create and feed our addiction. More money is spent advertising the automobile each year than any other product. Over the last decade, in the United States alone, the car manufacturers have spent approximately $40 billion to sell us the automobile. General Motors routinely spends over a billion dollars a year on advertising. The auto ad-men have used God, country, sex, animals (Jaguars, Skylarks, Broncos, et al.) to sell cars. Remarkably, they have succeeded in making many of us associate our self image and economic status with the automobiles we drive.

The phenomenal growth of the auto over the last few decades is not due solely to advertising. The auto industry and its allies have relentlessly and successfully lobbied for legislation promoting car use—and undermining public transit.

It is now becoming clear that after a century long experiment, the gasoline age is over. Whatever its allure, however much is spent to brainwash us, no matter the auto's political clout, its growing impact on the environment is no longer sustainable.

Of course, there are direct costs of the auto in human suffering. Automobile accidents have slain far more Americans than all the wars of the twentieth century combined. The car had cost its first million dead by 1952, its second million by 1975, and its third million is likely by 1994. Added to that total is the approximately ninety million Americans who have sustained disabling injuries in auto accidents since 1900.

Driving also takes a horrendous toll on the animal kingdom. Nearly one million animals are killed each day on United States roads (a conservative estimate). This makes road-kills second only to the meat industry in numbers of animal deaths. States routinely record more deer killed by cars than by hunters. Humans are killed and injured in these collisions as well. Each year about eight thousand humans are injured in car-animal accidents, with property damage each year at close to $40 million.

But the ultimate costs of the auto go well beyond these direct casualties. The car contributes to a variety of major air pollution problems including global warming, ozone depletion, acid rain, and smog. These environmental impacts cost thousands of lives each year and threaten the survival of the planet.

These concerns about the ultimate consequences of the car culture have governments, environmentalists, and scientists advocating major changes in society's automobile use. Whether by force or by choice, the days of the automobile are numbered.

Driving Ourselves to Death

Cars kill in many ways. Around the globe, motor vehicles are the dominant source of emissions for some of our most dangerous air pollutants. In the United States, transportation sources are responsible for 69 percent of the lead, 70 percent of the carbon monoxide, 45 percent of nitrous oxides, and 35 percent of the hydrocarbons released into the air. According to some estimates, vehicle emissions of these hazardous gases in the United States hasten up to 100 thousand deaths per year by contributing to the incidence of lung cancer, emphysema, and a variety of respiratory and pulmonary disorders. These gases also harm terrestrial and aquatic ecosystems, destroying wildlife and food crops. The United States National Crop Loss Assessment Program found that damage caused by car emissions resulted in annual yield losses of $1.9 billion to $4.5 billion for only four crops—wheat, corn, soybeans, and peanuts.

Of special concern is ozone pollution. Ozone at ground level is produced by the mixture of several of the compounds released by automobiles and causes

---

Troubled Transit

In 1900 there were about 8,000 registered cars in the United States, 150 miles of paved roads, and fewer than 100 motor vehicle deaths. By 1910 there were more than 500,00 autos on the road; in 1950 there were more than 40 million passenger cars. Then in 1956, the Federal Highway Act was passed, committing the nation to decades of highway construction at the cost of tens of billions of dollars. By the mid–1980s we were driving more than 135 million cars on 3,600,000 miles of paved roads.

This extraordinary growth was possible because the auto industry and its allies had successfully lobbied–at times in violation of the law–for legislation to promote car use and undermine public transit. For example, when the nation's trolley systems disappeared in the 1940s and 1950s most people saw it as simply a sign of progress. Far from it. During the decade of 1936–46, a holding company called National City lines (consisting of General motors, Firestone Tire, Standard Oil, and Mack Truck) cozied up to city officials across the nation and conspired to buy up and destroy trolley car systems. Street car systems were dismantled in over 45 municipalities. By 1955 almost 95 percent of street cars were gone from our cities.

In 1947, the conspirators were brought to trial. After almost ten years of litigation, they were found guilty. To the dismay of prosecutors, an accommodating judge fined individual defendants $1 each, and corporate defendants $5,000.

Now, ironically, nineteen gridlock-plagued American cities plan to spend hundreds of millions of dollars to rebuild their trolley systems–often along virtually the same routes taken by the street cars half a century ago.

lung and pulmonary disorders worldwide. In the United States, approximately eighty million Americans reside in areas with air quality standards, especially ozone concentrations, that are below the legal limit.

Internationally, the car pollution problem has also galvanized concern and action. From Los Angeles to New Delhi, where the number of automobiles is increasing by about ten thousand a month, smog takes an enormous toll on the environment and human lives. In Mexico City, children start out to school late in the day to avoid the suffocating morning smog. Athens has initiated significant restrictions on the number of cars entering the city. Singapore has introduced road pricing in an attempt to control auto congestion. There, drivers are sold daily permits to enter the central area during rush hour. In the United States, we are warned to stay indoors during certain summer days in many of our cities due to "unacceptable air quality" conditions.

The outlook for the future is not bright. While the worldwide trend towards adoption of various pollution-control technologies continues, the number of vehicles and miles travelled also continue to grow. Unhealthy conditions still persist throughout the globe and will likely deteriorate further unless drastic traffic reduction measures are quickly initiated.

Cars are also a major contributor to the greenhouse effect. While many fossil fuel burning activities create carbon dioxide (CO_2), cars and light trucks are the largest contributing sector—responsible for 33 percent of all carbon emission in this country. Each gallon of gas burned by vehicles releases twenty-two pounds of CO_2 into the atmosphere. Every year that amounts to an average of five tons of CO_2 being released into the atmosphere for each of the over 125 million cars used in the United States. That means that in the United States we're putting 600 million tons of CO_2 into the atmosphere annually, just by driving our cars. Continued CO_2 emissions at these levels could well lead to global environmental catastrophe.

Furthermore, automobiles contribute to the destruction of the ozone layer. While ozone at the ground level—created primarily by car pollution—can kill us, ozone in the upper atmosphere is essential for life to exist at all. The ozone in the upper atmosphere provides a vital shield that prevents hazardous ultra violet radiation emitted by the sun from reaching the earth. Increasingly, release of the chlorofluorocarbons (CFCs)—a car exhaust gas—is destroying our ozone protection.

Gaping holes in the ozone layer now exist. The National Aeronautics and Space Administration (NASA) predicts that ozone loss may expose the earth to dangerous levels of ultraviolet radiation. The Environmental Protection Agency

Over the last decade, in the United States alone, the car manufacturers have spent approximately $40 billion to sell us the automobile. General Motors routinely spends over a billion dollars a year on advertising.

(EPA) predicts hundreds of millions of skin cancer cases, cataracts, and significant harm to animal and plant life over the next several decades if ozone depletion goes unchecked.

Aerosol products and various cleansers and refrigerants contain CFCs (CFC–12). About 41 percent of the CFC–12 used for refrigerant in the United States is used by vehicle air conditioners. But because auto air conditioners are particularly prone to leaks and need frequent replacements of refrigerant, the largest sources of CFC emission in the United States are the approximately ninety-five million auto air conditioners in use in this country. The installation of each air conditioner causes a release of 2.5 pounds of CFCs. An annual air conditioner recharge releases another pound of CFCs. Thus, our use of automobile air conditioners is putting hundreds of millions of pounds of CFCs into the atmosphere each year. CFCs remain in the atmosphere for over 100 years and, besides destroying the ozone layer, also contribute to the greenhouse effect. The United States is the only major user of auto air conditioners.

Some action has been taken. Vermont, Oregon, and Hawaii have already passed legislation restricting the sale of CFCs. Recycling technology for auto air conditioner refrigerant is currently available and being used. Even the car manufacturers are getting involved. General Motors recently announced that by 1991 it would require its ten thousand dealers to recycle CFCs from car air conditioners undergoing service. At the same time, Nissan announced it would halt the use of CFCs entirely in its air conditioners by 1993. While these are laudable first steps, far more needs to be done to avert the destruction of the fragile ozone layer.

Few environmental problems have the visceral impact of acid rain. This global environmental problem decimates forests, eliminates fish populations in lakes and rivers around the world, and even eats away at the great outdoor sculptures and monuments of Europe. The major culprits in the production of acid rain are sulfur dioxide (SO_2) and nitrogen oxide (NO).

Acid rain is caused primarily by the burning of coal. However, automobile use also plays an important role. Automobiles account for 34 percent of NO emissions. If we are to cut down on the environmental costs of acid rain, estimated at $2.4 billion annually, we must curtail our use of automobiles.

Breaking the Habit

The automobile addiction will not be easy to overcome. The automobile's unique position in our culture, and increasingly in cultures

In the United States we're putting 600 million tons of CO_2 into the atmosphere annually, just by driving our cars.

throughout the world, is reinforced by government policies and an increasingly complex infrastructure that encourages car use rather than public transportation. Furthermore, the car is also entrenched in the world's economies. In the United States, according to one estimate, one in six workers is employed in car-related industries.

Additionally, the car habit is psychologically reinforced each day. We are inundated with print and electronic media messages by the auto manufacturers teasing our imaginations and appropriating our self-identity in order to promote the auto culture. But just as with cigarettes over the last few years, the self esteem of auto use is going to have to make way for survival concerns. Just as there is ultimately little that is sexy in the health effects of smoking, the seductive metaphors and messages of the car companies can't ultimately hide the horrors of death by car fumes, acid rain, cancer-causing ozone depletion, and the greenhouse effect.

The largest sources of CFC emission in the United States are the approximately ninety-five million auto air conditioners in use in this country.

Perhaps the best way to break the car habit is to just say no. We can begin by using public transportation whenever possible, taking short trips on foot or by bicycle, and avoiding city driving. Additionally, car pooling is a relatively easy step towards breaking the auto habit. Approximately 88 percent of Americans commute to work in automobiles. In the United States, thirty-three million gallons of gasoline would be saved each day and car air pollution would be significantly reduced if the average commuter passenger load were increased by one person.

Other intermediate steps that can help limit the many social costs of the car include greatly reducing or eliminating the use of air conditioners to avoid the release of ozone depleting CFCs. Government studies have demonstrated that light-colored cars with tinted glass stay cooler in hot weather and need less air conditioning. Additionally, driving at moderate speeds not only cuts down on highway deaths but also increases fuel economy up to 30 percent, with the resulting diminution in air pollution. And planning trips carefully can help avoid peak traffic hours in city areas.

The environmental impacts of driving can also be reduced through the use of highly fuel-efficient vehicles. European prototypes of such vehicles get over eighty miles per gallon (MPG) on highways. Unfortunately, relatively low oil prices discourage the production and use of such vehicles in the United States. Also, car manufacturers are once again encouraging consumers to purchase larger, more powerful, and less efficient cars. Due to increased demand for larger cars, the nation's fuel efficiency dropped in 1988 for the first time in over a decade.

While each individual can take steps to cut down or eliminate auto use, government leaders and policymakers around the world must also do their part. Most immediately, they should begin enacting legislation to discourage car use and encourage public transportation, including removing auto ads from the public media and charging auto and gas taxes (which reflect the true costs of the auto). Up to now, too many governments have ignored the looming cost of "auto-cracy." Perhaps seduced by the economic importance of the auto to their local economies, they have been reluctant to encourage the breaking of the car habit. We have reached a critical turning point in our understanding of the growing costs of the automobile. With the future of the planet in the balance, even more than drugs or smoking, cars are our most dangerous addiction.

Tips

- **Buy a fuel efficient car.** One of the most important steps you can take to use less fuel—and therefore emit fewer greenhouse gases—is to buy a fuel-efficient car. Purchase cars that get around 40 MPG. Keep in mind that heavier cars use up to 50 percent more fuel than lighter models—so don't buy a bigger car than you need.

  In general, before buying a new car, know its mileage rating. Ask your dealer for a copy of the current *Gas Mileage Guide* or write to *Gas Mileage Guide*, Pueblo, CO 81009. For further information on fuel efficiency and cars, consult your local library and ask for the periodical, *Consumer Reports*. The April edition traditionally focuses on automobiles. To order, contact the Consumers Union of the United States, Inc., 256 Washington Street, Mt. Vernon, NY 10553; (914) 667–9400.

- **Avoid buying optional equipment.** Convenience options such as power steering and air conditioning decrease fuel economy in two ways: by adding weight to the vehicle and by consuming power in operation.

- **Properly maintain your vehicle;** get it tuned up every five to ten thousand miles or every six months, whichever comes first. Vehicles that are properly maintained get better mileage than those that aren't. According to the EPA, the average car experiences a 5–8 percent fuel economy improvement after a tune-up.

- **Calculate your own gas mileage.** It's relatively simple to figure your gas mileage accurately. Write down the odometer reading to the nearest mile whenever you fill up the gas tank. At your next fill-up, note carefully the number of gallons purchased and the number of miles travelled. If you have traveled 300 miles and required ten gallons, your MPG is 30.

- **Make sure your brakes are properly adjusted.** Dragging brakes can rob a car of fuel efficiency. Keeping your brakes properly adjusted will save fuel and could help save your life.

- **Use unleaded gas and a quality multigrade oil.** Recent surveys indicate that approximately 14 percent of the drivers in this country use leaded gas in vehicles requiring unleaded gas.

In the United States, thirty-three million gallons of gasoline would be saved each day and car air pollution would be significantly reduced if the average commuter passenger load were increased by one person.

This fuel switching adds significantly to automotive emissions—including hydrocarbons, nitrous oxides, and lead. High levels of these materials not only contribute to the greenhouse crisis and acid rain, but also to brain diseases, colic, palsy, and anemia. Don't switch fuel. Use unleaded gas. Additionally, a quality multi grade oil (such as 10W–30 or 10W–40) helps to reduce engine friction and to increase fuel efficiency.

- **Use radial tires and check tire pressure regularly.** Radial tires generally improve fuel economy by 4 percent as compared to nonradial tires made by the same manufacturer.

    For long trips with heavy, vacation-type loads, or simply for optimal gas mileage, inflate your tires three to four pounds above the recommended pressure. Do not, however, exceed 32 PSI. When they're properly inflated, tires can save up to 10 percent on gas.

- **If your car is going to idle for more than sixty seconds, save gas by turning your engine off.** EPA tests have shown that energy can be saved if engines are turned off rather than left idling for over sixty seconds. On the average, an engine will use about a gallon of gas for every one to two hours it idles. So on short stops, remember the rule; over sixty seconds turn it off, under sixty seconds let it run.

- **Greatly reduce or eliminate the use of your air conditioner.** A major source of CFC emissions in America is car air conditioners. The installation of an auto air conditioner causes a release of 2.5 pounds of CFCs. Annual air conditioner recharges cause another pound of CFCs to be released. And an estimated ninety-five million automobile air conditioners are in use in the United States. Additionally, when in use, the air conditioner reduces fuel economy by as much as 2.5 miles per gallon.

- **Encourage your local auto service center to install and use CFC recycling equipment for auto air conditioning repair.** Relatively inexpensive machines are available that capture and recycle CFCs released during air conditioner service and repair.

- **Buy a light-colored car with tinted glass. It will need less air conditioning.** Government studies have shown that light-colored vehicles and cars with tinted glass stay cooler in hot weather and need less air conditioning.

- **Remove unnecessary articles from your car.** The lighter the car, the less fuel it burns. Each addition of 100 pounds decreases fuel economy by 1 percent.

- **Don't speed. Drive at a moderate pace.** As car speed increases, so does wind resistance—a big factor in gas mileage. So for optimum fuel economy, keep a steady pace near 50 MPH. Cruising at 70 MPH reduces fuel economy by 20–30 percent. Of course, speeding also creates a safety hazard for everyone on the road.

- **Drive smoothly; accelerate and slow down gradually.** To save fuel, slow down well in advance of traffic lights. Avoid quick stops and jackrabbit starts. If the traffic lights in your area are timed sequentially, try to drive at a constant rate of speed to avoid unnecessary stopping.

- **Plan your trips carefully. Choosing the shortest, least-congested route will save fuel.** Figure out which route will be most fuel-efficient. Try to travel during non-peak hours, using routes with the least number of stop signs and signals. Avoid urban areas whenever possible. Call

The best way to save fuel is to drive as little as possible. Take public transportation whenever possible.

AAA and ask them to map out the best route to your destination. They have studied the United States highway system and are experts at planning the most fuel-efficient routes.

- **Avoid short trips whenever possible. Walk or use a bicycle.** Short trips from a cold start result in much poorer fuel economy. One experiment done by the EPA demonstrated that such trips could result in a 100 percent decrease in fuel efficiency. Cold weather adds even more to the fuel cost because of longer warm-up time. Try making short trips by foot, bicycle, or public transportation. It's good exercise and can significantly reduce car use.

- **Try to avoid driving in cold, windy, or rainy weather and on poor road surfaces.** There's about a 1–3 percent fuel loss for each 10° F drop in the temperature. Driving into a wind also reduces mileage. Driving in the rain may reduce fuel economy by 10 percent. Poor roads can cause poor fuel economy. Broken asphalt causes a 15 percent drop in fuel efficiency at 40 MPH; gravel, a 35 percent loss; and dry sand a 45 percent decrease.

- **Try to avoid city driving.** City driving consumes twice as much fuel as highway driving. The average speed in a congested downtown area is often only 7 MPH. This results in a 57 percent loss in fuel economy.

- **Arrange or join a car pool for commuting.** In the United States, we'd save thirty-three million gallons of gasoline each day if the average commuter passenger load were increased by one person. Carpooling may be the single most significant step individuals can take to ease car use and the resulting air pollution.

  Many states have a car pool information number linked to a computer network of commuters who car pool to work in your area. Carpooling information is listed in the *Yellow Pages*. Another way to start a car pool is to post an announcement in the local paper or your place of work.

- **Use public transportation whenever you can.** The best way to save fuel is to drive as little as possible. Take public transportation whenever possible. Call your local transit authority and request bus and subway schedules. Attempt to arrange your schedule to coordinate with the bus and subway lines.

- **Don't tailgate.** Tailgating is not only dangerous, it wastes energy. Tailgating requires constant braking and accelerating, which require far more fuel than smooth driving.

- **Call ahead.** Whether shopping or going out, call ahead to the place of business. Make sure it is open and has what you want. Many trips could be avoided by this simple step.

- **Dispose of hazardous auto products safely.** Oil, gas, and auto air conditioner refrigerant should be disposed of or recycled safely.

- **Support local and federal mass transit funding.** Support local initiatives for mass transit and alternate transportation needs, including bicycle paths. More Americans traveled by mass transit in 1900 than do today. Under 5 percent of all travel is done by mass transit. Substantial increase in mass transit use and decrease in automobile use are key to reversing global environmental problems.

With the future of the planet in the balance, even more than drugs or smoking, cars are our most dangerous addiction.

- **Support restrictions on car use.** Even though it may be inconvenient, support restrictions on automobile use in your community. These may include High Occupancy Vehicle standards that require three or more persons in cars entering or leaving city areas during rush hour of a reduction of parking spaces in cities. Restrictions like these are essential if we are going to break the car habit.

Books, Articles, and Organizations

- *The Car Book*, by Jack Gillis (Harper & Row, New York, 1989).

- "Car Culture: Driving Ourselves Crazy," by Andrew Kimbrell (Outlook Section, *Washington Post*, September 3, 1989).

- "Rethinking Transportation," by Micheal Renner (Worldwatch Institute Report No. 84, June 1988, 1776 Massachusetts Avenue, NW, Washington DC, 20036, $4).

- "Steppin' Out/How to Lead a Car-Free Life," *Utne Reader* (No. 16, June/July 1986, pp. 98–108).

- **Transportation Alternatives**, PO Box 2087, New York, NY 10009.

- **International Bicycle Fund (IBF)**, 4247 135th Place, SE, Bellevue, WA 98006.

- **Institute for Transportation and Development Policy (ITDP)**, PO Box 56538, Washington, DC 20011

- **Rails-to-Trails Conservancy**, 1701 K Street, Suite 304, Washington, DC 20036.

Taking Charge of the Working Environment
by Kirk B. Smith

Though often overlooked, the office is a major participant in today's environmental crisis. In fact, from the standpoint of global ecology, today's office job has as much potential for environmental harm as the more visible destruction of strip-mining and the lumbering of virgin timber. The inefficient use of energy and other resources at the office contributes to a variety of environmental ills, from the greenhouse effect and acid rain to groundwater contamination and the solid waste glut.

Moreover, the office is now becoming a polluted environment itself, threatening its inhabitants with a frightening array of toxics, carcinogens, mutagens, and allergens. The United Nation's World Health Organization has recently stated that "there's probably more damage to human health from indoor pollution than from outdoor pollution."

From Greenhouse to Garbage

The office's use of energy, primarily through electricity and fuel oil use, is its most significant contribution to the greenhouse effect and our other urgent environmental problems. The office's consumption of manufactured goods and the disposal of trash and waste materials also adds to our environmental woes. Over the last century, the United States has undergone an economic and technological transformation whereby advertising, marketing, accounting, information management, and other office-related activities now employ more workers than farms and factories combined. The once "cushy" office job has become the nation's most common form of labor.

As the sum of office work has increased, so has the office's share of global energy resources. In 1986 alone, United States private offices consumed 641 trillion British thermal units (Btus) of electricity. This represents about 27 percent of all the electricity consumed by the American commercial sector. This dangerous trend has increased rapidly over the last decade—in 1983 the figure

> "There is an increasing realization that the cozy offices we've created may be as threatening to human health as are the outdoor environmental ills that have come to light during the past decade or so."
>
> — *Joel Makower*

was only 23 percent, and in 1979 only 21 percent. Furthermore, in 1986, United States private office heating and cooling systems burned an additional 468 trillion Btus as well.

The pollution costs of this energy use are high. Businesses and industry are responsible for almost half of all carbon dioxide (CO_2) pollution—the air pollutant most responsible for global warming. Commercial buildings (offices, stores, schools, hospitals, hotels, etc.) are the fastest growing sector of the economy in terms of energy use and CO_2 pollution.

The environmental impact of an office, however, goes far beyond that of the power generation required for heating and electricity. For example, the manufacture of paper and other products (including plastics, metals, and silicates) for office consumption requires vast quantities of water and electricity. This produces thousands of tons of toxic residues that all too often filter into lakes and streams (not to mention neighborhoods and schoolyards), wreaking ecological havoc. In addition, the production of office paper products claims untold thousands of acres of virgin timber each year in the Pacific Northwest and other regions of our nation. This contributes to the irretrievable loss of vast quantities of topsoil in other timber regions (including Maine, South Carolina, and Alaska), and fouls drinking water supplies in paper milling areas.

American throw away enough office and writing paper each year to build a wall twelve feet high stretching from Los Angeles to New York City.

Office activity also generates a vast array of solid wastes (trash), as well as sewage, toxic ambient particulates, and "electromagnetic scrim." Consider the solid-waste problem: Americans produce 300 billion pounds (or 150 million tons) of solid waste per year, more per capita than any other nation in the world. New York City alone produces 52 million pounds of trash per day, or seven pounds per person, per day. A large and rapidly growing percentage of this waste is generated by offices. Used envelopes, correspondence, copier paper, computer paper, fax paper, cardboard cartons, "styro-peanuts" used in packaging, plastic wrap, foam, plastic and paper coffee cups, soda cans and bottles, lunchtime leftovers, plastic containers of every description, spent pens, tape, glue, batteries—all of these things end up either in a landfill, or, via incineration, in a particulate haze somewhere over North America.

Many of the products consumed in the office also contain chlorofluorocarbons (CFCs). These include solvents, foam materials, packaging, air conditioning refrigerant, aerosol propellants, and fire extinguishers.

Rx for the Office Environment

By vigorously pursuing both energy conservation and recycling in the office, we can reduce the environmental toll. It is also no secret that the nation's economy could benefit substantially from energy conservation. According to a 1984 study published by the National Audubon Society, a national energy conservation plan could conceivably cut total energy use in residential and commercial buildings by thirty percent and save consumers $93 billion (in 1983 dollars) in the year 2000. If such a plan were implemented at an annualized capital investment of $47 billion, it would yield reductions in fuel bills double that ($93 billion).

Furthermore, within the next 30 years, using technologies that are either commercially available or under development, the American Council for an Energy-Efficient Economy (ACEEE) estimates that commercial sector end-use energy demand could drop by one-third, even while commercial floor area increases by one-half.

Ideally, all offices should have an energy audit conducted by either the local power utility or a private energy consultant. This is a proven money-saving—and eco-crisis addressing—process. The costs run from free to reasonable, and any cash spent will likely return via energy savings very quickly. Such audits have shown to be the best first step in assessing, planning, and implementing a full-range conservation and recycling program.

An office energy audit may point out some direct solutions to energy waste that require no equipment and overhaul to implement. For example, keeping an inactive photocopier on power-saving mode saves some 60 percent of its power requirement over the course of a work day. This saves money in reduced electric bills, wear on the machine itself, and helps cut down on the amount of CO_2 and nitrogen oxide (NO) expended to run it. The amount of time lost waiting for the copier to warm-up from the power-saver mode is insignificant when compared to the savings.

The same "greenhouse economics" applies to the personal computers and work station terminals that are so common in offices today. To save the 30–60 second warm-up time, computers are left running throughout the day, despite the fact that most terminal operators use them only one to two hours per day. Further, research shows that most office workers only need to access their terminals three to five times per day. It follows that, to save from one to five minutes of waiting time over the course of an entire workday, a desktop computer

EPA's Sick Building Headaches

Often when employees of the nation's Environmental Protection Agency (EPA) want to have a meeting they have to do it by conference call. The reason—sick building syndrome. This syndrome occurs in many office buildings when a combination of poor ventilation, overcrowding, and the presence of indoor toxics causes severe allergic-type reactions in workers. Now, because of the adverse health effects they suffer in the EPA facility, many workers have been working out of efficiency apartments or at home, and communicate to the main facility by phone.

Like many buildings constructed over the last two decades, the large EPA complex in Washington D.C. was built for energy efficiency. This unfortunately meant poor ventilation and sealed windows. The new offices were then filled with known sources of indoor pollution including furniture, particle board partitions, and rugs containing formaldehyde adhesives; copy paper and type writer fluids made with hydrocarbons; and xerox machines emitting a variety of toxics. Overcrowding also became a problems as over 5,500 workers filled the complex.

While there had been complaints about the complex for years, the problem climaxed in October 1987. New carpets were laid in one part of the EPA complex emitting a toxic odor traced to a byproduct of the rugs latex backings (phenylcyclohexane (4-PC)). Dozens of workers reported a number of respiratory and neurological problems. For over a year the workers complaints met indifference from management. Finally, after William K. Reilly became administrator in February of 1989, the EPA began to respond. Ten workers were place in nearby apartments and four others allowed to work at home.

(and its associated devices such as printers, modems, etc.) will needlessly run five, six, or more hours a day.

Office Heating and Cooling

Turning thermostats down a few degrees in the winter and up in the summer saves money on heating and cooling bills. This also cuts down on the amount of CO_2 and NO released by the boiler system or power plant during the combustion process and helps stem both acid rain and global warming.

An energy audit concentrating on the existing building or office heating and cooling system will clearly show where waste occurs—and how to address it. System modifications, called "retrofits," are usually in order. Offices gain their largest potential energy savings from so-called shell retrofits—that is, building or office-wide enhancements designed to keep heat in during the winter and out in the summer. Basic shell retrofits are not necessarily costly and often net significant energy savings.

Just as in the home, standard inside retrofits include the insulation of roofs, ceilings, basements, and walls. Some less extensive inside changes include installing and using window shades in the summer and heavy curtains in winter.

Outside modifications include the installation of storm windows and the weatherstripping of existing windows. Also useful is replacing single-glazed windows with double-glazed where possible. The use of exterior awnings and the planting of shade trees can greatly reduce summer cooling costs. Trees, as well, serve as wind breaks, helping to cut drafts in winter.

An energy audit will likely further recommend retrofits to both office- and building-wide heating and cooling systems. One of the biggest drains on power in the office is lighting, accounting for an average of one-third of the total electricity used in offices.

Fluorescent lighting has been shown to be the most efficient. By upgrading existing fluorescent set-ups, companies can save 60–80 percent on lighting costs. The key here is to get away from so called "grid lighting" where whole floors of office buildings are litup at the same time. "Task lighting" is the goal. Each office work station should have its own lighting switches and controls and use all available lighting sources optimally. To this end, a variety of new lighting controls have been developed recently. These range from daylighting and occupancy sensors to small-scale computer timing devices suitable for small offices.

The United Nation's World Health Organization has recently stated that "there's probably more damage to human health from indoor pollution than from outdoor pollution."

The cost of fixtures and installation involved in office lighting retrofits is often repaid within a year or two from reduced utility bills. Decreasing light energy consumption also lowers heat gains, which in turn cuts cooling needs.

You ought to install such energy conservation measures, not only for the environmental benefits, but for other reasons as well. First, saving energy saves money. Office conservation measures that pay for themselves within a few years can cut operation costs significantly—without cutting productivity. The dollar savings are extensively documented. In a Buildings Energy Performance Standards (BEPS) project conducted by the ACEEE, twenty-two buildings, ranging from a 3,800 square foot one story branch bank to a 637,000 square feet twenty-nine story office tower, were redesigned, and the energy-efficiency improvements were analyzed. Half of the sample were buildings with 50,000 square feet or less located in a wide range of climates. Redesign produced energy savings in excess of 40 percent, with an estimated 3.5 percent increase in the cost of construction. Similar gains were recorded in studies of retrofitted buildings.

Office Solid Waste

Commercial buildings (offices, stores, schools, hospitals, hotels, etc.) are the fastest growing sector of the economy in terms of energy use and CO_2 pollution.

Recycling is the single best way to fight the solid-waste problem—especially in the office. A successful office recycling plan will help the environment and also save—perhaps even make—money. The first step in implementing any office recycling plan is setting up separate receptacles for paper, plastics, glass, aluminum, and hazardous materials. Start by providing conveniently located collection stations for soda cans, bottles, and so on, and have wastebaskets set aside for copy and computer paper only.

It is worth noting that recycling is not only environmentally sound, energy efficient, and cost effective, but it is also legally binding in a growing number of states and communities. In the last several years, recycling laws affecting offices have passed in a number of states. For example, Rhode Island's Recycling Act of June 1986, the first mandatory source separation law passed in the country, mandates source separation of aluminum, glass, and metal food and beverage containers, newspaper, white goods, and plastic soda bottles and milk jugs from solid waste brought to state-owned disposal facilities. The law calls specifically for a commercial waste-recycling program, requiring businesses to separate corrugated cardboard, office paper, glass food and beverage containers, tin cans, aluminum, and newspapers from their solid-waste stream. Any generator of commercial solid waste with more than 100 employees must submit a source reduction and recycling plan.

Also, New Jersey passed the Mandatory Statewide Source Separation and Recycling Act in April 1987, which includes a 50 percent State Corporate Business Tax credit to industries purchasing new recycling equipment. The New York State Solid Waste Management Act of 1988 expands the existing state office paper recycling program to include all state facilities and public authorities and establishes a commercial and industrial audit program to help businesses identify and evaluate the potential to reduce, reuse, or recycle wastes. The act also provides $3 million in grants and low-interest loans for businesses to adopt new recycling technologies. And, according to the Maryland Energy Office, recycled paper accounts for between 42 and 47 percent of the state's paper procurement. The Maryland Recycling Act of 1988 requires the development of a plan to increase the state purchase of recycled materials. Similar laws on the books in Connecticut, Massachusetts, Florida, Pennsylvania, and Illinois cover office paper.

Americans produce 300 billion pounds (or 150 million tons) of solid waste per year, more per capita than any other nation in the world.

White Collar Pollution

A prerequisite to an environmentally oriented production system is a safe and environmentally sensitive workplace. As we retool our industries to respond to the growing environmental crisis, we must also ensure that workers are protected from environmental hazards at the workplace. For years, it has been known that, because of toxic chemicals in the workplace, certain factory and blue collar occupations carry higher risks of cancer.

Now the office has become the primary workplace for many Americans. We are becoming a predominantly white collar labor force. An estimated 50 percent of Americans have information-related jobs. Futurists regularly predict that 90 percent of American workers will have white collar jobs by the next century.

Just as with the factories and mines of the past, the office is becoming an increasingly toxic workplace. Air and toxic pollution at the office is becoming a major environmental and human health concern. Here is a list of a few of the worst pollutants in the office and how they affect workers and the environment:

Asbestos.   This may be the most potent killer in the office. Dr. Samuel Epstein, in his book *Politics of Cancer*, estimates that asbestos is responsible for 50 thousand cancer deaths per year—mostly cancer of the lungs, esophagus, stomach, colon, and rectum. The Environmental Protection Agency has not determined any "safe" level for exposure to this toxin. Approximately 50 percent of office buildings constructed between 1958 and 1970 used asbestos fibers, mostly for fireproofing and insulation. As the buildings age and are repaired, asbestos can be released. Asbestos is also a significant air and water pollutant.

Benzene. This toxic chemical is present in photography supplies, spot removers, and a variety of solvents and plastics. Benzene is a skin irritant and a carcinogen and can destroy the bone marrow's ability to produce blood cells. Offices should avoid buying products with this chemical.

Carbon Monoxide. This odorless, colorless gas starves the body and brain of oxygen. Symptoms include headache, dizziness, disorientation, and in extreme cases convulsions, coma, and even death. In offices, the biggest source of this gas is automobile exhaust sucked into buildings from ventilation systems.

Fiberglass. A common construction and insulation material, fiberglass particles can cause significant skin irritation, scratchy throat, severe rashes, and even become lodged in the lungs. In offices where these symptoms are common, potential fiberglass contamination should be investigated.

Formaldehyde. Also known as formalin, formal, and methyl aldehyde, formaldehyde is a known carcinogen, especially of the nose and throat. It also causes mucous membrane irritation, respiratory ailments, nausea, and dizziness. Formaldehyde is often used as a resin in adhesives for making plywood and particle board. This toxin is released as building materials deteriorate. It has already been demonstrated to create substantial symptoms in office workers. Offices should avoid buying insulation or wood products with formaldehyde.

Nitropyrenes. These are crystals that may be contained in Xerox brand or other photocopier toners. Though all the results are not in, they could be carcinogenic and mutagenic. When working with toner, use rubber gloves and protective clothing. Additionally, make sure your photocopier is in a ventilated area.

Trichloroethane. This solvent has been associated with liver cancer and a large number of gastrointestinal, heart, and liver problems. It has many industrial, medical, and home applications, ranging from cleaning machinery to decaffeinating coffee. It may be present in a variety of office products including typewriter and stencil cleaners and typewriter correction fluid.

Trinitrofluorenone (TNF). Also used in photocopiers, this chemical has been the center of some controversy between IBM, which asserts it is safe, and the EPA and others, who suspect it may cause cancer.

A successful office recycling plan will help the environment and also save—perhaps even make—money.

Tips

By upgrading existing fluorescent set-ups, companies can save 60–80 percent on lighting costs.

- **Encourage your company or office-building owner to get an energy audit** and implement all conservation measures recommended. Bigger companies are likely to have their own energy management department. Smaller companies can get an energy audit from the local utility or from a private company. Most businesses have not made saving energy a priority in recent years. This is surprising since audits not only reduce energy use but also substantially lower energy bills. Urge your company not to limit itself to implementing "quick payback" measures. Conservation measures with a payback of two to ten years are still a good investment—for the company and for the environment.

  A good office energy audit includes: (1) an assessment of current energy and water use, including how much electricity, heat, and water the office consumes and wastes; (2) an estimate of the actual costs of the energy consumed in the office; (3) and an estimate of the amount of energy wasted. Note: the following is a checklist of items that an energy auditor should be able to discuss with you.

- **Building Retrofits:** replace boiler burner and controls; Replace boiler/furnace; install vent damper; install stack heat reclaimer; replace electric resistance heater with heat pumps; install boiler turbolator; install setback thermostats; install enthalpy control; replace room air conditioning units; replace central air conditioning units; vary chilled water temperature; convert terminal reheat to variable air volume; reduce ventilation volume; install evaporative cooling system; replace air-cooled condenser with water-cooled; install fog cooling (evaporator coil spray); insulate ducts; insulate pipes; install two-speed fan motors; install adjustable radiator vents; reduce orifice size on furnace/boiler; install multifuel boiler; use condenser coil spray; install chiller bypass system.

- **And to save on water heating:** install summer domestic hot water boiler; install solar water heater for handwashing, etc.; provide flow control devices; insulate hot water storage; provide vent damper on heater; install hot water heat pump; reclaim refrigeration heat for hot water.

- **Develop a short-term plan for energy savings.** This may include such steps as installing flow restrictors on faucets, minor tune-ups to the heating and hot water system, insulating walls, and installing window curtains.

- **Plan and estimate costs for long-term solutions to energy waste.** Such plans may include major upgrades to the office cooling and heating plants and long-term retrofits of office and building interiors and exteriors.

- **Recommend that your company minimize its direct and indirect use of CFC–11, CFC–12, CFC–113, and halons.** Businesses and industries use these ozone depleting chemicals in solvents, foam materials, air conditioning equipment, aerosol propellants, and fire extinguishers. Many alternatives to the ozone-depleting CFCs are readily available, as are recycling systems. For example, recycling of CFC-based solvents is feasible, and new non-CFC solvents are available as are alternatives to CFC-based foam and aerosol propellants. Urge your company to recycle CFCs and to switch chemicals or processes.

- **Recommend that your company install more energy-efficient lighting.** A wide range of energy-saving lighting technologies have become available in recent years. Most companies have barely begun to take advantage of the cost-effective opportunities to reduce lighting electricity use. Some possibilities: maximize use of daylight, especially in fall and spring; install natural lighting control sensors; replace grid lighting with task lighting—overhead lights that cannot be turned off individually when not in use are a senseless waste; replace incandescent lamps with high-efficiency fluorescent lamps, or switch to high-efficiency incandescent bulbs; install more efficient lamp ballasts; install lighting control systems.

- **Start a comprehensive recycling program at your office.** Whether your an office of two or two hundred, start recycling. Paper, newspaper, aluminum, glass, and copier supplies should all be recycled.

- **Try to reduce office paper use and buy recycled office paper.**

- **Avoid using plastic or styrofoam cups.** Use ceramic mugs instead.

- **Organize an office-wide meeting to discuss the environmental crisis and how office energy savings and recycling can help.**

- **Set up an employee counseling system to educate and encourage everyone in the office to conserve energy and recycle at home.** Organize office-wide meetings to discuss energy and heating oil conservation at home, home recycling, household chemical hazards, etc.

- **If you suspect asbestos contamination in your office or office building, immediately contact local and state environmental departments.**

- **Offices should avoid buying products with the carcinogen Benzene.**

- **Investigate the possibility of carbon monoxide poisoning in your office.** Symptoms include headache, dizziness, disorientation, and in extreme cases convulsions, coma, and even death.

- **Offices should avoid buying insulation or wood products with formaldehyde.**

- **Avoid contact with Nitropyrenes.** They could be carcinogenic and mutagenic. If you must work with toner, use rubber gloves and protective clothing.

- **Avoid contact with Trichloroethane.** This solvent has been associated with liver cancer. It may be present in a variety of office products including typewriter and stencil cleaners and typewriter correction fluid.

- **Avoid contact with Trinitrofluorenone**, ad with other photocopier hazards. Always use photocopiers in a well ventilated area, avoid contact with toners, and have the machines maintained.

- **Consider job related stress when assessing office environmental conditions.** The major areas of concern are: (1) unnecessary noise from office equipment and machinery and (2) poorly designed office lighting. The first rule is to match lighting to the type of work. See to it that each office worker has adequate lighting.

Just as with the factories and mines of the past, the office is becoming an increasingly toxic workplace.

A Materials Policy from the Ground Up
by David Morris

*"No, not **New York's** garbage."*
> — An Arkansas official, when asked to
> consider accepting shipments of garbage
> from New York City.

Our extravagantly wasteful use of materials threatens the planet. Americans consume, on average, twice the quantity of fuels and industrial materials as the Japanese or Western Europeans, and ten to one hundred times as much as Third World nations. As a result, with less than 5 percent of the world's population, we generate 25 percent of its pollutants and more than 30 percent of its garbage. If other nations adopted our habits, the planet would quickly become uninhabitable.

To become a good citizens of the planet, we Americans must dramatically reduce our consumption of energy and virgin materials. That means, in part, using materials more efficiently and recycling them whenever possible.

By a happy coincidence, materials management is in large part a local concern. Cities and states regulate human, solid, and hazardous wastes. This localization of authority permits citizens an unusual opportunity to monitor and strengthen the enforcement of those regulations, and in doing so, to shape our environmental and economic future.

The garbage crisis arose in the late 1970s, when we discovered our so-called sanitary landfills leaking poisons into underground drinking water. During the next ten years, half of all garbage dumps were closed. Disposal costs soared. In response, desperate policymakers rushed to embrace an old waste-management technology—incineration. It seemed a convenient solution. No personal habits had to be changed and existing collection technologies could be used. Perhaps, most importantly, manufacturing processes and product design could remain untouched.

"Use it up, wear it out, make it do, or do without."
> — *New England Proverb*

However, citizens are increasingly opposing incinerators, citing concerns about mercury, lead, and dioxin pollution from the stacks and heavy metal pollution of the groundwater from incinerator ash. As the crisis of planetary pollution emerges, the incinerator is being criticized not just for the direct pollution that emerges from the plant itself, but also for the indirect pollution the existence of such a plant encourages. By destroying various materials, incinerators force us to excavate more materials.

Another strategy was to export our wastes. By the late 1980s, the single largest export from major United States ports was wastepaper. New Jersey exported its garbage to Ohio. When Long Island, New York, tried to export its garbage to Africa and the Caribbean, the seven thousand mile odyssey of its garbage barge attracted international attention.

Recently, developing nations have begun to prohibit unauthorized garbage imports. Nigeria forced Italy to recover wastes dumped in that country and return them to Italy. Mexico threatened to torpedo Long Island's wandering garbage barge if it came any closer to its shores.

The waste generated each year in the United States would fill a convoy of ten-ton garbage trucks 145,000 miles long—over half way from here to the moon.

While the attempt to burn or export our used materials galvanizes grass roots opposition around the world, recycling is increasingly being appreciated as an important response to the growing disposal crisis. Recycling a ton of steel prevents the release of two hundred pounds of air pollutants, a hundred pounds of water pollutants, almost three tons of mining waste, and about twenty-five tons of water. One ton of remelted aluminum eliminates the need for four tons of bauxite and almost a ton of petroleum coke and pitch. These savings multiply with each re-use. Refillable milk bottles are re-used on an average fifty to a hundred times. Newspaper can be recycled five to ten times before it must be composted.

In hundreds of communities across the globe, the struggles between those promoting materials destruction and those favoring materials recovery continue. Yet the trends are unmistakable. In 1987, for the first time, the number of incinerator proposals rejected in the United States exceeded the number accepted. Whereas in 1985 policymakers assumed they could recycle only 10 percent of their waste stream, by 1990 cities and states had already achieved 40 percent recycling and many had raised their objectives to 60 percent or more.

Environmental concerns are spurring us to accept responsibility for our own wastes. But the economic opportunities that arise from accepting that responsibility constitute an important and not fully understood argument for recycling.

Urban areas are a treasure trove of used materials. As environmental regulations raise the cost of pollution, the value of used materials rises, and most of that value potentially lies within our community. Cities can now view themselves as mines and forests. San Francisco, for example, disposes of more paper than can be extracted from a good-sized commercial timber stand, more aluminum than from a small-sized bauxite deposit, more copper than from a medium-sized copper mine.

Recovering these materials is economically efficient. A ton of wastepaper sells for about $25, the price of wood pulp is about $600 a ton, and the price of printing and writing paper is about $1000 a ton.

City economic development departments now find common cause with sanitation departments. Sanitation departments strive to guarantee a reliable supply of quality used-materials to processors. Economic developers attract scrap-based manufacturers and encourage existing firms to change their internal processes to allow for higher proportions of scrap.

To guarantee a reliable supply of materials, hundreds of communities have made recycling mandatory. Manufacturers have responded by developing production technologies capable of handling large quantities of scrap. In the 1970s, glass mills used 10 to 20 percent collet or scrap in the melt. By 1989, 60 percent was not unusual. At least one glass mill has operated on 100 percent scrap. There are 100 percent newsprint-to-newsprint mills and 100 percent scrap-based steel mills.

Manufacturers can be convinced to use scrap materials if they know there is a market for their final products. Thus, to promote that market, governments have developed, and must continue to develop, government procurement standards that require high proportions of scrap when buying products—from rubber mats to paper.

As ecologists remind us, everything is connected to everything else. What begins as a simple recycling effort soon branches out into many parts of the economy. To facilitate recycling, communities have become involved in product design. Denmark, for example, requires soda bottles to be refillable and also requires uniform bottle sizes to facilitate recovery. Saint Paul and Minneapolis banned squeezable ketchup bottles because their numerous plastic resins make the jars almost impossible to recycle. Communities that require yard-waste composting soon develop closer links to surrounding farmers. They quickly discover the advantages of combining yard waste with human waste. The nitrogen from sludge and the carbon from organic wastes make the combination an excellent soil builder and fertilizer. Once again environmental regulations determine the value of the end-product.

"Sexy" Composting

The Connecticut town of Fairfield was in trouble. In 1988, the state ordered the town's overfilled landfill closed. Fairfield was in danger of drowning in its own garbage, including 4,000 tons of sludge a year.

While the town could find a place for much of its garbage, no one would take the sludge. Since neighborhood incineration was viewed as politically unfeasible, the town was stuck.

Enter the simple miracle of composting. Using up-to-date composting technology, Fairfield turned its problem into an opportunity. The town bought a composting system designed to turn sewage sludge into a usable product—compost. The compost center, consisting of six troughs each about 70 yards long, mixes the sludge with leaves, grass, and branches. And in about 20 days out comes clean, odor free compost. Fairfield is the first town in New England to institute composting on this massive a scale.

The town has plans to use the compost to cap its eighteen acre landfill, transforming the fill into a recreational park. At the dedication of the composting center, a citizen of Fairfield was heard to comment, "Composting may not be sexy, but its getting sexier by the minute."

Every Sunday, more than 500,000 trees are used to produce the 88% of newspapers that are never recycled.

As communities ban the introduction of heavy metals into the sewage system, the sludge becomes much more useful. Estimates of the quantity of fertilizer available from municipal compost varies greatly. On a national basis, it can displace only a modest amount of conventional fertilizer, but in densely populated states, it could displace the majority of agricultural fertilizers, which themselves have become a significant pollution problem.

We can never completely close the materials loop, though we should note that scrap-based manufacturing processes require 25 to 95 percent less energy than virgin-based processes. Recycling also loses materials and requires some new energy at every cycle. However, with recycling, we can dramatically reduce the amount of materials we consume. And in doing so, we may create a locally based, environmentally sensitive industrial sector.

The garbage crisis, and our reaction to it, reflects a healthy relationship between politics and economics. Before 1980, we valued convenience and the throwaway society and ignored the mounting solid waste problem. In the 1990s, we have adopted new values and in doing so have changed the economic rules governing our use of materials. That this has been done community-by-community in nation after nation reflects the democratic nature of this decision-making process. The new rules reward those technologies and techniques that promote a clean planet.

Through the actions of millions of people worldwide, we have changed the rules of the marketplace. And in so doing, we have sparked a fever of entrepreneurialism. Waste management is already the fastest growing industry in the world. By designing new rules that reflect dearly held values, we are channeling human ingenuity in a new direction. The end result may be not only a cleaner planet but also a new economic structure. As one sage observer recently mused, "We ain't just talking garbage here."

Tips

- **Start separating recyclable waste into appropriate categories.** Separate your waste material into six basic groups: newspaper, other paper, glass, aluminum, organic wastes, and plastics.

- **Contact local recycling centers.** You can find out about recycling programs in your community by calling the state recycling numbers below.

  For further information about recycling, please refer to: *Coming Full Circle: Successful Recycling Today*, **Environmental Defense Fund**, 257 Park Avenue South, New York, NY 10011; (212) 505–2100. **The Institute for Local Self-Reliance**, 2425 18th Street, NW, Washington, DC 20009; (202) 232–4108. **Reynolds Aluminum Recycling Co.**; (800) 228–2525. Reynolds' toll free number will put you in touch with information on aluminum recycling in general as well as where you can find an aluminum recycling center in your area. **Alcoa Recycling Co., Inc.**, 1501 Alcoa Building, Pittsburgh, PA 15219; (412) 553–4645. Alcoa can guide you to a recycling contact in your area and provide information as to how to go about beginning an aluminum or complete recycling program. **Conservatree Paper Company**, 10 Lombard Street, Suite 250, San Francisco, CA 94111; (415) 433–1000. Conservatree offers recycled paper for every office and personal use. Its catalog features office letterhead, computer paper, and copy paper, as well as stationery, and other paper products. **Earth Care Paper, Inc.**, PO Box 3335, Madison, WI 53704; (608) 256–5522. Earth Care's catalog contains recycled wrapping paper, stationery, and paper for office use, as well as biodegradable cellulose food storage bags. Educational material on recycling and the environment may also be ordered through this catalog.

- **Contact local officials and urge them to begin roadside pick-up of separated recyclable waste and household toxic materials.** If a pick-up service is not yet available in your community, pressure local officials to establish one. The easier it is for people to recycle, the greater the participation.

    Hazardous products, including paints, solvents, furniture polishes, pesticides, and oven cleaners should be separated from other wastes; they can cause serious pollution problems if they aren't disposed of safely and responsibly (see chapter 2).

- **Recycle all household goods, not just the obvious items.** You can recycle and reuse many materials, from plastic containers to virtually all metals, motor oil to clothing, even appliances like refrigerators and air conditioners. Your local recycling center can provide further information.

    There are several resources to turn to in order to find out how and where to recycle plastic. **Council for Solid Waste Solutions**, 1275 K Street, NW, Washington, DC 20005; (202) 371–5319. This organization can provide complete information on both the recycling aspects of plastic as well as general information on biodegradability and aspects of solid waste disposal. **National Association for Plastic Container Recycling**, PO Box 7784, Charlotte, NC 28241; (704) 357–3250. Information on how to recycle plastic and how to set up a plastic recycling program is available by writing or calling this group. **Webster Industries**, PO Box 3119, 58 Pulaski Street, Peabody, MA 01960; (508) 532–2000. Webster Industries manufactures a garbage bag of recycled and biodegradable plastic with the brand name **Good Sense**.

- **Encourage family, friends, colleagues, neighbors, and local organizations to recycle and to sponsor recycling efforts.** Recycling drives are an excellent source of income for local organizations. Collecting paper and aluminum cans can support everything from the local high school band to youth service organizations. Look in the *Yellow Pages* under "Recycling" to find recycling centers.

- **Insist that local fast food chains stop current packaging procedures and instead opt for environmentally sound, recyclable packaging.** Packaging accounts for 13 percent of food costs and 50 percent of waste disposal costs. Sensibly packaged products are those with less packaging, and should always use recyclable packaging material. Paper, aluminum, and glass are all recyclable packaging materials—plastic and foam are not.

Recycling one aluminum can saves an amount of energy equivalent to half that can full of gasoline.

- **Organize local community letter-writing campaigns to convince retailers to use recyclable packaging.**

    Additionally, up to twenty tons of waste are generated in the extraction, processing, and transportation of final products that end up as one ton of garbage generated at the household level. More than half the energy in the country is used to mine, process, and transport materials.

State recycling phone numbers

Alabama: 205-271-7700
Alaska: 907-465-2666
Arizona: 602-255-3303
Arkansas: 501-562-7444
California: 916-323-3508
Colorado: 303-320-8333
Connecticut: 203-566-8895
Delaware: 302-736-5742
District of Columbia: 202-767-8512
Florida: 904-488-0300
Georgia: 404-656-3898
Idaho: 208-334-2789
Illinois: 217-782-6761
Indiana: 317-232-8883
Iowa: 515-281-3426
Kansas: 913-296-1500
Kentucky: 502-564-6716

Louisiana: 504-342-1216
Maine: 207-289-2111
Maryland: 301-974-3291
Massachusetts: 617-292-5962
Michigan: 517-373-0540
Minnesota: 612-296-8439
Minnesota: 612-536-0816
Mississippi: 601-961-5171
Missouri: 314-751-3176
Montana: 406-444-2821
Nebraska: 402-471-4210
Nevada: 702-885-4420
New Hampshire: 603-224-6996
New Jersey: 201-648-19789
New Mexico: 505-827-2780
New York : 518-457-7336
North Carolina: 919-733-7015

North Dakota: 701-224-2366
Ohio: 614-265-6353 or 614-644-2917
Oklahoma: 405-271-7519
Oregon: 503-229-5826
Pennsylvania: 717-787-7382
South Dakota: 605-773-3153
Tennessee: 615-741-3424
Texas: 512-458-7271
Utah: 801-538-6170
Vermont: 802-244-8702
Virginia: 804-786-8679
Washington, DC: 202-939-7116
West Virginia: 304-348-3370
Wisconsin: 608-267-7565
Wyoming: 307-777-7752

State Recycling Hotlines

Alabama 1-800-392-1924
California 1-800-RECYCAL
Colorado 1-800-438-8800
Delaware 1-800-CASHCAN
Maryland 1-800-345-BIRP
Minnesota 1-800-592-9528
New Jersey 1-800-492-4242

Ohio 1-800-282-6040
Rhode Island 1-800-RICLEAN
Tennessee 1-800-342-4038
Texas 1-800-CLEANTX
Virginia 1-800-KEEPITT
Washington 1-800-RECYCLE

Source:
Coming Full Circle,
Environmental Defense Fund, 1988

Section Two/Chapter 7

Choose to Eat Low on the Food Chain
by Frances Moore Lappé

What we put into our mouths is our most direct, daily link to the earth. That much is obvious. What many still do not know is that *which* foods we choose can make that link either wasteful and destructive or efficient and life-enhancing.

In 1971, I made a very simple discovery that changed my life. The experts were telling us that famine was inevitable because people were stretching the limits of the earth's food-producing capacities. Yet I learned that my own country's food system had become a giant protein-disposal machine. Half of our harvested acreage was and is funneled into the production of livestock. It takes sixteen pounds of cattle feed to turn out just one pound of meat.

Besides, nutritionists tell us that we don't even need to eat meat to be healthy. Human metabolic systems evolved on largely plant-centered diets. Eating the meat-centered diet of the late twentieth century, Americans typically ingest more than twice the protein their bodies can use.

That discovery was almost twenty years ago. I wanted to shout to the world that there is enough food for all of us. In grain alone there is enough food produced to provide roughly 3,500 calories daily for every man, woman, and child alive. I wrote a one-page handout, which became *Diet for a Small Planet*, to explain to the world that the problem of hunger is less about nature's limits than about human habits. In a world in which the gap between rich and poor continues to widen—both within and among most countries—each year about one billion people go without adequate food. This scarcity could be labeled "scarcity of democracy," because the majority of people in the world lack power to claim the land or jobs they need to grow or buy food.

Because the roots of hunger have not been addressed on a global scale, the misery of hunger is spreading. A single world food system has emerged in the post-war era. It includes far more than the original monoculture luxury crops (like coffee and cocoa) of the colonial era. In today's global food trade, the

"Forty thousand children starve to death on this planet every day."
— *Institute for Food and Development Policy*

Relative safety of common food additives

Avoid the following:

Orange B (hot dogs)—causes cancer in animals.

Red #40 (soda, candy)—causes cancer in mice.

Red #3 (cherries, candy)—may cause cancer.

BHT (in some cereals, potato chips)—may cause cancer.

Saccharin (soda, diet foods, toothpaste)—causes cancer in animals.

Sodium nitrite (bacon, ham, luncheon meats)—can be chemically transformed into cancer-causing nitrosamines, especially in fried bacon.

Use with caution:

Artificial flavoring (soda, candy, gum, breakfast cereals)—may cause hyperactivity in children and some adults.

BHA (cereals, potato chips)—needs testing.

EDTA—may leach minerals from the body.

Gums (ice cream, beverages)—poorly tested, probably safe.

Monosodium glutamate (soups, sauces, some Chinese food, Italian sauces)—damages brain cells in mice; causes headache and burning in head, neck, and arms in some people.

Propyl gallate (soups)—poorly tested.

American "steak religion" is now promoted worldwide. Thus, in many Third World countries, landowners devote more and more of their agricultural resources to grain-fed livestock production. In 1971, approximately one-third of the world's grain was grown to feed livestock; currently the proportion is over 40 percent.

Ironically, the fastest growing demand for grain-fed meat is not in the industrial countries but in the Third World, where the total percentage of hungry people is growing. There, on average, demand for feed-grain to produce meat for the wealthy is growing twice as fast as demand for the grain that poorer people eat directly. Traditional, mixed agricultural systems—growing food for local consumption—are giving way to new monocultures of livestock feed in countries ranging from Mexico to Thailand. Yet the consumption of animal foods by the poor, worldwide, is in decline.

Grain-fed meat production has become a symbol and symptom of the irrational destructiveness of the contemporary market-economy food system. On one level, grain-fed meat is the food equivalent of the Cadillac, the most expensive and inefficient way to get from here to there. On another level, consumption of grain-fed meat is an inevitable result of putting the laws of the marketplace and unlimited property accumulation above all other values.

Farmers are forced to run on the treadmill of ceaseless competition, to eke every possible bushel of grain from the land without considering long-term consequences such as topsoil erosion and groundwater depletion. The more they grow, the cheaper the grain; and as real prices fall per acre of production, farmers must plant ever more acreage just to end up with the same income. When the grain is so cheap, it makes economic sense in the short term to feed it to livestock. The result is "factory farming" of livestock, where cattle, hogs, and chickens are subjected to unnatural and cruel conditions.

Actually, when all the hidden costs are counted, grain used for feed is not cheap at all. For example, the production of just one pound of steak requires as much water as a typical household uses in a whole month. Including grain production for feed, livestock production accounts for one-half of all water consumed in the United States. The energy costs are also enormous: to produce a one-pound steak that provides approximately 500 food calories requires the expenditure of 20,000 calories of fossil fuel energy. Furthermore, feedlot wastes are a significant source of water pollution.

The most difficult part of my effort to communicate what I have learned about diet and hunger is that most Americans assume that we have so much and they, "over there," have so little. It seems obvious that our task is to share more—to send our surplus grain abroad to end hunger. In reality, however, our "surplus" is in part the result of forced overproduction that is destroying our agricultural land. Moreover, virtually *all* countries have the capacity to meet basic food needs using their own resources. Thus the key to helping the Third World (including China and the USSR) is for us to stop impoverishing our own agricultural lands, and to encourage the powerful elites in those countries to do the same.

Unfortunately, the prevailing ideology in our country teaches us to identify our interests with those of the same elites who are preventing the necessary changes. There is, however, a contrary development that has gained momentum over the past twenty years: hundreds of citizen groups, spearheaded by Food First, are putting North Americans directly in touch with realities abroad. We now have the opportunity to begin viewing ourselves as allies, not colonial benefactors of the Third World.

Consciously linking food choices to what we learn can be liberating. In my case, I have learned that I can make real choices based on what is best for my body and for the earth. Yes, we *can* transform the world and improve our health simply by changing our diet. When we eat for health, we see that the planet's resources are truly bountiful.

Probably safe:

Alginate, Seaweed gel.
Alpha Tocopherol (vitamin E).
Ascorbic acid (vitamin C).
Beta carotene (vitamin A).
Calcium propionate, preservative.
Calcium stearoyl lactylate, dough conditioner.
Citric acid, natural flavoring.
Ferrous gluconate, iron.
Gelatin, thickener made of animal by-products.
Glycerin, natural fat.
Lactic acid, natural acidifier.
Lecithin, natural thickener.
Polysorbate 60, 65, 80, synthetic emulsifiers.
Sodium benzoate, preservative.
Potassium sorbate, natural preservative made from berries.
Vanillin, synthetic flavoring.

Adapted from *Well Body, Well Earth,* Sierra Club Books (1983).

Tips

Along with the impact of their production on the environment, fat, salt, refined sugar, and processed foods have been associated with cancer, obesity, diabetes, atherosclerosis, angina, heart attacks, strokes, kidney disease, gallstones, arthritis, high cholesterol and high blood protein levels, chronic constipation, diverticulosis, and cancer.

- **Reduce intake of fat and cholesterol.** Switch from meat and eggs to cereals and salads. If you eat meat, trim the fat, remove the skin, and do not fry. Cook with water rather than oils, and reduce your intake of milk products.

- **Reduce intake of salt.** Avoid salting food during cooking and at the table. Also avoid anchovies, bacon, bologna, corned beef, hot dogs, salted snacks (potato chips, for example), and sausage.

- **Eat less processed sugar.** Desserts, sodas, and even ketchup contain large amounts of sugar.

- **Avoid additives and processed foods.** Approximately 3,000 chemicals are added to foods during processing. Packaging and spraying are thought to be responsible for 10,000 more chemicals entering into our foods. These include familiar chemical compounds such as saccharin, cyclamates, butylated hydroxytoluere (BHT), vinyl chloride, and acrylonitrile.

The production of just one pound of steak requires as much water as a typical household uses in a whole month.

- **Read food labels carefully.** Unprocessed whole foods—oranges, for example—do not require labeling. Processed foods generally do. Ingredients are listed on labels according to weight. What there is most of comes first; what there is least of comes last. If your breakfast cereal lists sugar as its first ingredient, then that cereal contains more sugar than anything else. Reviewing ingredients is one of the best ways to know what you are buying and eating.

  Note, however, that if fat is less than 10 percent of the product, the manufacturer can list several fats that the package may (or may not) contain. For example, the label may state "oil (contains one or more of the following: soybean, partially hydrogenated corn, palm or coconut)." This leaves the consumer ignorant about whether the oil is highly saturated (palm, coconut), hydrogenated, or polyunsaturated (soy, etc.).

  If any artificial flavor or color is used, it must be listed. FD&C Yellow #5 must be mentioned specifically, because of a high incidence of allergic reaction. Other colorings do not have to be specified (even though studies suggest their safety varies widely). Because of strong lobbying, dairy products are *exempt* from the regulations on colorings. Processors may add natural or artificial coloring to cheese, ice cream, and butter without troubling the consumer with that information. Nutrition labeling is mandatory when a processor makes a nutritional or dietary claim on the label or in advertising, when a food is fortified with a nutrient, or when the food is intended for children under four (baby and junior foods). This labeling is important for people monitoring calories, fat, protein, sodium, etc.

  Perhaps the trickiest part of reading a food label is deciphering the words it contains. Some have specific definitions established by the Food and Drug Administration (FDA), but others derive their meaning solely from the creative imaginations of advertising copywriters. In several areas that consumers care about, there is confusion. For instance, the word "natural" has no legal definition; almost anything goes. "Natural" cheeses, for example, can contain artificial coloring and preservatives; "natural" ice creams are not only loaded with sugar but often include vegetable gums and mono- and diglycerides; "natural" cereals are more highly sweetened than processed ones; and foods that are "naturally flavored" may also contain artificial flavoring, preservatives, thickeners and colorants.

- **Avoid a "chemical feast."** To avoid some of the worst chemical tampering, ask two basic questions about the fruit you buy: "Is it fresh?" and "Has it been grown organically?"

- **Fight for the right to eat.** Why is this not a basic right for every citizen in our society?

- **Support legislation to discourage factory farming and the consolidation of farmland holdings.** Also, as consumers, we can use our buying power to support family-run organic farms where we live. Patronize farmers' markets and food cooperatives that distribute locally-grown foods.

Personal Investments: Casting a Vote for Social Responsibility
by Cindy Mitlo

Environmentalists have long advocated actions we can all take to help solve the environmental crisis. These include such steps as energy conservation, recycling, reduction of auto use, and reforestation. Now, we have another important strategy—investing in companies that are fighting environmental degradation.

Financial planning is always worthwhile, whatever your resources. A good plan, when followed through, can help you realize your personal dreams and goals, or can prepare you for weathering tight financial times.

But careful financial planning can also benefit society. Our money holds power—we vote with it every day when we make decisions about how to spend it. And in our economic system, money has particular power when it comes to our savings and investments.

Too often, we see our money used in destructive ways—by industries that pollute the environment and companies that treat workers and communities unfairly. Increasingly, concerned consumers are realizing that by carefully choosing where our money goes, we can express our concerns for the environment, peace, human rights, economic development, and humane workplaces.

The social investment movement is growing. Over $400 billion of securities are being invested with social criteria in mind. This figure includes the assets of institutional investors, such as universities, states and cities, and insurance companies. A much smaller amount is channeled toward companies or funds that are doing socially positive work, such as providing low income housing or researching renewable energy. For example, nearly $50 million is currently invested in local community funds.

You can make socially responsible investments whether you are an individual of modest means or of wealth, whether your plan is a simple one or a complex investment strategy. Moreover, the field of social investment in the environment offers a wide range of opportunities. This socially responsible field

Over $400 billion of securities are being invested with social criteria in mind.

is backed by extensive research, competent professionals, and innovative thinking. It also offers investment safety and return competitive with the traditional options you may be currently using. But while your money works for you, it can also work to affect corporate and public policy and to protect the environment.

There are three major socially responsible investment strategies:

(1) Divert capital AWAY FROM destructive uses by refusing to invest in businesses or institutions that violate socially responsible investment criteria. Corporations that pollute the environment, create greenhouse gases, destroy the ozone layer, create acid rain, waste energy, and contribute to the destruction of rain forests, promote nuclear energy, contribute to species extinction and germplasm loss are deleted from an investor's plan or portfolio.

Companies that are now manufacturing products from recycled materials are also responsible and potentially profitable investments.

(2) Channel capital TOWARD socially responsible purposes by investing in companies and institutions whose products, services and practices contribute to a just, healthy, and peaceful society. Using this strategy, concerned consumers build their portfolio with the securities of businesses that are environmentally sound. Waste management is one such area. Recycling, for example, makes big money for small companies and for investors. Upgrading their image from scrap dealers to recyclers, many companies are helping the environment by recycling a wide variety of materials including glass, paper, aluminum, and other metals. Companies that are now manufacturing products from recycled materials are also responsible and potentially profitable investments. Finding methods for recycling and utilizing metals, plastics, rubber, and other difficult to reuse materials is a growing industry.

Cleaning-up existing environmental hazards is the other side of recycling our waste. In large part, environmental statutes demand that private industries use state-of-the-art clean-up technologies. There are now over 200 companies currently in existence that produce such clean-up equipment.

Alternative energy companies can also be a part of positive investment. Many small companies have devoted themselves to the development of solar, geothermal, photo-voltaic, wind, and biomass power.

In all these areas, socially responsible investors can purchase stocks or bonds in individual companies or invest in mutual funds that specialize in environmental cleanup or recycling. Concerned consumers can also keep their money with banks, loan funds, and financial instruments that lend money for environmentally responsible purposes.

(3) Make small investments in companies that violate socially responsible criteria in order to influence the direction of the business. Using this strategy, investors use shareholder actions to get other stockholders to join with them. As

owners, they pressure the company's officers to change their destructive policies. Activist investors often work together—through organizations—to accomplish their objectives. For example, investors in several large oil companies have put pressure on those companies to adopt more environmentally sound procedures.

Environmentally concerned investors can choose to follow one strategy or combine them. As a concerned consumer, it helps to establish clearly the environmental criteria that reflect your values and your own personal and financial goals. Your environmental criteria and financial objectives will become your guidelines for developing a socially conscious financial plan.

Today's environmental investor has a multitude of options. You can focus on one or two areas, like alternative energy or recycling, and seek ways to reinvest your money solely for those concerns. You can set a range of environmental criteria and invest in one of the many responsible investment vehicles that diversifies your portfolio and addresses a number of environmental concerns. If you would rather manage your own plan, you can consult publications that monitor companies, environmental investment issues, and responsible financial products. If not, you can consult the growing list of certified responsible professionals to help you devise and implement your plan.

Many small companies have devoted themselves to the development of solar, geothermal, photo-voltaic, wind, and biomass power.

Investment Counseling Sources

Advest, Inc., 124 Mount Auburn Street, Cambridge, MA 02138; (800) 876–6673, (617) 876–5700 in Massachusetts.

Boettcher and Co., 828 17th Street, Denver, CO 80202; (800) 525–6482, (303) 628–8314 in Colorado.

Calvert Social Investment Fund, 1700 Pennsylvania Avenue, NW, Washington, DC 20006; (800) 368–2748.

Financial Alternatives, 1514 McGee Avenue, Berkeley, CA 94703; (415) 527–5604.

Interwest Financial Advisers, Inc., PO Box 790, Salem, OR 97308; (503) 581–6020.

PAX World Fund, 224 State Street, Portsmouth, NH 03801; (603) 431–8022.

Prescott, Ball & Turben, 230 West Monroe, 28th Floor, Chicago, IL 60606; (800) 621–6637, (312) 641–7800 in Illinois.

The Social Responsibility Investment Group, Inc., The Candler Building, Suite 622, 127 Peachtree Street, NE, Atlanta, GA 30303; (404) 577–3635.

Solid Investments, Inc., 101 West Street, Hillsdale, NJ 07642; (201) 358–1212.

United Services Fund, PO Box 29467, San Antonio, TX 78229–0467; (512) 696–1234.

Working Assets Funding Services, 230 California Street, Suite 500, San Francisco, CA 94111, (415) 989–3200. Largest socially responsible money market fund in the United States screens out companies with a history of environmental violations and does not invest in nuclear power.

Working Assets VISA, 230 California Street, San Francisco, CA 94111; (800) 52–APPLY. Each time this credit card is used, five cents is donated to environmental, peace, or human rights organizations.

Information Sources

Catalyst, 64 Main Street, Montpelier, VT 05602; (802) 223–7943.

Clean Yield Publications, Box 1880, Greensboro Bend, VT 05842; (802) 533–7178.

Co-Op America, 2100 M Street, NW, Suite 310, Washington, DC 20036; (800) 424–COOP, (202) 871–5307 in Washington, DC.

Council on Economic Priorities, 30 Irving Place, New York, NY 10003; (212) 420–1133.

The Data Center, 464 19th Street, Oakland, CA 94612; (415) 835–4692.

Envest, Energy Investment Research, Inc., 2 Greenwich, Suite 100, Greenwich, CT 06830; (914) 937–6939.

Financial Alternatives, 1514 McGee Avenue, Berkeley, CA 94703; (415) 527–5604.

Funding Exchange, 666 Broadway, 5th Floor, New York, NY 10012; (212) 529–5300.

Good Money Publications, Box 363, Worcester, VT 05682; (802) 223–3911.

Interfaith Center on Corporate Responsibility (ICCR), 475 Riverside Drive, Room 566, New York, NY 10115; (212) 870–2295.

Investor Responsibility Research Center, 1755 Massachusetts Avenue, NW, Suite 600, Washington, DC 20036; (202) 939–6500.

The National Boycott Newsletter, 6506 28th Avenue, NW, Seattle, WA 98115; (206) 523–0421.

Nukewatch, 315 West Gorham Street, Madison, WI 53703; (608) 256–4146.

Social Investment Forum/Franklin Research & Development, 711 Atlantic Avenue, 5th Floor, Boston, MA 02111; (617) 423–6655.

Strub/Dawson, Inc., 45 West 45th Street, Suite 402, New York, NY 10036; (212) 302–8802.

In Praise of Idleness
by Jay Walljasper

*It is possible that progress might be nothing
more than the development of an error.*
— Jean Cocteau

Healing the earth involves more than just flicking off a few light switches and bundling up your newspapers for recycling. Minimizing the damage that each of us inflicts on the environment is important, but we also need to take a serious look at the deeper reasons why the earth is in such dire need of healing today.

A few wasted kilowatts of electricity is not what brings us the threat of acid rain. It's the restless nature of our society—constantly building new things, tearing down old things, and seeking salvation through higher and higher technology—that incites America's ravenous demand for resources. A few too many newspapers isn't what sparked our worsening garbage crisis. It's the throw-away mentality—the notion of "out of sight, out of mind" practiced on a massive scale—that's behind the junk washing up on our beaches and the poisons leaching out of landfills. To ensure a healthy planet for our children and their children, we need to take a long, hard look at the philosophical and political underpinnings of modern life. In other words, we must break loose from the widespread belief that *bigger, faster, newer,* and *more* is always better.

The critical need for a new, more ecological lifestyle is perhaps seen most clearly in how we spend our leisure time. To begin with, most of us could stand a bit more leisure time. According to a Harris Poll, Americans now have about one-third less leisure time than they had in 1973. The increasing workaholism seen in almost all sectors of American society, and the resulting time pinch in everyone's schedules, spawns the need for all sorts of shortcuts and conveniences in our daily lives, many of which carry a high ecological price-tag.

The *New York Times,* for instance, attributes the recent rise in telephone use and sales, especially cellular and car phones, to people's attitudes "that time

"We are so trapped in this frenetic world of clocks and computers, schedules and programs, that most of us are counting the days until our next vacation."

— *Jeremy Rifkin,* Time Wars

should always be used for purposeful activity." This is the kind of thinking that propels people to shopping malls on bright Saturday afternoons rather than allowing them to enjoy the summer's warmth, the winter's snow, the spring's blossoms, or the autumn's colors. Look back on some of your more pleasurable moments over the last few months. Didn't they spring more often from some happy happenstance—a scenic spot discovered on a stroll, an old acquaintance encountered in an unexpected place—than from some programmed activity?

You may wonder how this all fits into the big job of mending our environment. What does a walk in the woods have to do with reversing global warming trends? Well, if we don't take the time to appreciate our environment, we will feel less inclined to preserve it. Hence, outdoor entertainment like camping, canoeing, cross-country skiing, backpacking, bird-watching, bicycling, mushroom hunting, snowshoeing, fishing, snorkeling, rock climbing, and—perhaps the most underrated pleasure of modern times—walking, can help us celebrate the importance of ecology in our lives.

Motorized recreation, on the other hand, distances us from nature and diminishes the aesthetic enjoyment and environmental stability of the outdoors. And if land is scarce, especially wilderness, we should not motorize it. Motorized vehicles shrink distances, whereas legs lengthen and enlarge precious wild lands. Have you ever heard a water skier rhapsodize about the beauty of a lake or an off-road vehicle driver discuss wildflowers? Before making a big investment in money and fuel by jetting or driving to some faraway garden spot, you might consider taking a closer look at your own backyard. Can you honestly say that you know intimately all the neighborhoods, parks, historical sites, hiking trails, museums, woods, and other attractions of your own town? Nearly all communities have unique charms of their own, even if they aren't sunny Caribbean islands or glamourous big cities. It's a sad commentary on modern life that so many people believe that a good time can only be had a long way from home.

Of course travel can be one of life's most inspiring and enriching experiences, especially if it's done in a spirit of exploration rather than escape. A trip to Europe or the Third World, especially, can offer an interesting perspective on how America uses its land and resources.

> "I hope the leaders of the YMCA start a campaign to induce good young men to do nothing."
>
> — *Bertrand Russell*

Tips

- **Assess the environmental impact of any recreation you undertake.** Downhill skiing, for instance, does more damage to the landscape than cross-country skiing.

- **Plan a vacation in your own town, doing all the things you never find time for otherwise.**

- **Go on a socially responsible vacation tour, and experience another culture first-hand while helping with ecological or archeological projects.** Steer clear of vacations that threaten the environment—big-game safaris, for instance, or snowmobile tours.

    Western tourists vacationing in Third World countries have a profound impact on their ecosystems and economies. As tourism in these countries has increased, rainforests and farming lands have been sacrificed to construct golf courses, and parks and hotels and resorts are built with development funds intended for economic and agricultural improvement for the country. Here are several organizations that offer trips geared toward the experience of nature and the respect for other cultures:

    Center for Responsible Tourism, 2 Kensington Road, San Anselmo, CA 94960. This organization can provide information on how tourism affects the third world, to help you with your travel plans. Membership is $10.

    Earthwatch, 680 Mount Auburn Street, PO Box 403, Watertown, MA 02172; (617) 926-8200. Earthwatch coordinates volunteer "vacations." Volunteers help with field work for universities and organizations. No training is necessary.

    Biological Journeys, 1867 Ocean Drive, McKinleyville, CA 95521; (415) 527-9622. This group offers the more serious environmentalist whale watching and other expeditions on the West Coast and Mexico.

    The Cousteau Society, 930 West 21st Street, Norfolk, VA 23517; (804) 627-1144. The Cousteau Society provides summer jobs for divers as well as those interested in studying the ecology.

    University Research Expedition Program, c/o University of California at Berkeley, Desk G-8, Berkeley, CA 94720; (415) 642-6586. Sponsors field research expeditions worldwide in areas such as archaeology, marine study, and zoology.

- **Consider wilderness schools**, including:

    Boulder Outdoor Survival School (BOSS), PO Box 905, Rexburg, ID 83440. The oldest, most challenging survival school in the country.

    Reevis Mountain School, HCO2, Box 1534, Globe, AZ 85501. Instruction in stone masonry, herb study, natural remedies, navigational skill, desert survival, and meditation.

    The Tracker School, PO Box 173, Asbury, NJ 08802. The largest wilderness survival and tracking school in the country.

    National Outdoor Leadership School, PO Box AA, Lander, WY 82520. Concentrates on minimum-impact camping and outdoor leadership skills—talents necessary to take yourself safely and comfortably into the wilderness.

    Outward Bound Schools, 384 Field Point Road, Greenwich, CT 06830. There are now thirty-five Outward Bound schools teaching wilderness skills on five continents.

- **Pitch in on local campaigns to preserve historical sites, establish pedestrian zones, and create new parks or trails.**

"Drink your tea slowly and reverently, as if this activity is the axis on which the whole earth revolves. Live the moment. Only this actual moment is life."
— *Thich Nhat Hanh*

Cruelty-Free Living
by Dr. Michael W. Fox

*I think I could turn and live with animals, they are so placid
and self contained. . . . Not one is dissatisfied, not one is de-
mented with the mania of owning things.*
— Walt Whitman

How difficult it is to find that middle way of living gently so as
to minimize harming our fellow creatures and the environment. While it is easy
to avoid buying furs of wild animals caught in traps or raised on cruel factory
fur ranches, it becomes increasingly difficult to avoid other animal products in
the things we buy and consume. This is because society has become dependent
upon animal exploitation for a multitude of purposes, processes, and products.
But as we begin to change our own consumer habits and seek a cruelty-free
life-style, this dependence may be gradually broken.

Around the home and garden, we can all avoid the use of pesticides,
detergents, and other chemicals that have been tested pointlessly on laboratory
animals and which are a hazard to one's family and animal companions, as well
as to wildlife. "Pest" problems, from fleas and cockroaches to rats and termites,
can be dealt with by more humane, integrated pest-management programs. Using
weedkiller on the lawn, hanging sticky fly paper from the ceiling, and having an
electric bug zapper on one's patio are thoughtless practices that should be
abandoned.

In most restaurants, "vegetable" soup contains chicken stock, and baked
goods contain eggs and dairy products, making the vegan way a challenge. The
film and phonograph records we buy include gelatins and other slaughterhouse
by-products, as does our bone china. Most protein-enriched shampoos and skin
creams contain animal by-products and even fetal fluids and glandular extracts
(which in Europe are injected into people, and sometimes their pets, purportedly
to rejuvenate them and alleviate chronic disease). Soap sometimes contains the
tallow not only of exhausted dairy cows and over-fattened chickens, pigs, and

"In the relations of man
with animals, with the
flowers, with the objects
of creation, there is a
great ethic, scarcely
perceived as yet, which
will at length break forth
into the light and that will
be the corollary and
compliment to human
ethics."

— *Victor Hugo*

cattle, but also of the estimated 7.5 million cats and dogs that are exterminated each year in animal shelters across the United States.

It is little wonder that pesticide residues have been found in face creams, since animal fat and almost the entire food chain, including our drinking water, is contaminated with these and other agrichemical and industrial chemicals. Lanoline-based cosmetics have been found to be contaminated with pesticides in which the rendering sheep have been dipped. The moral of these findings is that, by our wholesale misuse of pesticides, without regard for the harm caused to other creatures, we ultimately harm ourselves.

In response to my syndicated newspaper column "The Animal Doctor," I have received dozens of letters from cat owners whose pets relish licking their hair and skin after the owners have had a shampoo or applied skin cream. Clearly, they are attracted to the taste of animal remains in these products. Dogs have been sexually aroused by certain hand creams. These creams contain a chemical like the one female dogs secrete when they are in heat. Cats have gone berserk soon after their owners have put on expensive perfumes. One spry Siamese actually cornered his owner in the bathroom for four hours. These perfumes contain the musk of wild civet cats, who are kept under deplorable conditions in Ethiopia to have their anal glands curetted at intervals to collect this high-fashion secretion.

There is an American Indian teaching for the novice hunter that advises, "Kill the deer swiftly with one arrow, otherwise you will feed its fear to your family." In contemporary times, we feed more than fear to our families: aflatoxins from moldy feed mean cows' milk is contaminated with dioxins, a most potent class of carcinogens; toxic cadmium is in their livers and lead in their bone meal; pesticides and other fat-soluble poisons are concentrated in the fat of farm animals, and thus in hamburger, bacon, egg yolks, and butter. (For more details read John Robbins' *Diet for a New America*, or my own book *Agricide: The Hidden Crisis that Affects Us All*.)

The conscientious consumer, like the conscientious objector, sees that in harming the earth and fellow creatures, we harm ourselves.

Increasingly, these conscientious individuals are working together to assert their economic power, seeking and demanding products and services that have not entailed animal exploitation or destruction of the environment. This quest for a cruelty-free life-style represents a growing public concern over the fate of the earth and is a major step toward adopting a more humane ethic of planetary stewardship.

Soap sometimes contains the tallow not only of exhausted dairy cows and over-fattened chickens, pigs, and cattle, but also of the 7.5 million cats and dogs that are exterminated each year in animal shelters across the United States.

Cruelty Free Resources

For companies that practice animal testing, see specific listings in the "Current Boycotts" section in chapter 17.

Seven Steps towards Cruelty-Free Living:

(1) Buy only products that are made without harm to animals. Usually, these products have positive health and environmental effects as well.

(2) Speak up. Let your friends know about cruelty-free alternatives to products they use, and ask your local store managers to carry these products.

(3) Let companies that conduct animal testing know that you have stopped supporting them. Write letters about why you have decided to switch to other brands.

(4) Contact your representative in Congress and ask him or her to support *H.R. 1635*, the *Consumer Products State Testing Act*, which could provide protection to many animals. Your representative can be contacted at the United States House of Representatives, Washington, DC 20515; (202) 224–3121.

(5) Get your name on the National Action Phone Tree of People for the Ethical Treatment of Animals (PETA). Learn more about the cruelty-free campaign and help out with events in your area. Call a Compassion Campaign Coordinator at (202) 726–0156.

(6) Help support PETA with a tax-deductible donation. Your contribution helps PETA print flyers to make others aware of the cruelty-free cause.

(7) Call consumer hotlines to let companies know what you think about their use of animal testing. Many large companies have toll-free numbers to hear your concerns. See the "Animal Testing" boycott section of chapter 18 for a listing of companies and phone numbers.

"Whenever people say 'we mustn't be sentimental,' you can take it they are about to do something cruel. And if they add, 'we must be realistic,' they mean they are going to make money out of it."

— *Brigid Brophy*

Cruelty-Free Products Sources

Products that are not tested on animals are available at most health food stores and food cooperatives and at an increasing number of drug store chains, grocery stores, and department stores. Sometimes, however, consumers have trouble finding these products at their local stores. Here are the addresses and phone numbers of cruelty-free companies followed by a sample list of distributors that carry cruelty-free products.

Cruelty-Free Manufactures

Abracadabra, Inc., PO Box 1040, Guerneville, CA 95446; (707) 869–0761.

Most protein enriched shampoos and skin creams contain animal by-products and even fetal fluids and glandular extracts.

A. J. Funk and Co., 1471 Timber Drive, Elgin, IL 60120; (312) 741–6760.

Alexandra Avery, Northrup Creek, Clatskanie, OR 97016; (503) 755–2446.

Allens Naturally, PO Box 514, Farmington, MI 48332–0514; (313) 453–5410.

Aloegen (see Levlad, Inc.)

Alva-Amco Pharmacal Companies, Inc., 6625 Avondale Avenue, Chicago, IL 60631; (312) 792–0200.

Andalina, Tory Hill, Warner, NH 03278–0057.

Aura Cacia, PO Box 3157, Santa Rosa, CA 95402; (707) 584–5115.

Auromere, 1291 Weber Street, Pomona, CA 91768; (714) 629–8255.

Autumn-harp, Inc., 28 Rockydale Road, Bristol, VT 05443; (802) 453–4807.

Avanza Corp. (see Nature Cosmetics, Inc.)

Aveda, 321 Lincoln Street, NE, Minneapolis, MN 55413; (612) 379–8500.

Beauty without Cruelty, Ltd., 451 Queen Anne Road, Teaneck, NJ 07666; (201) 836–7820.

Biotene H–24 (see CARME).

Body Love, PO Box 7542, Santa Cruz, CA 95061; (408) 425–8218.

Borlind of Germany, PO Box 1487, New London, NH 03257; (603) 526–2076.

Carme, 84 Galli Drive, Novato, CA 94949; (415) 883–8844.

Chenti Products, Inc., 21093 Forbes Avenue, Hayward, CA 94545; (415) 785–2177.

Clientele, 5207 NW 163rd Street, Miami, FL 33014; (305) 624–6665.

Come to Your Senses, Inc., 321 Cedar Avenue South, Minneapolis, MN 55454; (612) 339–0050.

Comfort Manufacturing Co., 1056 West Van Buren Street, Chicago, IL 60607; (312) 421–8145.

Community Soap Factory, PO Box 32057, Washington, DC 20007; (202) 347–0186.

Country Comfort, 28537 Nuevo Valley Drive, PO Box 3, Nuevo, CA 92367; (714) 657–3438.

Country Roads (see CARME).

Desert Essence Cosmetics, PO Box 588, Topanga, CA 90290; (213) 455–1046.

D+P Products, Inc., PO Box 5601, 2810 E Long Street, Tampa, FL 33605–5601; (813) 248–6640.

Dr. Bronner's, PO Box 28, Escondido, CA 92025; (619) 743–2211.

Earth Science, PO Box 1925, Corona, CA 91718; (714) 630–6720.

Ecco Bella, 125 Pompton Plains Crossroads, Wayne, NJ 07470; (201) 890–7077.

Fashion Two Twenty, Inc., 1263 South Chillicothe Road, PO Box 220, Aurora, OH 44202; (216) 562–5111.

4–D Hobe Marketing Corp., 201 S McKemy, Chandler, AZ 85226; (602) 257–1950.

Fruit of the Earth, Inc., PO Box 727, Bensenville, IL 60106; (312) 766–5400.

Golden Star, Inc., 400 East 10th Avenue, PO Box 12539, North Kansas City, MO 64116; (816) 842–0233.

Gruene, Inc., 1621 West Washington Blvd., Venice, CA 90291; (213) 392–2449.

G.T. International, 1800 South Robertson Blvd., Suite 182, Los Angeles, CA 90035; (213) 551–0484.

Hawaiian Resources Co., Ltd., 1123 Kapahulu Avenue, Honolulu, HI 96816; (808) 737–8726.

Heavenly Soap, 5948 E 30th Street, Tucson, AZ 85711; (602) 790–9938.

Home Service Products Co., 230 Willow Street, Bound Brook, NJ 08805; (201) 356–8175.

Humane Alternative Products, 8 Hutchins Street, Concord, NH 03301; (603) 228–1929.

Humphreys Pharmacal, Inc., PO Box 256, 63 Meadow Road, Rutherford, NJ 07070; (201) 933–7744.

Ida Grae Products (see Nature's Colors Cosmetics).

Ilona of Hungary, Inc., 3201 East Second Avenue, Denver, CO 80206; (303) 320–5991.

Image Laboratories, Inc., PO Box 55016, Metro Station, Los Angeles, CA 90055; (213) 623–9254.

Institute of Trichology, 1619 Reed Street, Lakewood, CO 80215; (303) 232–6149.

International Rotex, Inc., PO Box 20697, Reno, NV 89515; (702) 356–8356.

Internatural, PO Box 463, South Sutton, NH 03273; (603) 927–4776.

Jason Natural Products, Inc., 8468 Warner Drive, Culver City, CA 90232–2484; (213) 838–7543.

John Paul Mitchell Systems, PO Box 10597, Beverly Hills, CA 90213–3597; (818) 407–0500.

Jojoba Farms (see Carme).

Jurlique Cosmetics, 16 Starlit Drive, Northport, NY 11768; (516) 754–3535.

Kimberly Sayer Skin Care System, 61 West 82nd Street, Suite 5A, New York, NY 10024; (212) 362–2907.

Kiss My Face Corp., PO Box 804, New Paltz, NY 12561; (914) 255–0884.

KMS Research Laboratories, Inc., 6807 Highway 299 E, Bella Vista, CA 96008; (916) 549–4472.

KSA Jojoba, 19025 Parthenia Street, Northridge, CA 91324; (818) 701–1534.

Lady Finelle Cosmetics, 137 Marston Street, PO Box 5200, Lawrence, MA 01842–2808; (617) 682–6112.

Levlad, Inc., 9183–5 Kelvin Avenue, Chatsworth, CA 91311; (818) 882–2951.

Loanda Herbal Soaps (see Carme).

Magic American Corp., 23700 Mercantile Road, Cleveland, OH 44122; (216) 464–2353.

Marie Lacoste Enterprises, Inc., 1059 Alameda de Las Pulgas, Belmont, CA 94002; (415) 361–1277.

Micro Balanced Products, 25 Alladin Avenue, Dumont, NJ 07628; (201) 387–0200.

Mild And Natural (see Carme).

Mountain Ocean, Ltd., PO Box 951, Boulder, CO 80306; (303) 444–2781.

Natural Research People, Inc., South Route, PO Box 12, Lavina, MT 59046; (406) 575–4343.

Nature Cosmetics, Inc., 881 Alma Real, Suite 101, Pacific Palisades, CA 90272; (213) 459–9816.

Nature's Colors Cosmetics, 424 Laverne Avenue, Mill Valley, CA 94941; (415) 388–6101.

Nature's Gate Herbal (see Levlad, Inc.)

New Age Creations, 219 Carl Street, San Francisco, CA 94117; (415) 564–6785.

Neway, 150 Causeway Street, Boston, MA 02114; (617) 227–5117.

Nexus Products Co., PO Box 1274, Santa Barbara, CA 93116; (805) 968–6900.

No Common Scents, King's Yard, Yellow Springs, OH 45387; (513) 767–4261.

North Country, 7888 Country Road, Suite 6, Maple Plain, MN 55359; (612) 479–3381.

Nutri-Metics International, Inc., 3530 Pine Valley Drive, Sarasota, FL 34239; (813) 924–3251.

The film and phonograph records we buy include gelatins and other slaughterhouse by-products, as does our bone china.

Optikem International, Inc., 2172 South Jason Street, Denver, CO 80223; (303) 936–1137.

Oriental Beauty Secrets (see G. T. International).

Orjene Natural Cosmetics, 5–43 48th Avenue, Long Island City, NY 11101; (718) 937–2666.

Pagrovian Research (see Pro-Life Natural).

Panache (see Marie Lacoste Enterprises, Inc.)

Patricia Allison, 4470 Monahan Road, La Mesa, CA 92041; (619) 444–4879.

Paul Penders (see D+P Products, Inc.)

Pro-Life Natural, PO Box 13, Pacific Grove, CA 93950; (408) 373–7536.

Rachel Perry, Inc., 9111 Mason Avenue, Chatsworth, CA 91311; (818) 888–5881.

Rainbow Research Corp., PO Box 153, Bohemia, NY 11716; (516) 589–5563.

Reviva Labs, 705 Hopkins Road, Haddonfield, NJ 08033; (609) 428–3885.

Shahin Soap Co., PO Box 2413, 427 Van Dyke Avenue, Paterson, NJ 07509; (201) 790–4296.

Shikai, PO Box 2866, Santa Rosa, CA 95405; (707) 584–0298.

Sierra Dawn Products, 8687 Graton Road, Sebastopol, CA 95472; (707) 823–3920.

Sirena Tropical Soap Co., PO Box 31673, Dallas, TX 75231; (214) 243–1991.

Sleepy Hollow Botanicals (see Carme).

The Soap Opera, 319 State Street, Madison, WI 53703; (603) 251–4051.

Sombra Cosmetics, Inc., 5600–G McLeod, NE, Albuquerque, NM 87109; (505) 888–0288.

Sparkle (see A. J. Funk and Co.)

St. Ives Laboratories, Inc., 8944 Mason Avenue, Chatsworth, CA 91311; (818) 709–5500.

Sunshine Fragrance Therapy, 1919 Burnside Avenue, Los Angeles, CA 90016; (213) 939–6400.

Tom's of Maine, Railroad Avenue, PO Box 710, Kennebunk, ME 04043; (207) 985–2944.

Tri Hair Care Products (see Institute Of Trichology).

Velvet Products Co., PO Box 5459, Beverly Hills, CA 90210; (213) 472–6431.

Vita Wave Products, 7131 Owensmouth Avenue, Suite 94D, Canoga Park, CA 91303; (818) 886–3808.

Weleda, Inc., 841 South Main Street, PO Box 769, Spring Valley, NY 10977; (914) 352–6145.

Cruelty-free Distributers

Beauty Naturally, 57 Bosque Road, PO Box 426, Fairfax, CA 94930; (415) 459–2826.

The Body Shop, Inc., 45 Horsehill Road, Hanover Technical Center, Cedar Knolls, NJ 07927–2003; (800) 541–2535.

Bodywares, 2000 Pennsylvania Avenue, NW, Washington, DC 20006; (202) 785–0716.

Bonne Sante, 462 62nd Street, Brooklyn, NY 11220; (718) 492–3887.

Carole's Cosmetics, 3081 Klondike Avenue, Costa Mesa, CA 92626.

A Clear Alternative, 8707 West Lane, Magnolia, TX 77355; (713) 356–7031.

The Compassionate Consumer, Inc., PO Box 27, Jericho, NY 11753; (718) 445–4134.

Heart's Desire Mail Order Co., 1307 Dwight Way, Berkeley, CA 94702.

Humane Street USA, 467 Saratoga Avenue, Suite 300, San Jose, CA 95129; (408) 243–2530.

My Brother's Keeper, Inc., PO Box 1769, Richmond, IN 47375; (317) 962–5079.
Panacea, PO Box 294, Columbia, PA 16512.
Sunrise Lane Products, Inc., 780 Greenwich Street, New York, NY 10014.
Vegan Street, PO Box 5525, Rockville, MD 20855; (301) 869–0086.

Household Products Sources

Faultless Starch/Bon Ami Company, 1025 West Eighth Street, Kansas City, MO 64100; (816) 842–2939.
Golden Lotus, PO Box 19366, Denver, CO 80219; (303) 761–0174.
Home Service Products Co., 230 Willow Street, Bound Brook, NJ 08805; (201) 356–8175.
JLM Enterprises Ltd./Naturall Products, PO Box 593, Keego Harbor, MI 48033, (313) 624–3311.
Magic American Chemical Corp., 23700 Mercantile Road, Cleveland, OH 44122; (216) 464–2353, or (800) 321–6330.
The Murphy-Phoenix Company, PO Box 22930, Beachwood, OH 44122; (216) 831–0404.
Sparkle, A. J. Funk And Co., 1471 Timber Drive, Elgin, IL 60120; (312) 741–6760.

Cosmetic and Household Product Sources—Mail–Order

The Body Shop, Inc., 45 Horsehill Road, Hanover Technical Center, Cedar Knolls, NJ 07927–2003.
The Compassionate Shopper, Beauty Without Cruelty USA, 175 West twelfth Street, New York, NY 10011–8275.
Amberwood, Route 1, PO Box 206, Milner, GA 30257; (404) 358–2991.
My Brother's Keeper, PO Box 1769, Richmond, IN 47375; (317) 962–5079.

Personal Health and the Environment
by Larry Dossey, MD

Strictly speaking, there is no such thing as "personal" health. This may seem a quarrelsome way to begin an essay about healthiness and its relationship to our environment, but the problem is that this "person" we wish to be healthy is only an abstraction. Although each of us seems to be bounded by his or her skin, this is a sheer illusion. When we view our physical boundaries with pinpoint accuracy, they are so fuzzy as to be nonexistent. With each bodily movement, we trail such a haze of chemicals, vapors, and gases behind us that we resemble out-of-focus images.

Not only are we constantly blending physically into the world and our environment, we are blending into each other. Quite literally, we are sharing bodies. How? As writer Guy Murchie has shown, each breath of air we inhale contains a quadrillion or 10^{15} atoms that have been breathed by the rest of mankind within the past few weeks, and more than a million atoms breathed by each and every person on Earth. These atoms don't just shuttle in and out of our lungs, they enter our blood and tissue and make up the actual stuff of our bodies. This means that human bodies are constantly being interchanged with those of any and all things that breathe—not just the bodies of humans but those of cows, crocodiles, serpents, birds, fish, etc. These exhaled "pieces" of our bodies remain after we die to be taken in by other bodies. Yet our roots in the world go even deeper, even to the stars themselves. Many of the elements that comprise our bodies were not born on Earth but were recycled through lifetimes of several stars before becoming localized on our planet. Thus, not only are our roots in each other, they are also in the stars. We are, literally, star stuff.

As we are a constant blur, with roots in each other and in the distant universe, our bodies are more like ghosts than things. Each year, 98 percent of the atoms in our bodies are replaced by other atoms from the environment. Some of the organs in the body are especially dynamic, such as bone, liver, and the lining of the gastrointestinal tract, which are replaced every few weeks. Others are more tenacious and have more staying power. But by the end of five years, 100 percent

> The assumption of being merely individuals is our greatest limitation.
>
> *— Pir Vilayat Khan*

of the atoms in our body are replaced, down to the very last one. This means that five years ago the body you now have did not exist; and if you live five more years you will have another, completely new one, albeit in roughly the same pattern that now exists. And if you are curious where your old body went, look around you. It is part of other bodies—those of plants and animals—already a partner in the "biodance," the endless round of life on Earth.

Of course, our linkages with the Earth and with each other are really deeper than whatever atoms we may share. We are connected to the world and to others by more than molecules; we are bound together by mind and consciousness. The idea that we could share consciousness with the Earth would have, until recently, been considered lunacy. But many eminent scientists have increasingly entertained the possibility that consciousness is a quality not just of humans but of the world itself, down to the level of atoms and electrons. For example, the respected British physicist Paul Davies hads said, "[T]he universe has organized its own self-awareness . . . [there is] powerful evidence that 'something is going on' behind it all. The impression of design is overwhelming. . . . [A] meaning behind existence."

Freeman Dyson, one of the most eminent physicists of our century, agrees: "Mind is already inherent in every electron, and the processes of human consciousness differ only in degree but not in kind from the processes of choice between quantum states which we call 'chance' when they are made by electrons." Anthropologist and philosopher Gregory Bateson, one of the most original thinkers of our century, also believed that mind is not limited to humans but is loose in the world. "The individual mind is immanent but not only in the body," he observed. "It is immanent also in pathways and messages outside the body; and there is a larger Mind of which the individual mind is only a sub-system. This larger Mind is comparable to God and perhaps what some people mean by 'god,' but is still immanent in the total interconnected social system and planetary ecology."

If we are to succeed in going beyond the environmental problems we have created, and if we are to create health for ourselves and for the Earth, it will be necessary for us to identify with the world-soul, the global mind, and to realize—deeply realize—that this is not just a metaphorical, poetic way of thinking about our connection with the Earth. Again, this means going beyond the person. It means giving up the precious notion that our consciousness is limited to the self, the ego; the I—unconfined to specific points in time and space—is unbounded. And if unbounded, it is ultimately one, not many. This means that there are not five billion minds inhabiting the Earth today, with a

Each breath of air we inhale contains a quadrillion or 10^{15} atoms that have been breathed by the rest of mankind within the past few weeks, and more than a million atoms breathed by each and every person on Earth.

one-to-one ratio between minds and brains, but a single, unitary mind—what we can call the One Mind or the Universal Mind, borrowing a term that was in favor in centuries past.

This unified view of consciousness has been affirmed by one of the greatest physicists of this century, Erwin Schrodinger, whose wave equations lie at the heart of modern quantum physics. Schrodinger observed, "Mind by its very nature is a singular tantum. I should say: the over-all number of minds is just one. . . . [The] thinking ego . . . is identical with the whole. . . . [T]he self-consciousness of the individual members are numerically identical both with each other and with that Self which they may be said to form at a higher level. . . . There is really no before and after for mind."

The view that we are infinite, nonlocal creatures leads to the vision that we constitute a unified Whole—or it would not be the whole—not even the Earth. This implies that we and our Earth are one. Physicist Erwin Schrodinger, mentioned above, was struck by our oneness with the Earth and left this ecstatic description of his vision:

> Thus you can throw yourself flat on the ground, stretched out upon Mother Earth, with the certain conviction that you are one with her and she with you. You are as firmly established, as invulnerable as she, indeed a thousand times firmer and more invulnerable. As surely as she will engulf you tomorrow, so surely will she bring you forth anew to new striving and suffering. And not merely 'some day': now, today, every day she is bringing you forth, not once but thousands of times, just as every day she engulfs you a thousand times over. For eternally and always there is only now, one and the same now; the present is the only thing that has no end.

Those persons who experience for the first time the ideas of nonlocal consciousness and Earth-unity sometimes feel as if the ground has shifted beneath their feet. They may not want to give up the notion of being a self-contained person with a stable, fixed body and a mind they can call their own. They may resist the evidence for their nonlocality and the implications that their minds are infinite in time and space and thus omnipresent, eternal, and one. Furthermore, the idea of inner divinity may stir within them an uncomfortable sense of blasphemy. They may overwhelmingly want to remain "local."

But this fear of nonlocality, of infinity in space and time, is nothing less than spiritual agoraphobia. It is analogous to the psychological fear of those persons who are terrified of wide spaces and great distances in real life. Yet if we are to be honest and responsible in our relationship with the Earth, we must overcome this spiritual agoraphobia; only then can we realize our affinity and identify with her, and know that our mind and that of the Earth are ultimately one.

Each year, 98 percent of the atoms in our bodies are replaced by other atoms from the environment. Some of the organs in the body are especially dynamic, such as bone, liver, and the lining of the gastrointestinal tract, which are replaced every few weeks.

James Hillman, the brilliant "depth psychologist," has affirmed this idea of the oneness of the mind of humans and that of the Earth, the anima mundi, which is akin if not equivalent to the Universal Mind. Hillman: "[T]he soul of the individual . . . [and] the soul of the world . . . are inseparable, the one always implicating the other. . . . Any alteration in the human psyche resonates with a change in the psyche of the world." The message, again, is that our minds extend beyond ourselves, and are interlocked in a give-and-take relationship not only with those of other persons but of the Earth itself.

What is the relation to personal health? It is true that we should devise strategies that are important to the health of persons, for we do exist as individual bodies at a gross, macroscopic level. If I develop melanoma from excessive ultraviolet irradiation and a thinning of the protective ozone layer, the surgeon will remove the cancer from me, not you. If you suffer heat stroke from soaring greenhouse temperatures, you will be taken to the hospital, not me. Almost all measures of health care are based on these implicit assumptions: health is fundamentally related to persons, and health care measures must be individual in nature.

So why claim that there is no such thing as personal health, the words with which this essay began? If we can look beyond the obvious, perhaps now we can see why. Because we are essentially nonlocal beings, we are the world; personal health is thus the health of the world, and the health of the world is that of ourselves. Unless we are extraordinarily mindful, we can quickly become unconscious of our extended being, and our infatuation with "personal" health can suddenly degenerate into a narcissistic, selfish concern, if not downright fear, about the welfare of the body.

Recognizing our affinity with the Earth can transform us into Green clinicians whose personal health is identified with that of Mother Earth. Looking after her health becomes as important as focusing on our own. What could be more true? We can exist without air for only minutes, without water for days, without food for weeks—all of which depend on a healthy Earth. Even the medications we rely on are Earth-based—whether penicillin, herbs, or acupuncture needles. Even synthetic drugs and the stainless steel in the surgeon's knife have their origins in Mother Earth. The greatest urgency for proper health care cannot then be the person; it must be the progenitor of the person, the sustained sense of the individual: Earth herself.

But in caring for the health of the Earth, we must stop thinking of ourselves as "custodians"—as persons who are in charge of something external to us, something "out there." The Earth is not a house we live in; it is ourselves. If we

We are connected to the world and to others by more than molecules; we are bound together by mind and consciousness.

forget this important fact, we shall never understand why efforts to restore the health of the Earth are actions also toward personal health.

Following this essay there are many tips on how personal and environmental health are interrelated—all from the vantage point that persons are real and that bodies are important. That is not a negation of what I have said above, only an approach from a complementary point of view. I have emphasized only one side of this complementarity because I think it is the most important. Now it is time to acknowledge the importance of the other aspect. To deny that bodies need care is simply silly; to ignore them as if they did not exist dishonors the Earth that birthed them. Indeed, I have spent much of my life as a physician attempting to make bodies healthier. Yet I have come to believe that our greatest empowerment to act as individuals in making our bodies healthy comes when we realize that we are essentially and fundamentally not individuals.

Lao Tzu, the ancient Taoist sage, observed,

> The universe is deathless,
> Is deathless because having no finite self,
> It stays infinite.

If we understand our unity with the universe, the Earth, and each other, we will know that we, too, are deathless; and if deathless, then in some sense our health must be inherently perfect. This recognition can be freeing. It can liberate us from focusing too much on the body, chronically worrying about whether it is going to survive the latest onslaught of toxins, chemicals, pesticides, or foul air. And, importantly, it can also free us to work against these onslaughts.

When we catch the spirit of our nonlocal nature, this can issue in a great ecstasy. But let us remember that there is much work to be done. Thus the Zen saying, "After ecstasy, the laundry."

To work!

Sure, we all hate pills and surgery and x-rays, but the best treatment for acute appendicitis is still surgery, and mammograms do detect breast cancers while they're curable.

Notes

1. Guy Murchie, *The Seven Mysteries of Life* (Boston: Houghton Mifflin, 1978), p. 320.

2. Larry Dossey, "The Biodance," *Space, Time and Medicine* (Boston: New Science Library, 1982), p. 72 ff. For a complete discussion of the nonlocal nature of human consciousness that follows, see my *Recovering the Soul: A Scientific and Spiritual Search* (New York: Bantam, 1989).

3. Paul Davies, *The Cosmic Blueprint*, p. 203.

4. Freeman Dyson, *Disturbing the Universe* (New York: Harper & Row, 1979), p. 249.

5. Freeman Dyson, *Infinite in All Directions* (New York: Harper & Row, 1988), pp. 119–120.

6. Gregory Bateson, *Steps to an Ecology of Mind* (San Francisco: Chandler Press, 1972), p. 467.

7. Robert G. Jahn and Brenda J. Dunne, *Margins of Reality* (New York: Harcourt Brace Jovanovich, 1987).

8. Randolph G. Byrd, "Positive Therapeutic Effects of Intercessory Prayer in a Coronary Care Unit Population," *Southern Medical Journal*, 81:7, July 1988, pp. 826–9.

9. Erwin Schrodinger's views on human consciousness can be found in his books, *What is Life? and Mind and Matter* (Cambridge: Cambridge University Press 1967), and *My View of the World* (Woodbridge, CT: Ox Bow Press, 1983).

10. Henry Margenau, "A Universal Mind?", *The Miracle of Existence* (Woodbridge, CT: Ox Bow Press, 1984), p. 106 ff.

11. Erwin Schrodinger, op. cit., *What is Life? and Mind and Matter*, p.22.

12. James Hillman, "Anima Mundi and the Imagination of Post-Modern Therapy," paper presented to the conference, "Toward a Post-Modern World," The Center for a Post-Modern World and the Center for Process Studies, Santa Barbara, CA, January 16–20, 1987.

13. Lao Tzu, *The Way of Life*, Witter Bynner, trans. (New York: Perigee Books, 1980), p.28.

Tips

- **Biofeedback.** Uses thoughts, images, and visualizations to change the body. Extremely well-validated scientifically. Electronic instruments measure subtle changes in the body that are usually unnoticed, which are "fed back" to conscious awareness; this makes it possible to gain control over many bodily processes. As a result, many nasty symptoms can be eliminated such as headaches, insomnia, pain syndromes, etc. To locate a certified, well-trained therapist in your area, contact the Biofeedback Certification Institute of America (BCIA), 10200 West 44th Avenue, Suite 304, Wheat Ridge, CO 80033.

- **Music.** "Music therapy" has come of age and, like biofeedback, can be used by skilled therapists to improve health and eliminate pesky problems. Contact the Institute for Music, Health and Education (Don G. Campbell, Director), PO 1244, Boulder, CO 80306.

- **Volunteerism.** Studies have confirmed that altruism and volunteer work lead to what's been called the "helper's high," a state of good feelings probably related to an increase in the brain's endorphin chemicals. Also reported is a decrease of physical ailments in volunteers. Volunteering not only helps "them," it helps you: Interconnectedness in action. For information on the "helper's high," contact Allan Luks, Executive Director, Institute for the Advancement of Health, 16 East 53rd Street, New York, NY 10022.

- **Meditation.** Practitioners of some forms of medication, particularly Transcendental Meditation, have less illness, make fewer trips to the doctor, and spend less for health care. Contact your local TM chapter. See "The Maharishi Effect" in *Recovering the Soul* by Larry Dossey (New York: Bantam, 1989).

- **Exercise.** Aerobic exercises strengthen the muscles of respiration, improves efficiency of the heart, tones up body muscles, and increased total amount of blood circulating through the body. Moreover, mind-body connections are **real**, and vigorous exercise can help you become aware of them. In some spiritual traditions, exercising the body plays an important role (e.g., Sufi dancing and tai chi). Need advice? A fine place to start is Joan Borysenko's book *Minding the Body, Mending the Mind.* Need instruction? We're not talking marathons, and you may not find what you're looking for from your aerobics instructor. Shop around.

- **Crafts.** Sound too old-fashioned and time-consuming? That's the point. Doing methodical, intricate work makes you slow down, reflect, turn inward. Crafts are a splendid antidote to what Jeremy Rifkin has called the "nanosecond culture." Can be done in isolation or in groups. Focus on making something that *lasts*—a fine piece of needlepoint, a quilt, metalwork, or jewelry. Passing your work along as an heirloom helps you realize your extension through time, your connections with others.

- **Educate yourself.** Stay informed about the latest mind-body approaches to health care. Two fine sources can help you stay abreast: Marilyn Ferguson's legendary *Brain/Mind Bulletin*, a monthly publication (PO Box 42211, 4717 North Figueroa Street, Los Angeles, CA 90042) and a quarterly journal, *Advances*, published by the Institute for the Advancement of Health (16 East 53rd Street, New York, NY 10022). Both publications are suitable for both laypersons and professionals.

- **Traditional, orthodox medicine.** Sure, we all hate pills and surgery and x-rays, but the best treatment for acute appendicitis is *still* surgery, and mammograms *do* detect breast cancers while they're curable. Besides, there are an increasing number of "green-aware" doctors around. Do yourself a favor and find one *before* you need her/him. How? Best technique: ask friends.

- A final tip: **Be skeptical.** Not everything that sounds "green" is good for you. Ask for evidence, not anecdotes. Before doing anything to your body, check it out. It's still O.K. to use your intellect.

The Role of Religion
by Thomas Berry

i thank You God for most this amazing
day: for the leaping greenly spirits of trees
and a blue true dream of sky; and for everything
which is natural which is infinite which is yes
        — e.e. cummings

The divine presence to the human is primarily through the natural world about us. If we lose the radiance and the exciting qualities of the woodlands and meadows and flowers, of birds and butterflies and the multitude of living creatures about us, we lose our experience of the divine. There is a reciprocal relation between the vigor of religion and the splendor of the natural world. If we lose one, we will certainly lose the other. We can only restore one by restoring the other.

Presently we need to emphasize rituals that celebrate the earth in all its manifestations as modes of divine presence. Our western religious traditions have never been fully adequate in this regard. We have been so concerned with salvation that we seldom appreciate our positive role in creation. We have set the God of Redemption against the God of Creation.

Too often our religious songs are overladen with longing for redemption out of this world. We love too much the pathos in songs such as that expressed in the hymn "Swing low sweet Chariot, coming for to carry me home." While we do indeed need such comforting sentiments to help alleviate our earthly miseries, excessive emphasis in this direction only increases our miseries and eventually leads us to wreck the earth in search of some better mode of existence.

The entire natural world in its beauty proclaims the joy of the divine for which we are created and which alone can heal and console us in our sorrow as well as raise us up to ecstatic joy. The supreme expression of this delight is found in the Canticle of Canticles. "Come then, my love, my lovely one, come. For see, winter is past, the rains are over and gone. The flowers appear on the earth. The season of glad songs has come, the cooing of the turtledove is heard in the land.

If God were dead, so would nature be—and humans could be no more than embattled strangers, doomed to defeat, as we have largely convinced ourselves we in fact are.

— *Erazim Kohák*

The fig tree is forming its first figs and the blossoming vines give out their fragrance."

The psalms also—especially the 104th Psalm, the great Creation code—proclaim the grandeur of our human existence amid the various forms of life that surround us. These psalms, communicated through a divine revelation, are our best Western-derived guide to a religious attitude to the natural world.

In association with the ritual expression and moral commitments that should arise from our religious sources, we need formal statements from our religious authorities. We have in this country representation from many of the religious traditions of the world. Our main establishments however are Protestant, Catholic, and Jewish. Each of these has significant influence.

The Cathedral Church of John the Divine in New York, an Episcopal center, has committed itself throughout all of its activities to a role of defending, healing, and fostering the integrity of the earth. A few years ago their series of Lenten services dealt with "The Passion of the Earth" as the present mode in which the Christ-Passion is being experienced in these times. This is a model of what can be done. Also, one of their Advent seasons celebrated the Sun, the Earth, the Water, and the Wind, since these are integral aspects of the Incarnation itself.

A new movement toward ecological concerns is also finding expression in the Jewish tradition based on the scriptural directives and celebrations concerning human presence to the earth. These especially relate to the nourishment of the land that nourishes the human. Most powerful in this tradition is the covenant made by God after the flood, a covenant signed with the Rainbow: "When I gather the clouds over the earth and the bow appears in the clouds, I will recall the Covenant between myself and you and every living creature of every kind."

The Catholic bishops, with such a large religious membership in this country, could appropriately issue a pastoral letter on the ecology of the North American continent. This could be done along the model presented by the Philippine bishops in their pastoral letter entitled "What is happening to our beautiful land."

There are other traditions also, from the indigenous peoples of this continent as well as from Asia and Africa. All of these have a greater sense of intimate rapport with the natural world than is generally found in our Western traditions, especially as these western traditions have existed in these past few centuries. The most common attitude is that of universal compassion that exists in relation to every living being upon the earth. We often feel uncomfortable with these peoples precisely because of this wider concern for the natural world. Yet we

> "Any religion which is not based on a respect for life is not a true religion. . . . Until he extends his circle of compassion to all living things, man will not himself find peace."
>
> — *Albert Schweitzer*

might now recognize them as contributing to our own appreciation of the spiritual qualities found in the flourishing world about us.

A special opportunity for all our religious traditions to give expression to our concern for the well being of the planet is provided by the United Nations Environmental Program with its designation of the first weekend in June each year as the occasion for an Environmental Sabbath. This includes Friday as the Moslem holy day, Saturday as the Jewish Sabbath, and Sunday as the Christian Sabbath. This project provides well designed literature to assist local groups in their celebration of the earth in its sacred aspects.

Until recently, religious people have been distracted in their concern for the nonhuman world because of their overwhelming concern for the pathos of the human. Once we recover our sensitivity to the earth and recognize the need of all earthly creatures for their own nourishment, their habitat, and their freedoms, a new florescence of the earth will come about, and our capacity to alleviate the human pathos will be vastly increased.

We are awakening to a new moral sense in our religious institutions, a moral sense that is finding expression in the doctrine of stewardship of the human in relation to the entire planet. While this concept of "stewardship" is much needed it needs to be completed with the doctrine of "communion" with the natural world. A complete moral consciousness should bring about a mutual intimacy of the human with the entire community of living beings. This new intimacy is finding expression through our natural history writers and our poets who are awakening new religious sensitivities throughout our societies. The best of all our guides to such intimate association with the natural world, however, is found in the traditions and practices of the native peoples of this continent.

We might enhance our sense of the natural world in its religious meaning through adoption of the Omaha Indian ritual of presenting a newborn child to the universe or through some similar ritual developed out of our own religious thinking. This would enhance our traditional Christian baptismal ritual. The difficulty with the baptismal ritual is that it introduces the child to the divine world and to the human religious community but does not introduce the child to the natural world through which the divine providence functions in its care for the child.

This Omaha ritual addresses the various realms of the natural world with an invocation, an announcement, and a petition. First there is the invocation: "Ho! Ye Sun, Moon, Stars, and ye that move in the heavens, I bid you hear me! Into your midst has come a new life. Consent ye, we implore! Make its path smooth so that it may reach the brow of the first hill." Then in sequence, the other realms

If our earth were barren, our imagination would be as empty as the moon, our sensitivities as dull, our intelligence as limited.

are addressed, "Ye Winds, Clouds, Rain, and ye that move in the air/ Ye Hills, Rivers, Trees, and ye of the Earth/ Ye Birds, great and small, that fly in the air; Ye Animals, great and small, that dwell in the forests; Ye insects that creep among the grasses." To each of these the announcement is made that "[A] new life has come into their midst." The petition follows that they would each care for the child throughout its life so that it might reach its proper destiny.

This recognition of the larger spiritual community is of enormous importance, since a lack of reverence for the sacred role of the natural world is among the basic causes for our assault on the living forms about us. In our work of renewing the earth, we need the psychic energy evoked by religious commitment. Economic motivation is not adequate to the task before us. If we do not feel the inspiration of a religious commitment, we will hardly sustain the efforts at renewal that are needed.

The urgency of the moment can be appreciated by reflection on the lunar landscape. If our earth were barren, our imagination would be as empty as the moon, our sensitivities as dull, our intelligence as limited. If we have a glorious sense of the divine, if we have such exalted feeling in our poetry and music, if we have a sensitive awareness of each other, if we have such highly developed intelligence, it is because we live on such a gorgeous planet. As we dim the luster of the earth, we dim our own interior radiance. There is no way in which this consequence can be avoided.

Of special significance is the responsibility that we bear toward our children. We hold their world in sacred trust. What we do to the world around us. we do to them. Our prodigal living is their deprivation. None of the generations that come after us will ever see any of the species that we extinguish. There is a single earthly heritage for everyone on the earth and for all the generations that will ever be. The florescence of the planet that we protect and enhance is beyond question the most sublime gift that we can bestow upon them.

"Woe to those who
add house to house
and join field to field until
everything belongs to them
and they are
the sole inhabitants of
the land."

— *Isaiah*

Tips

- Form an environment committee on your parish council to coordinate environmental justice and education projects.

- To make your chapel, temple, parish hall, rectory and other buildings environmentally sound, implement the conservation measures suggested in the home and office chapters.

- When teaching and preaching, rabbis, priests, and ministers might give special emphasis to the goodness of God's creation, and on the sinfulness of its abuse and destruction.

- Integrate a "Respect for Creation" component in your parish religious education program.

- In your daily life, honor God by avoiding extravagance and excessive reliance on "conveniences." Simple living is a respected tradition in all the world's major religions.

Information Sources

North American Conference on Christianity and Ecology (NACCE), 3019 4th Street, NE, Washington, DC 20017; (202) 269–3462. The umbrella group for Christian environmentalism offers the published proceedings of last summer's conference for $12 postage paid and its central document for $2.

Appalachian Science in the Public Interest (ASPI), Route 5, Box 423, Livingston, KY 40445; (606) 453–2105. ASPI publishes a quarterly newsletter ($5 a year), various helpful manuals (write for a listing), the popular "Simple Lifestyle Calander" ($7 each) and "Earthen Vessels: an Environmental Action Manual for Churches" ($10).

11th Commandment Fellowship, 1555 Rose Avenue, Santa Rosa, CA 95407. Small local groups follow what founder Vincent Rossi calls the 11th Commandment: "The Earth is the Lord's and the fullness thereof; Thou shalt not despoil the Earth, nor destroy the life thereon."

New Creation Institute, 518 South Avenue W., Missoula, MT 59801; (406) 721–6704. This center runs programs "to convert the church by its own gospel for saving God's creation and building human wholeness." It offers a free introductory brochure and, for $12.95 postage paid, A Worldly Spirituality, Wesley Granberg-Michealson's scripture-based analysis of the case for Christian environmentalism.

Epiphany, PO Box 14727, San Francisco, CA 94114. Three issues, Fall 1985, Fall 1987, and Winter 1988, of this theologically conservative Christian journal contain Vincent Rossi's clear explanations of eco-Christianity (along with various writers' attacks on Creation Spirituality). Back issues are $6 each plus $1 shipping for one copy, and $.25 for each additional copy.

Thomas Berry and the New Cosmology, 23rd Publications, 185 Willow Street, Mystic, CT 06355. This introduction to "earth's first geologian" costs $9.20 postage paid.

Section Three/Chapter 13

Organic Gardening for a Healthier Planet
by Robert Rodale and Maria Rodale

What is organic gardening? Organic gardening is gardening in accord with the natural rhythms of the earth, without the chemical "fix" of artificial pesticides and fertilizers. Using chemicals both simplifies and weakens a garden. While chemical applications often increase yields in the short run, many beneficial plants and insects die in the process, impairing the long-term capacity of the garden.

Artificial pesticides and fertilizers act on the garden just as certain addictive drugs act on humans. They speed up biological processes—allowing a garden to do more in less time. And, just as drugs can eventually destroy our lives, chemicals can ruin a garden and harm even the gardener. The best way to garden is nature's way.

During World War II, many Americans planted "victory gardens." These gardens supplied families with food at a crucial point in our national history. Though not in the midst of a world war, we still need victory gardens: this time, to combat the environmental crisis and regenerate the earth.

Planting a garden, no matter what size, benefits the environment and you. Vegetation of all sorts absorbs carbon dioxide (CO_2) and slows the greenhouse effect. Also, vegetables grown organically require no energy for transport and can be raised without chemical fertilizers. What's more, organic produce tastes better than store-bought produce and contains no preservatives or chemical pesticides. It's no wonder that, according to a 1987 Harris poll, gardening is now America's number one recreational activity.

But before you go out the back door to start digging and planting, you should know the three fundamental principles of organic gardening. First, a garden is more than just a twelve by twelve foot box of dirt where geraniums or tomatoes grow. Your *whole* yard is a garden that can produce not just vegetables and fruits but also vital nutrients for the soil and pure oxygen for the atmosphere. Gardens also provide homes for birds and insects that will help your garden grow.

God Almighty first planned a garden; and indeed it is the purest of human pleasures.

— *Francis Bacon,* Essays, 1625

93

Artificial pesticides and fertilizers act on the garden just as certain addictive drugs act on humans.

Second, the organic gardener must learn to *see the connections*. A garden is part of an ecosystem—an incredibly complex and wonderful web of biotic diversity. *We* are part of the same ecosytem, no matter how much we try to disguise this fact with our clothes, homes, and automobiles. The biosphere is our home, and we must live according to its patterns and limitations to survive in health and happiness. Human separateness and "dominion" have been wrongfully absolutized over the centuries, at an enormous cost to the well-being of the earth and to our own health.

Look at your landscape. Do you see any birds? Why are they there? They certainly please the eyes and ears, but they also support plant life by carrying seeds and eating harmful insects. They have a *purpose* beyond aesthetics. Birds are an integral, indispensable, and beautiful part of any healthy landscape, and they should not be threatened or replaced by chemical pesticides.

On a crisp fall day, observe leaves falling quietly to the ground. Should we admire them merely for their colors and then stuff them into Glad Bags and haul them off to a landfill? Or do they have a further role to play? Wouldn't it be better to compost them and reintegrate them into the landscape? Even in death, leaves, grass clippings, and other yard debris have value as natural fertilizers, helping to bring forth new life—where before there was only "waste." Inorganic, chemical fertilizers are superfluous, poisonous to groundwater, and generally not as beneficial to the soil as organic fertilizers.

Examine a bucket of freshly turned soil. Can you find any earthworms? Do earthworms do more than make good bait for bluegill? By ceaselessly ingesting and excreting soil, earthworms keep the soil loose enough to allow for the necessary flow of water, oxygen, nitrogen, carbon dioxide, and various nutrients. This allows a protective vegetation cover to flourish. Many pesticides threaten the earthworm, and the use of heavy machinery compresses the soil again, making it less productive and more susceptible to erosion.

The third principle of organic gardening is the principle of extended regeneration. The healing effects of organic gardening go well beyond the garden itself. Nature, left to its own devices, usually heals itself. As organic gardeners and healers of the earth, we should allow this self-regeneration to happen, and we should also assist the process where the natural healing capacity has been diminished by pollution. When we promote this regenerative process in our gardens, seven things usually occur in the plant and soil system. In accord with the principle of extended regeneration, these effects have parallels in our own lives and in our communities:

1. Greater Diversity. In a healthy garden, there's plenty of room for differences. As a garden regenerates, you'll start to notice more birds, animals, insects (good ones!), and plants.

- More plant and animal species in your garden.

- A more varied, tastier diet for you.

- With less dependence on "agribusiness," more local color and flavor in the market.

2. Increased Resistance. Nature needs a skin. As any gardener can tell you, weeding can become a major occupation. But "weeds" are simply nature's way of healing her wounds. The solution is simple—provide a skin for her of either mulch or ground cover.

- Greater self-regulation of and resistance to natural pests.

- Stronger resistance to disease and injury through healthier eating. More personal hardiness and ability to withstand crisis.

- Increased resistance to economic and demographic fluctuations because of greater agricultural self-sufficiency and a more diverse economic base.

3. Purification. Using organic methods protects soil, groundwater, air, wildlife, and people from contamination by dangerous chemicals.

- Natural purity for plants and other life.

- Less buildup of toxins in body tissues.

- A healthier community.

4. Increased Stability. Our agricultural system is based almost entirely on annual crops. But in a healthy system, nature prefers to stay for a while. Annuals are not all bad, just less efficient and harder on the soil. Nature prefers more of a balance.

For more permanence in your own garden, plant margins of perennials like asparagus, raspberries, rhubarb, and grapes. Fruit and nut trees will provide homes for birds and animals and bring you considerable pleasure for years. Watching a garden over time connects you to the earth and helps you to understand your relationships with nature.

- Vigorous root systems develop, protecting and conditioning the soil.

- Lasting sense of partnership with the land.

According to a 1987 Harris poll, gardening is now America's number one recreational activity.

- Strengthened sense of responsibility for the environment.

5. Greater Harmony. A regenerative system reaches a state of sustainable equilibrium after a while. When this happens in your garden, no single pest—Japanese beetles or thistles—can wipe out the whole garden because diversity provides a buffer.

- Past patterns of weed and pest interference are neutralized.

6. Realization of Potential. Nutrients naturally tend to move upward in the soil profile. In this "trickle up" garden economy, plants receive the nourishment they need.

- Vegetation becomes fuller and thicker, without artificial stimulation.

7. Real Progress. Healthy soil is like a sponge. Progress occurs when rainwater is absorbed. Soil drain off takes all that's valuable with it.

- Soil structure improves, increasing water-retention capacity.

Organic gardening teaches us how to heal the earth. We cannot impose health from without (by adding chemical fertilizers and pesticides). A healthy garden and planet must develop within its own capacity and according to its own guidelines. Our job is to learn and respect those guidelines, helping the earth along at times, leaving it be at others.

During World War II, many Americans planted "victory gardens." Though not in the midst of a world war, we still need victory gardens: this time, to combat the environmental crisis and regenerate the earth.

Tips

- **Start a garden.** Start small and then slowly expand your garden as space and time allow. If you are interested in a vegetable garden, some good "starter" crops include beans, carrots, corn, cucumbers, greens, lettuce, peas, potatoes, squash, and tomatoes.

  For information on how to start a community garden, request a "Community Gardens Organizer's Kit" through the National Gardening Association, 180 Flynn Avenue, Burlington, VT 05401.

  Here are some seed sources: **Allen, Sterling & Lothrop**, 191 Route 1, Falmouth, ME 04105. **Becker's Seed Potatoes**, RR 1, Trout Creek, Ontario, Canada P0H 2L0. **Bountiful Gardens**, c/o Ecology Action, 5798 Ridgewood Road, Willits, CA 95490. **Burpee Seeds**, 300 Park Avenue, Warminster, PA 18991. **D. V. Burrell Seed Growers Co.**, Rocky Ford, CO 81067. **The Cook's Garden**, Box 65, Londonderry, VT 05148. **William Dam Seeds**, PO Box 8400, Dundas, Ontario, Canada L9H 6M1. **DeGiorgi Co., Inc.**, Box 413, Council Bluffs, IA 51502. **Early Seed & Feed Ltd.**, Box 3024, Saskatoon, Saskatchewan, Canada S7K 3S9. **Fisher's Garden Store**, PO Box 236, Belgrade, MT 59714. **Garden Import**, Box 760, Thornhill, Ontario, Canada L3T 4A5. **Gaze Seed Co.**, Box 640, St. Johns, Newfoundland.,

Canada A1C 5K8. **Good Seed**, Box 702, Tonasket, WA 98855. **Hastings: Seedsman to the South**, PO Box 4274, Atlanta, GA 30302–4274. **Ed Hume Seeds**, Box 1450, Kent, WA 98032. **Johnny's Selected Seeds**, 305 Foss Hill Road, Albion, ME 04910. **Le Marche Seeds, International**, PO Box 190, Dixon, CA 95620. **Letherman Seed Co.**, 1221 Tuscawaras Street E., Canton, OH 44704. **Liberty Seed Co.**, PO Box 806, New Philadelphia, OH 44663. **McFayden Seeds**, Box 1800, Brandon, Manitoba, Canada R7A 6N4. **Meyer Seed Company**, 600 South Caroline Street, Baltimore, MD 21231. **Midwest Seed Growers**, 10559 Lackman Road, Lenexa, KS 66219. **Park Seeds**, Cokesbury Road, Greenwood, SC 29647–0001. **Pinetree Garden Seeds**, New Gloucester, ME 04260. **Porter & Son Seedsmen**, Box 104, Stephenville, TX 76401. **S & B Seed Sales**, Box 278, Nash, TX 75569. **Seeds Blum**, Idaho City Stage, Boise, ID 83707. **Seedway, Inc.**, Hall, NY 14463–0250. **Shepherd's Garden Seeds**, 7389 West Zayant Road, Felton, CA 95018. **Stokes Seeds**, PO Box 548, Buffalo, NY 14240. **T & T Seeds**, Box 1710, Winnipeg, Manitoba, Canada R3C 3P6. **Territorial Seed Co.**, Box 27, Lorane, OR 97451. **Thompson & Morgan**, Box 1308, Jackson, NJ 08527. **Tillinghast Seeds**, Box 738, LaConner, AK 98527. **Tomato Growers Supply Co.**, Box 2237, Fort Myers, FL 33902. **Otis Twilley Seed Co.**, PO Box 9000, Houlton, ME 04730–0829.

- **Try intensive gardening.** Cultivate small plots in which a variety of vegetation can grow. Use a compost pile and intensive soil conservation techniques.

- **Save seeds and exchange seeds and seed information with other gardeners.** These seeds will have been climatically tested so their growth potential is known. When exchanging seeds, remember that the more diversity we have in our seed germplasm, the more productive plants we will have available to deal with climate change and diminishing resources. The easiest seed-saving crops include beans, eggplant, escarole and endive, lettuce, okra, peas, peppers, sunflowers, and tomatoes. Flower seeds to collect include balsam, California poppy, columbine, flax, hollyhock, larkspur, marigold, morningglory, snap dragon, and zinnia. Whatever seed you are collecting, be sure to pick it when it's dry, not green. For further information, send a self-addressed stamped envelope to Seed Savers Exchange, RR 3, Box 239, Decorah, IA 52101.

- **Grow items you'd normally buy at the store.** By doing so, you save on energy that would be used in the production and transport of commercially grown produce. You also help reduce the emissions of CO_2 into the atmosphere. Home grown vegetables and fruits also do not require preservatives, pesticides, and other contaminants.

- **Subscribe to an organic gardening magazine and consult government information resources.** In planning your garden, consider subscribing to gardening publications, such as *Organic Gardening*. You can also consult valuable information sources like local nurseries and the United States Department of Agriculture.

- **Buy plants with vigorous leafing patterns.** These plants supply oxygen better than others and absorb CO_2 efficiently. The following plants are recommended by government information sources. Golden Pothos Vine (*scindapsus Aureus*); Lacey Tree Philodendron (p. *Selloum*); Alicean Ear Philodendron (p. *Domesticum*); Chinese Evergreen (*agilnema modestum*); Flowering Chrysanthemums; Gerbera Daisies.

- **Actively support organic gardening and sustainable agriculture.** Become a member of local and national organizations working to promote organic gardening and sustainable agriculture. To obtain information on such organizations, contact **The International Alliance for Sustainable Agriculture**, 1701 University Avenue, SE, Minneapolis, MN 55414; (612) 331–1099.

- **Consult your garden nursery on the best native plants and plants from similar climates, that require little or no watering.** These plants also require less time to maintain.

- **Don't use chemical fertilizers on your lawn.** Avoid chemical-intensive lawn care services if you have a lawn. Instead, if necessary, use organic fertilizers, a mixture of grass varieties, and proper lawn care maintenance to ensure a healthy lawn.

  For information on environmentally sound lawn care practices, contact **The National Coalition Against the Misuses of Pesticides (NCAMP)**, 530 Seventh Street, SE, Washington, DC 20003; (202) 543–5450.

  Please note: Chemical fertilizers require significant energy to produce, and they emit nitrous oxide, a greenhouse gas.

- **Plant a garden instead of grass.** Rather than planting an extensive lawn, plant a variety of trees and vegetables. This provides a food supply while absorbing more CO_2. For further information on starting a garden, consult *The 1977 Yearbook of Agriculture, Gardening for Food and Fun*, Superintendent of Documents, United States Government Printing Office, Washington, DC 20402.

Pest Control

- **Don't use chemical pesticides or herbicides.** These contaminate water and require energy to produce. To control pests in your home (from cockroaches and termites to fleas and plant mites) by using nontoxic methods, contact **The National Coalition Against the Misuses of Pesticides (NCAMP)**, 530 Seventh Street, SE, Washington, DC 20003; (202) 543-5450.

Some of these books are no longer in print and must be obtained through your local public or university library. Please consult the publisher before ordering. Book codes: **G** = General Information; **I** = Insect Identification; **C** = Control Measures.

The Audubon Society Field Guide to North American Insects and Spiders, Louis Milne and Margery Milne (**I**) (Alfred A. Knopf, Inc., 1980). Includes 702 full-color photographs arranged by shape and by color, making identification quick and easy.

Biological Pest Management for Interior Plantscapes, Marilyn Y. Steiner and Don P. Elliott (**I, C**), 30 pp. (Alberta Environmental Centre, 1983). Provides information on the use of biological control agents or organisms in areas such as homes, shopping malls, office buildings, schools, hospitals and other environmentally sensitive areas where it is difficult to control pests.

The Encyclopedia of Natural Insect and Disease Control, ed. Roger B. Yepsen, Jr. (**I, C**), 440 pp. (Rodale Press, Inc., 1984).

Good Neighbors: Companion Planting for Gardeners, Anna Carr (**C**), 379 pp. (Rodale Press, Inc. 1985).

Handbook in Biological Control of Plant Pests, The Brooklyn Botanical Garden (**C**), 97 pp. (Special Printing of Plants and Gardens, Volume 16, No. 3, 1960. Reprinted 1976). Discusses the importance of biological control and gives specific examples of predators, parasites, and pathogens for use against certain pests.

Insects, Herbert S. Zim, Ph.D. and Clarence Cotton, Ph.D. (**I**), 157 pp. (Western Publishing Co., Inc. 1951). A guide to familiar American insects with color illustrations; pocket size; general.

1001 Questions Answered about Insects, Alexander B. Klots and Elsie B. Klots (**G**), 260 pp. (Dover Publications, Inc., 1961. Second printing in 1977). A useful introduction to the world of insects.

Rodale's Color Handbook of Garden Insects, Anna Carr (**I, C**), 241 pp. (Rodale Press, Inc., 1979, paperback and hardcover). Over 300 full-color photographs including all life stages of the insects.

Simon and Schuster's Guide to Insects, Dr. Ross H. Arnett Jr. and Dr. Richard L. Jacques Jr. (**I**), 511 pp. (Simon and Schuster, a Division of Gulf and Western Corp., 1981). An easy-to-use guide to 350 species, with more than 1,000 spectacular full-color illustrations; information on insect anatomy and behavior, species' primary activity, habitat, ecological significance, and more.

What's Eating Your Houseplants?, William H. Jordan, Jr. (**I, C**), 229 pp. (Rodale Press, Inc., 1977). How to use predatory and parasitic insects and mites to protect your plants from indoor plant pests.

- **Shop for beneficial organisms.** Manufacturers and suppliers source-key list:

1. **ABBOTT LABORATORIES**, Dept. D–44C, 1400 Sheridan Road, North Chicago, IL 60064; (312) 937–7909. Manufacturers of BTI (trade name Vectobac) strain of Bacillus thuringiensis specifically for mosquitoes.

2. **AEROXON PRODUCTS, INC.**, PO Box 249, 3 Cottage Place, New Rochelle, NY 10802. Aeroxon Giant Fly Catcher; Greenhouse Yellow Fly Traps; Revenge Home Exterminator Kit contains silica gel and pyrethrum to control roaches, ants, fleas, ticks, and other household pests; and Revenge Wasp and Hornet Killer with pyrethrum and rotenone.

3. **ALMAC PLASTICS, INC.**, 6311 Erdman Avenue, Baltimore, MD 21205; (301) 485–9100. Insect netting, Sticky Stakes for whiteflies, bird control netting.

4. **BIOCHEM PRODUCTS**, PO Box 264, Monchanin, DE 19710; (302) 654–0325. Manufacturers of Bactospeine, Bacillus thuringiensis var. kurstaki for caterpillar control; and Bactimos Bacillus thuringiensis var. israeliensis for control of mosquito and blackfly larvae. Contact for distributors in your area.

5. **BIOLOGIC**, 418 Briar Lane, Chambersburg, PA 17201; (717) 263–2789. ScanMask—a nematode-based biological insecticide that kills soil- and boring-insect pests without harming plant roots.

6. **BIO-RESOURCES**, PO Box 902, 1210 Birch Street, Santa Paula, CA 93060; (805) 525–0526. Beneficial insects and decollated snails.

7. **BOMA ENTERPRISES, INC.**, 600 Railway Street, Williamsport, PA 17701; (717) 326–2061. Dead-End Roach Killer, diatomaceous earth and inert ingredients.

8. **BURGESS SEED & PLANT CO.**, 905 Four Seasons Road, Bloomington, IL 61701. Dipel, animal traps, netting, dormant oil, 20 percent sabadilla dust in limited quantities when available.

9. **W. ATLEE BURPEE CO.**, 300 Park Avenue, Warminster, PA 18974; (215) 674–4900. Dipel, 1 percent rotenone, animal traps, netting, Tanglefoot, French marigolds, green lacewings, fly parasites, insecticidal soap.

10. **COPPER BRITE, INC.**, 5147 West Jefferson Boulevard, Los Angeles, CA 90016; (213) 933–9331. Roach Prufe boric acid, available in True Value and ACE Hardware Stores, or contact for distributors.

11. **WILLIAM DAM SEEDS, LTD.**, PO Box 8400, Dundas, Ontario, Canada L9H 6M1. FOR CANADA ONLY: Thuricide, rotenone, DE, DE and pyrethrin or rotenone, insecticidal soap, Tree Tanglefoot, netting, mesh.

12. **ECOSAFE LAB**, PO Box 8702, Oakland, CA 94662; (415) 655–9996. Line of herbal pet-care products, includes flea collars and flea and insect repellents; diatomaceous earth; pure pyrethrin extract—contains no synergists.

13. **ELLISCO, INC.**, American & Luzerne Streets, Philadelphia, PA 19140; (215) 223–3500. Contact for a list of distributors for their Japanese beetle traps.

14. **FAIRFAX BIOLOGICAL LABORATORY, INC.**, Clinton Corners, NY 12514. Manufacturers of Doom Milky Spore Disease and Japidemic. Can buy directly from them or through their distributors.

15. **FARMER SEED & NURSERY CO.**, 818 NW 4th Street, Faribault, MN 55021; (507) 334–1623. Thuricide, Grasshopper Spore, 1 percent rotenone, animal and insect traps, netting, Tanglefoot.

16. **FRANK FOSBENNER**, 371 New Street, Quakertown, PA 18951; (215) 536–6589. Perma Guard, Fossil Shell Flour, DE.

17. **GARDENER'S SUPPLY CO.**, 128 Intervale Road, Burlington, VT 05401; (802) 863–1700. Dipel, 5 percent retenone, Safer's Insecticidal Soap, sabadilla, DE, SEEK parasitic nematodes bird netting, BTI for mosquitoes, dusters and sprayers.

18. **GENERAL BIO-LAND CORP., INC.**, PO Box 2993, Conroe, TX 77305; (409) 756–6351. Roach Free boric acid with inert ingredients; Rug Guardian, kills fleas and deodorizes rugs and air. Can be used on pets.

19. **GREAT LAKES IPM**, 10220 Church Road, NE, Vestaburg, MI 48891; (517) 268–5693. Insect Monitoring Systems; pheromone and sticky traps for wide array of pests; hand nets monitoring tools; Tanglefoot.

20. **GROWING CRAZY**, PO Box 8, Tawas City, MI 48764–0008; (517) 352–4201. 1 percent and 5 percent rotenone, pyrethrin concentrate, rotenone-pyrethrum blend, ryania, blend, sabadilla, Thuricide, Dipel, Milky Spore, biological mosquito control, Grasshopper & Mormon Cricket Spore, insect traps, pheromone traps, Tanglefoot, sulfur, dormant oil, Fossil Shell Flour (DE), insecticidal soap, and a complete line of pest controls for pets and livestock.

21. **GURNEY SEED & NURSERY CO.**, 3916 Page Street, Yankton, SD 5707. Dipel, Thuricide, Grasshopper Spore, DE-pyrethrin blend, dormant oil, netting, animal and insect traps, Tanglefoot, beneficial organisms.

22. **HARMONY FARM SUPPLY**, PO Box 451, 4050 Ross Road, Graton, CA 95444; (707) 823–9125. Thuricide, Teknar, Grasshopper Spore, 5 percent rotenone, powder, DE, fungcidal, cryptocidal and insecticidal soaps, dormant and summer oils, pheromone traps, fly traps, Tree Tanglefoot, IPM monitoring tools, ryania, sabadilla, pyrethrum, mosquito rings, BTI, Milky Spore, animal traps (gophers, rats, and Havahart for larger animals), insect netting, predatory nematodes, yellow sticky traps, apply maggot sphere traps, wasp traps, Hinder deer and rabbit repellent, mouse sticky traps, copper strips for snail control, beneficial organisms.

23. **KENCO CHEMICAL MFG. CORP.**, PO Box 6246, Jacksonville, FL 32236; (904) 359–3005. Product line: Bag-A-Bug traps for Japanese beetles and gypsy moths, and Bt sprays for leaf-chewing insects.

24. **KING'S NATURAL PEST CONTROL**, 224 Yost Avenue, Spring City, PA 19475; (215) 948–9261. Safer's Insecticidal soap concentrate, Milky Spore, and predatory and parasitic organisms.

25. **MEADOWBROOK HERB GARDEN**, Route 138, Wyoming, RI 02898; (401) 539–7603. Insecticidal soap, soap-based wetting agent, rotenone-pyrethrum blend, pyrethrins-rotenone-ryania blend, chamomile flowers.

26. **MELLINGER'S**, 2310 West South Range Road, North Lima, OH 44452; (216) 549–9861. Dipel, Thuricide, Mormon Cricket Spore, Grasshopper Spore, Milky Spore, 1 percent rotenone, pyrethrum-rotenone blend, dormant oil, insecticidal soap, mesh, netting traps, Tanglefoot, Sticky Stakes, repellent plants, phero mone sex lures, diatomaceous earth, beneficial organisms.

27. **NATURAL GARDENING RESEARCH CENTER**, PO Box 300, Sunman, IN 47041; (812) 623–3800. Predatory nematodes, BTI, sticky traps, Japanese beetle traps, Milky Spore, nicotine sulfate, insecticidal soap, ryania, 1 percent & 5 percent rotenone dust, pyrethrum-rotenone dust, pyrethrum-rotenone-ryania blend, sabadilla dust, dormant oils, beneficial organisms.

28. **NATURAL PEST CONTROLS**, 8864 Little Creek Drive, Orangevale, CA 95662; (916) 726–0855. Formulations of Bacillus thuringiensis israeliensis for mosquito control; breeder of Gambusis Affinis, a mosquito eating fish; and beneficial organisms.

29. **NATURE'S WAY PRODUCTS**, Earlee, Inc., 726 Spring Street, Jeffersonville, IN 47130; (812) 282–9134. Diatom Shell Flour, Bt, Doom Milky Spore Powder, rotenone, insecticidal soap, dormant oils, Tanglefoot, tobacco dust, pyrethrum-rotenone-ryania blend, insect traps.

30. **THE NECESSARY TRADING CO.**, 602 Main Street, New Castle, VA 24127; (703) 864–5103. Dipel, Grasshopper Spore, Mormon Cricket Spore, Milky Spore, DE-pyrethrin blend, rotenone, rotenone-pyrethrum blend, 1 percent liquid pyrethrin concentrate, DE- and pyrethrin-based pet products, dormant oil, insecticidal and cryptocidal soaps, Tanglefoot, traps, pheromone monitoring traps, pheromone monitoring traps, Pent-A-Vate for nematodes, herbs and herbal oils, plus a good selection of beneficial insects, sabadilla, pure pyrethrin flowers, and preventative pest management systems.

31. **NICHOLS GARDEN NURSERY**, 1190 North Pacific Highway, Albany, OR 97321; (503) 928–9280. Thuricide, rotenone, netting, pyrethrum powder, Safer's Insecticidal Soap and Flea Soap for pets.

32. **OFF-LAND**, PO Box 53431, Lafayette, LA 70705; (318) 984–4427. Earth Guard diatomaceous, boric acid for roach control.

33. **ORGANIC CONTROL, INC.**, 5132 Venice Boulevard, Los Angeles, CA 90019; (213) 937–7444. Bt; Anti-Roach boric acid; Botanic: a pyrethrum-rotenone-ryania blend, available when they can get it.

34. **PARK SEED CO., INC.**, Highway 254 North, Greenwood, SC 29647; (803) 374–3341. Grasshopper Spore, insecticidal soap, netting.

35. **PEACEFUL VALLEY FARM SUPPLY**, 11173 Peaceful Valley Road, Nevada City, CA 95959; (916) 265–FARM. BTI; DE; 60+ types of pheromone traps; sticky traps; Japanese beetle, gypsy moth and fly traps; insect and bird netting; reflective mulch film; DE-pyrethrins blend; Dipel and Thuricide; dormant and summer oils; sabadilla; boric acid; pyrethrum; rotene; ryania; insecticidal soap; Milky Spore; Mormon Cricket & Grasshopper Spore; neem; repellent plants; Pent-A-Vate herbs and herbal oils; yucca extract; havahart traps; IPM monitoring equipment; snail bar; NPV; BXN fungi; predaceous upon nematodes; BX bacterial culture; Tanglefoot.

36. **PENT-A-VATE**, 966 West Palm Street, Lindsay, CA 93247; (209) 562–2839. Fish emulsion and yucca extract for nematodes.

37. **PROGRESSIVE AGRI-SYSTEMS, INC.**, 201 Center Street, Stockertown, PA 18083; (215) 759–5911. Ryania and rotenone-pyrethrum-ryania blend.

38. **J. L. PRICE PRODUCTS, INC.**, PO Box 9, South Milwaukee, WI 53172; (414) 764–4670. Big Stinky and Wee Stinky fly traps, insect traps.

39. **R VALUE, INC.**, PO Box 2235, Smyrna, GA 30081; (800) 241–3897. Manufacturers of the three boric-acid-based insecticides Roach Kill; Drax, a gel formulation for Pharaoh and other sugar-feeding ants; and Mop Up, a water-soluble formulation for use against roaches in commercial kitchens. Call or write for products representative in your area.

40. **W. A. RAPP & SON, INC.**, 2031 South Eastwood Street, Santa Ana, CA 92705; (714) 540–5808. Slug and bug traps

41. **REUTER LABORATORIES, INC.**, 8450 Natural Way, Manassas Park, VA 22111; (800) 368–2244, (703) 361–2500 in Virginia. Manufacturer of Grub Attack, Japanese Beetle Trap Attacj, Gypsy Moth Trap Attack (Bt), Grasshopper Attack, Whitefly Attack, Caterpillar Attack (Bt), Sod Webworm Attack, Vegetable Insect Attack, Aphid-Mite Attack, and Mosquito Attack (BTI).

42. **RICHTERS**, Goodwood, Ontario, Canada L0C 1A0; (416) 640–6677. FOR CANADA ONLY: Thuricide, rotenone dust and spray, pyrethrin-DE blend, dormant-oil spray, insecticidal soap, Tree Tanglefoot, repellent plants, sulfur, some beneficial insects in Canada and United States.

43. **RINGER RESEARCH**, 6860 Flying Cloud Drive, Dept. PC, Eden Prairie, MN 55344–3429; (612) 941–4180. Extensive line of organic pest control materials: Bt, diatomaceous earth, pyrethrum, milky spore, insecticidal soap, and more.

44. **SAFER AGRO-CHEM, INC.**, PO Box 649, Jamul, CA 92035; (619) 464–0775. Manufacturer of Safer's insecticidal, fungicidal, cryptocidal, and pet-flea soaps, and a family of effective, safe pest control and related products, including Caterpillar Killer, a BTI product.

45. **THE TANGLEFOOT CO.**, 314 Straight Avenue, SW, Grand Rapids, MI 49504; (616) 459–4139. Tangle-Trap for insects, Tree Tanglefoot, Bird Tanglefoot, Rat and Mouse Tanglefoot, Tanglefoot Roach and Ant Killer, Tanglefoot Grafting Compound, Tanglefoot Difuso, glue traps. Some products are available in paste, paint, or aerosol form.

46. **TRECE, INC.**, PO Box 5267, Salinas, CA 93915; (408) 758–0204. Contact for list of distributors of Pherocon (pheromone-lure) traps and attractants, and Storgard traps for monitoring stored-products insects.

47. **WOOD STREAM CORP.**, Front & Locust Streets, Lititz, PA 17543; (717) 626–2125. Manufacturers of Havahart traps, Rodent Control traps, insect traps, hand dusters, etc.

48. **ZOECON CORP.**, 975 California Avenue, Palo Alto, CA 94304; (800) 227–8929, (415) 857–1130 in California. Contact for list of distributors of Thuricide (Bt) and Javelin (Bacillus thuringiensis spondoptera), especially effective against armyworm species. Also: **Zoecon Corp.**, 12200 Denton Drive, Dallas, TX 75234; (800)

527–0512. Contact for list of distributors of Bti, and pyrethrin-based flea and tick shampoo, concentrated dip and spray for dogs and cats.

- **Index to specific products:**
  I. DISEASE ORGANISMS/MICROBIAL INSECTICIDES.
  Bacillus thuringiensis (Bt, Dipel, Thuricide, etc.). Source-keys: 4, 8, 9, 11, 15, 17, 20, 21, 22, 23, 26, 27, 29, 30, 31, 33, 35, 41, 42, 43, 44, 48.
  Bacillus thuringiensis spodoptera (Bts). Source-keys: 1, 4, 17, 20, 22, 28, 35, 41, 48.
  Bacillus thuringiensis spodoptera (Bts). Source-key: 48.
  Bacillus popilliae (Milky Spore, milky disease, Doom, Japademic). Source-keys: 14, 20, 22, 24, 26, 27, 29, 30, 35, 41, 43.
  Nosema locustae (Grasshopper Spore). Source-keys: 15, 20, 21, 22, 26, 30, 34, 35, 41.
  Anabrus simplex (Mormon Cricket Spore). Source-keys: 20, 26, 30, 35.
  Nuclear Polyhedrous Virus (NPV). Source-key: 35.

  II. TRAPS.
  Insect Traps. Source-keys: 2, 3, 15, 19, 20, 21, 22, 23, 26, 27, 29, 30, 35, 38, 40, 41, 46, 47.
  Pheromone Sex Lures. Source-keys: 19, 20, 22, 26, 30, 35, 46.
  Animal Traps. Source-keys: 8, 9, 15, 21, 22, 26, 30, 35, 47.
  Tanglefoot. Source-keys: 9, 11, 15, 19, 20, 21, 22, 26, 30, 35, 42, 45.

  III. ASSORTED PRODUCTS.
  Dormant and Summer Oils. Source-keys: 8, 20, 21, 22, 26, 27, 29, 30, 35, 42.
  Netting/Mesh (for birds, insects, bats). Source-keys: 3, 8, 9, 11, 15, 17, 21, 22, 26, 31, 34, 35.
  Soap Sprays (insecticidal, fungicidal, cryptocidal for mosses/algae, and flea soap for pets). Source-keys: 9, 11, 17, 20, 22, 24, 25, 26, 27, 29, 30, 34, 45, 42, 43, 44.
  Boric Acid (Roach Free, Anti-Roach, Roach Prufe, Roach Kill). Source-keys: 10, 18, 20, 32, 33, 35, 39. NOTE: Use with care around children.
  Pent-A-Vate (yucca-plant extract). Source-keys: 30, 35, 36.
  Miscellaneous items (scarecrows, rubber/plastic snakes, owls, reflective mulch, etc.). Source-keys: 9, 15, 21, 26, 35.
  Predatory Nematodes. Source-keys: 5, 17, 22, 27.

BXN (fungi predaceous upon nematodes) and BX (a bacterial culture). Source-key: 35.
Repellent Plants (herbs, herbal oils, marigolds, etc.). Source-keys: 9, 25, 26, 30, 31, 44, 48.
Beneficial Organisms (predatory insects, mites, snails, mosquito-eating fish, disease organisms, etc.) See "Suppliers of Beneficial Organisms" above.

IV. DIATOMACEOUS EARTH (DE, Perma Guard, Earth Guard, Fossil Shell Flour, Diatomite, etc.)
Plain DE. Source-keys: 11, 12, 16, 17, 20, 22, 26, 29, 30, 32, 35, 43.
DE + Pyrethrum. Source-keys: 11, 21, 30, 35, 42.
DE + Rotenone. Source-key: 11.
DE + Inert Ingredients. Source-key: 7.

V. BOTANICAL POISONS
Rotenone. Source-keys: 9, 11, 15, 17, 20, 22, 26, 27, 29, 30, 31, 35, 42.
Pyrethrum. Source-keys: 2, 20, 22, 30, 31, 35, 43.
Pyrethrum-Rotenone Blend. Source-keys: 2, 20, 25, 26, 29, 30, 35.
Pyrethrum-DE Blend. Source-keys: 11, 21, 30, 35, 42.
Rotenone-DE Blend. Source-key: 11.
Pyrethrum-Rotenone-Ryania Blen (Botanic; Tri-Excel DS) when available. Source-keys: 20, 25, 27, 29, 33, 37.
Sabadilla. Source-keys: 8, 17, 20, 22, 27, 30, 35.
Nicotine (tobacco dust). Source-keys: 27, 29, 35.
Neem Extract. Source-key: 35.

- **Use Homemade alternative pest control whenever possible.** There are several types of pest controls you can make or grow:

  TYPE ONE: General All-Purpose Insect Spray. This spray makes use of the repellent qualities of garlic, onion, and hot peppers. The soap makes it cling to plant leaves. Use: 1 garlic bulb, 1 small onion, 1 tablespoon cayenne pepper, 1 quart water, 1 tablespoon liquid soap (preferably non-detergent). Chop or grind garlic and onion, add cayenne, and mix with water. Let steep one hour, then add liquid soap. Store in a tightly covered jar in the refrigerator up to one week.

  TYPE TWO: Pyrethrum. Chrysanthemum cinerariifolium is the flower from which this poison is made. Be forewarned: some people are highly allergic to pyrethrum flowers and crude extracts. Seeds are available from: **CASA YERBA GARDENS**, Star Route 2, Box 21, Days Creek, OR 97429; (503) 825–3534. **J. L. HUDSON, SEEDSMAN**, PO Box 1058, Redwood City, CA 94064. **PEACEFUL VALLEY FARM SUPP-**

LY, 11173 Peaceful Valley Road, Nevada City, CA 95959; (916) 265–FARM. **REDWOOD CITY SEED CO.**, PO Box 361, Redwood City, CA 94064; (415) 325–7333. **RICHTERS**, Goodwood, Ontario, Canada LOC 1A0; (416) 640–6677.

To make pyrethrum dust, pick the flowers while the petals are still fresh and the pollen in the center is beginning to be released. Dry the flowers out of direct sunlight and then grind up the flower heads.

To make a spray, soak the ground flower heads overnight in methyl alcohol (the pyrethrum toxin is water-insoluble), then dilute this solution with approximately 100 times as much water before spraying.

Because commercial preparations of pyrethrum usually contain a chemical synergist like piperonyl butoxide, which can increase the potency of pyrethrum fourfold, they will work more effectively than the pyrethrum you make at home. Homemade preparations will knock down insects very well but may not kill them.

Both the dust and the spray described above break down quickly when exposed to light and air. They should be stored in dark, airtight containers.

TYPE THREE: Marigolds. Only the French marigolds (*Tagetes petula*) have been shown to be an effective control nematodes if the entire area is planted with them for a full season or if they are heavily interplanted. They are also said to repel many others types of garden pests. Seed for French marigolds is available from: **NICHOLS GARDEN NURSERY**, 1190 North Pacific Highway, Albany, OR 97321; (503) 928–9280. **PEACEFUL VALLEY FARM SUPPLY**, see above. **RICHTERS**, see above.

TYPE FOUR: Mole repellents.

A. Castor beans (*Ricinus communis*) are reputed to be good mole repellents. CAUTION: This is a poisonous plant. It should never be planted where small children play. The entire plant is toxic, especially the seeds. One to three of the mottled black, brown, and white glossy seeds can be fatal to a child. In addition, handling the leaves and seeds of this plant can produce severe allergic reactions in some people. Seeds are available from: **HARRIS SEEDS**, Moreton Farm, Rochester, NY 14624. **MELLINGER'S, INC.**, 2310 W. South Range Road, North Lima, OH 44452; (216) 549–9861. **PEACEFUL VALLEY FARM SUPPLY**, see above. **RITCHERS**, see above.

You can also make a liquid mole repellent with castor oil, which is non-poisonous: 1/4 cup castor oil, 2 tablespoons liquid soap, 6 tablespoons water. In a blender, whip together castor oil and liquid soap until the resultant mixture is like shaving cream. Add the water and whip again. Take a regular garden sprinkling can, fill it with warm water, and add 2 tablespoons of the oil mixture. Stir and sprinkle the liquid immediately over the areas of the greatest damage. For best results, apply after a rain or a thorough watering.

B. Euphorbia Lathyris (mole plant, caper spurge, gopher spurge) also drives moles and gophers from the neighborhood. CAUTION: this is a poisonous plant. Although not as toxic as the castor bean above, the stems contain a milky sap the can irritate the skin, and the fruit has been mistaken for the true caper and has been eaten by children, producing severe digestive symptoms. Seeds are available from: **LAKELAND NURSERIES SALES**, 340 Poplar Street, Hanover, PA 17333. **PEACEFUL VALLEY FARM SUPPLY**, see above. **TAYLOR'S HERB GARDENS, INC.**, 1535 Lone Oak Road, Vista, CA 92083; (619) 727–3485.

- **Bibiography.**

"Organic Sprays and How to Use Them," by Tony DeCrosta. Appeared March 1980. Describes the uses of four botanical insecticides, BTI, Milky Spore disease, diatomaceous earth, oil sprays, and sulfur.

"Insect Emergence Times," by Barbara Yoder. Appeared April 1980. In chart format, tells when to expect twenty-four common problem insects in sixteen regions of the United States.

"Best Ideas for Companion Planting," by Anna Carr. Appeared February 1985. An overview of current research with suggestions for beneficial plant combinations in the garden. Includes a bibliography.

"Flower Power," by John Warde. Appeared May 1985. An in-depth look at the botanical insecticide pyrethrum, with sources for seeds, flowers, and products.

"The Ultimate Pest Control," by Ellen Cohen. Appeared June 1985. People who work with natural pest controls discuss creative strategies for balancing the garden environment to reduce pests.

"Flea Killers You Can Live With," by Warren Schultz. Appeared July 1985. Suggestions and sources for safer flea controls for pets.

These reprints of *Rodale Organic Gardining* articles are available for twenty-five cents apiece and a self-addressed, stamped envelope (we have bulk rates for orders of fifty or more). Send requests to "Pest Reprints," *Rodale's Organic Gardening*, Research and Reader Service Dept., 33 East Minor Street, Emmaus, PA 18049. For descriptions and prices of Rodale Press books on pest control, ask for the listing "R&RS Recommends: Pest Books."

How to Grow Vegetables Organically, by Jeff Cox and the editors of *Rodale Organic Gardening*. Professional horticulturists at the Rodale Research Center provide hundreds of pointers on growing healthy vegetables without using harmful chemicals.

- **Organizations.**

  National Coalition Against the Misuse of Pesticides (NCAMP), 530 Seventh Street, SE, Washington, DC 20003; (202) 543–5450. Comprising 300 groups plus hundreds of individual members, NCAMP is the primary national organization working on pesticide issues. They promote public policy reform and provide referrals to local pesticide action groups and other contacts. A staff toxicologist also helps answer pesticide questions. Quarterly newsletter, *Pesticides and You*, $10.

  Natural Resources Defense Council (NRDC), 25 Kearny Street, San Francisco, CA 94108; (415) 421–6561. A source for referrals and legal advice on pesticide issues. NRDC also publishes studies on pesticides in food and provides information on the EPA's regulatory structure and national pesticide legislation. Also publishes *The Amicus Journal*, a quarterly magazine, and *NRDC Newsline* six times yearly. Both included with $20 membership fee.

  NRDC Toxic Substances Information Line, (800) 648–NRDC, (212) 687–6862 in New York. The hotline fields questions on toxic substances and their health effects. If they don't have the answer, staff members will try to refer inquiries to appropriate organizations.

  Pesticide Education and Action Project: The North American Regional Center for Pesticide Action Network (PAN) International, PO Box 610, San Francisco, CA 94101; (415) 771–PEAP. This group answers questions and provides information on international pesticide issues and policy reform. Newsletter, *PAN NA*, published three times yearly, $10.00.

  Pesticide Hotline: (800) 858–7378. The National Pesticide Telecommunications Network (NPTN). Funded by an EPA grant and located at Texas Tech University, NPTN answers pesticide questions twenty-four hours a day, seven days a week. They provide technical, chemical, and regulatory information; toxicity and health data; and referrals to residue testing labs, poison control centers, and local doctors experienced with pesticide poisonings.

  Bio-Integral Resource Center (BIRC), PO Box 7414, Berkeley, CA 94707. BIRC prescribes integrated pest management (IPM) strategies for controlling pests of the human body, building structures, plants, or pets. Membership benefits include a detailed written consultation on a pest problem and a subscription to the *IPM Practitioner* or *Common Sense Pest Control Quarterly*. For membership details and a catalog of IPM publications and audiovisual materials, send $1 and a self-addressed, stamped envelope.

  Concern, Inc., 1794 Columbia Road, NW, Washington, DC 20009; (202) 328–8160. An environmental-education organization that publishes concise, readable, community action guides on pesticides, hazardous wastes, and ground- and drinking-water contamination. They also provide answers and referrals for pesticide questions.

- **Suggested reading on health and environmental aspects of pesticide use:**

  CIRCLE OF POISON: Pesticides and People in a Hungry World, D. Weir and M. Schapiro (Institute for Food and Development Policy, 1981), 99 pp. Available from IFDP, 1885 Mission Street, San Francisco, CA 94103

  GUIDE TO THE FREEDOM OF INFORMATION ACT, Federal, California, Oregon, Washington, and Idaho Northwest Coalition for Alternatives to Pesticides (NCAP), 1983, 7 pp. Available from NCAP, PO Box 375, Eugene, OR 97440.

  THE HEALTH DETECTIVE'S HANDBOOK: A Guide to the Investigation of Environmental Health Hazards by Nonprofessionals, M. Legator, B. Harber and M. Scott. The Johns Hopkins University Press, 701 West 40th Street, Baltimore, MD 21211.

  ON THE TRAIL OF A PESTICIDE: A Guide to Learning about the Chemistry, Effects, and Testing of Pesticides, Mary O'Brien (NCAP, 1984), 166 pp., 1984. Available from NCAP, PO Box 375, Eugene, OR 97440.

- **Learn about organic gardening methods.**

  Here are some resources:

  AGROECOLOGY PROGRAM, University of California, Santa Cruz, CA 95064; (408) 429–4140. Located on UC Santa Cruz's twenty-five-acre farm and four-acre garden, six month (April-October) residential apprenticeship offers instruction in traditional organic horticulture.

  ALCYONE LIGHT CENTER, 1965 Hilt Road, Hornbrook, CA 96044; (916) 475–3310. Community hosts three-month internships and weekend workshops in organic gardening, etc.

  BIOLOGICAL URBAN GARDENING SERVICES, PO Box 76, Citrus Heights, CA 95611–0076; (916) 726–5377. International membership organization concerned with reducing the use of toxic chemicals in urban landscaping. Quarterly newsletter and a catalogue of publications on natural pest management.

  CAMP JOY, 131 Camp Joy Road, Boulder Creek, CA 95006; (408) 338–3651. Nonprofit organization and family farm. Hosts short courses, workshops, classes and tours.

THE MEADOWCREEK PROJECT, INC., Fox, AR 72051; (501) 363–4500. Nonprofit environmental education facility on 1,500 acres conducts conferences, internships, research, and demonstrations.

PEACEABLE KINGDOM SCHOOL, PO Box 313, Washington, TX 77880; (409) 878–2353. Nonprofit school with 152 acres of farmland sponsors programs in organic gardening, land management, and herbal medicine.

The Tree of Life
by R. Neil Sampson

The quality of life for most Americans is framed by the quality of their city or town. That quality is, in turn, defined by many aspects—economic, social, and environmental. In too many cases, however, our pre-occupation with jobs, economic growth, crime prevention, education, and similar urban issues cause us to overlook the importance of environmental quality in urban life.

As a result, most of our communities are far more polluted, hotter, and less pleasant than they need to be. Improving those conditions can make life better for everyone, and working to improve the environment is a job that anyone can undertake, with only a modest investment of time, money, or skill.

Planting trees is a good way to improve an urban environment. Anyone can do it, and everybody loves it. Planting a tree is a spiritual as well as physical act—helping set forth a new life in a new place—a life that could, with luck, run hundreds of years and affect many generations of people. This is not an act one does randomly, or thoughtlessly, or without joy.

To get the full value from planting a tree, it helps to know some basics about how trees affect the environment, what kinds of conditions trees need in order to thrive, and how to plant and care properly for trees.

THE ROLE OF TREES. Plants take CO_2 and other elements from the atmosphere, along with mineral nutrients and water from the soil, and convert these elements into cellulose and other organic compounds through photosynthesis, a process in which the action of sunlight on a green compound called chlorophyll drives the chemical reactions that form the basis of all life on earth.

The biological process is essentially the same whether the plant is a microscopic algae or a huge redwood tree, but the effect on the atmosphere and environment differ significantly. For example, in countering global warming, the tree is far more valuable. This is true for several reasons. First, trees store much of the material they produce in the form of wood. A fast-growing yard or street

> He that plants trees loves others beside himself.
>
> – *Thomas Fuller,*
> Gnomologia, 1732

tree can add up to four cubic feet of wood in its trunk, limbs, and roots each year. For every cubic foot of wood it grows, a tree locks up 17.5 pounds of carbon. If that tree lives for 100 or 200 years, the carbon contained in its wood will not be added to the growing problem of atmospheric CO_2 buildup—the principle cause of global warming. Even if harvested, some of the tree may end up in a house, bridge or book that will extend its carbon storage value for many years, perhaps centuries. Thus, trees and forests become a critical "storage reservoir" of carbon that mitigates the excess buildup caused by burning fossil fuels. Currently, an estimated 90 percent of the carbon bound up in the earth's living organisms is contained in the world's forests.

In rural forests, approximately one acre of fast-growing, healthy forest can absorb 1.4 tons of CO_2 each year. In addition, forest soils absorb methane (another greenhouse gas), using it as a nutrient. Recent research indicates that forest soils not artificially fertilized by humans, or affected by the excess fallout of nitrogen from "acid rain," absorb methane more efficiently. Thus, the health of trees and forests are a major concern to environmentalists studying the greenhouse effect and its possible causes and cures. Clearly, obtaining millions of acres of fast-growing new forest may be an important part of offsetting the greenhouse effect.

In far too much of the world, forests are simply burned and the land converted to crops or pastures—or barren deserts. Deforestation has become a major international concern. In the past, it was Europe and North America that suffered the most significant deforestation. Today, it is the tropics, where an estimated twenty-seven million acres of forest are destroyed each year by land clearing, and another thirteen million acres are affected by logging in ways that may be permanently harmful. In addressing the global environmental crisis, it is critical that we halt this destruction of forests. Just as important, however, is that both new and existing forests are healthy and fast-growing. Tree growth rates, not just the existence of trees, affects the amount of CO_2 absorbed by trees. Therefore, people must not just plant trees, but must also manage existing forests properly and protect them from air pollution that affects forest health and growth.

Trees also help address urban environmental degradation. Trees act as living air conditioners that cool the earth by evaporating water into the atmosphere. In addition, by shading streets, buildings, and soil, trees prevent heat buildup. This shading and cooling can result in energy savings that mitigate the effects of CO_2 on the environment. Through the reduction of air conditioning needs, a city tree saves electricity, which means less coal or oil burned in a power plant, which means less CO_2. It has been estimated that a properly placed city shade tree can

Planting a tree is a spiritual as well as physical act—helping set forth a new life in a new place—a life that could, with luck, run hundreds of years and affect many generations of people.

save fifteen times as much CO_2 production through energy savings as it consumes in its annual growth. Less air conditioning also means release of less ozone depleting CFCs from refrigerants.

Trees also reduce pollution. They filter some air pollutants directly from the air, although this capacity is limited, and air that is too polluted harms the tree itself. In addition, the cooling effect of trees is directly tied to reduction in ozone depletion and smog formation—a major urban pollution problem. Smog and ozone form as the result of sunlight's action on airborne chemicals, many of which are produced by automobiles and power plants. This chemical reaction speeds up as heat rises. Research at the Lawrence Berkeley Laboratory in California has indicated that approximately 25 percent of the air pollution in cities may be the direct result of the warmer temperatures increased by the urban "heat island" phenomenon. Those same studies showed clearly that the most cost-effective way to lower inner-city temperatures is by planting additional trees and painting black surfaces a lighter color wherever possible.

TREES NEED SPACE TO GROW. In planting a tree, it is easy to forget how large it can become when full size. Trees planted too close to houses, sidewalks, or streets, or under power and telephone lines are trees out of place—trees that cannot fulfill their promise as environmental fighters. They may become a nuisance or hazard in the process.

There are two aspects of tree space—above and below the ground—and both are important. The above-ground space needs are the most obvious. Tall trees should not be placed under overhead obstructions like power lines or building overhangs. Trees should be kept at least ten feet away from building foundations, and that distance should depend on the ultimate size and shape of the tree.

Underground space is a little more difficult for most people to envision. Trees do not have huge, deep taproots, as is commonly assumed. Research has demonstrated that almost all roots grow within the top foot of soil. Rarely do any roots grow deeper than three feet. The horizontal reach of roots can be more than twice as wide as the tree is tall. When fully grown, the whole tree might have the same profile as a wine glass set on a dinner plate. This means that trees around buildings and streets must be given far more root space than has often been the case in the past. Where sidewalks run close to street curbs, with only a foot or two of soil between them, trees should be planted inside the sidewalk on the yard, not in the narrow strip between sidewalk and street. Trees planted too close to impenetrable barriers like foundations or streets develop one-sided root systems that are less effective in absorbing needed water and nutrients and less able to anchor the tree against heavy storms.

Clear Cutting and Quarter Pounders

Tragically, deforestation has reached crisis proportions. Since 1967, the rate of deforestation in this country has exceeded one acre every five seconds. Moreover, the worldwide deforestation rate is approximately 27 million acres a year. Much of the deforestation is taking place in Brazil, Indonesia, and Zaire, which contain nearly half of all tropical forests. The worldwide rate of deforestation is ten times the rate of reforestation.

Contributors to this rate of deforestation might surprise you. For every acre that we use for parking lots, houses, and roads, seven acres of forest are made into land for grazing livestock and growing livestock feed.

The Central American rain forests are being depleted at an even faster rate, also primarily for cattle grazing. Central Americans countries now export over 138 million pounds of beef each year. And just one quarter-pound of imported beef, enough for one fast-food burger, requires the clearing of 55 square feet of tropical rain forest. When the trees are burned, they emit 500 pounds of CO_2 into the atmosphere.

Deforestation causes 25 percent of all worldwide CO_2 emissions. Therefore, scientists see reforestation as one of the most critical tasks in reducing global warming. To reverse the effects of the greenhouse crisis, we must plant enough trees to cover an area approximately equal to the land mass of Australia. We must all begin the crucial task of reforesting the planet.

In rural forests, approximately one acre of fast-growing, healthy forest can absorb 1.4 tons of CO$_2$ each year.

Thus, in planting trees for maximum environmental impact, give the tree the right kind of space—both above and below ground. Carefully plan where to put each tree, and get the right kind of tree in the right place. Seek locations that create maximum shade like the south and west sides of buildings, parking areas, driveways, and streets. For the best energy conservation, plant deciduous trees (those that lose their leaves in winter) on the south, southeast, and west sides of a home. That will provide summer shading, but in the winter, when the sun is low on the horizon and the leaves have fallen, the sun's rays can come through to help reduce heating needs. Plant evergreens on the north and northeast, so that they will help shield the building from winter winds.

PLANTING AND CARING FOR TREES. Planting a tree is largely a matter of preparing the soil correctly. Loosen the soil with a shovel or Rototiller in an area at least twice as wide as the tree root ball. This loosens the soil so roots can grow horizontally with less resistance and mixes the soil so roots will not be confined to any one area. Dig a hole as deep as the root ball, but no deeper, and about twice as wide. Place the tree in the hole and gently separate the roots and spread them in the planting hole. Do not allow any roots to circle the rest of the roots or the tree stem, because as it grows, that root will strangle the tree. Fill the hole with soil, and lightly pack soil around the roots. Spread a two to three inch layer of mulch over the entire area where the roots will grow. Stake the tree so it can flex with the wind, and water the tree thoroughly. Do not flood it, but water it frequently for several days so that the new roots can establish themselves. Summer watering will be critical for tree survival during the first season after planting.

Tips

Obviously their are many more aspects of planting and caring for trees than can be listed here. Don't be bashful about seeking help. Written guidelines on tree-planting and tree care are available at minimal cost from a variety of sources, including city forestry offices, local garden and nursery centers, county extension offices, and soil conservation districts. Members of local garden clubs, horticultural societies, and professional groups such as the American Society of Arboriculture and the Society of American Foresters also provide information and assistance. Tree-planting guides, tree care handbooks, and a wide variety of literature on trees, forests, and how they affect the environment can be obtained by joining the American Forestry Association (AFA), a citizen's conservation group that can be reached at PO Box 2000, Washington, DC 20013.

The AFA sponsors a campaign called Global ReLeaf, whose goal is to educate people about environmental improvement and fight the greenhouse effect by improving trees and forests. Global ReLeaf hopes to encourage Americans to plant new trees in the estimated 100 million tree spaces that exist around America's homes and businesses.

Planting trees is not an environmental panacea, but it isone small step in the right direction. It is the epitome of thinking globally and acting locally, as urged by ecologist Rene Dubos. It offers a simple, positive response to the most commonly asked question that comes from people who have been told that the world is suffering serious environmental abuse. "What can I do?" they ask. "Plant a tree," Global ReLeaf responds.

The potential environmental impact is significant. Planting 100 million trees could result in an annual savings of some $4 billion in air conditioning costs each year. Urban heat island effects would be reduced, energy resources would be conserved, and a small step toward reducing the greenhouse effect would be in place.

Trees act as living air conditioners that cool the earth by evaporating water into the atmosphere.

Perhaps even more important for the long-term, however, will be the effect on public attitudes and political constituencies of getting so many people involved in the task of environmental repair and enhancement. People and companies who have been involved in planting trees and improving forest management in their own neighborhoods will be more insistent that local, state, and national leaders take appropriate policy and program actions as well.

The result could be a future in which individuals, companies, communities, and national governments cooperate in joint efforts to assure that the productive ecosystems essential to the survival of the earth are managed, maintained, and used wisely.

- **Plant shade trees next to your home.** Planting shade trees near your home helps reforestation and also cuts down on the use of air conditioning—a major contributor to the greenhouse effect and ozone depletion. In colder climates, strategically plant evergreens to provide a wind break and to save on heating energy consumption.

- **Landscape your lawn with trees and shrubbery.** Because trees and bushes are many times more effective than lawns in absorbing CO_2, plant many trees when landscaping your yard.

- **Involve your family in tree planting activities.** The tree has always captured the imagination of young people. Planting trees is a wonderful way to raise kids' environmental consciousness and to involve the entire family in healing the earth. For birthday and holiday gifts, give the gift of life—buy a tree. Contact your local nursery and buy a tree gift certificate.

- **Call your local environmental organization and get involved with tree-planting projects.** Many environmental organizations are becoming more involved in tree-planting projects, and they need volunteers. So contact the groups in your community and get involved.

- **Improve your schools, churches, and other public areas by planting trees.** Reforestation efforts shouldn't be restricted to the home. Even if you don't own a home, you can become involved with church groups, parent/teachers associations, and other community organizations in planting projects throughout the community.

- **Maintain your trees.** Many trees require periodic pruning and other care to stay healthy. The Global ReLeaf Program is a national campaign with the specific goal of reducing the level of CO_2 build up in the atmosphere through reforestation. Several excellent resources on the program and how to become involved may be obtained by writing to **Global ReLeaf**, The American Forestry Association, PO Box 2000, Washington, DC 20013; (202) 667–3300.

  In addition to the Global ReLeaf campaign, the American Forestry Association offers detailed information on tree planting and tree care in several other publications. For brochures, booklets, and workshop information on how to plant at home, at school, in the community, and on how to organize neighborhood forestry projects, please write to **Tree People**, 12601 Mulholland Drive, Beverly Hills, CA 90210; (818) 769–2663.

- **Join with your neighbors in surveying the condition of trees along your streets, or in your community parks.** If there are lots of vacant spaces, or the trees aren't healthy, go to community leaders and ask why. (A workbook to lead you through this process and produce credible assessments is available from the American Forestry Association.)

- **Help teach students by assisting in school programs, Arbor Day celebrations, Global ReLeaf plantings, and other forms of environmental education.**

- **Urge passage of local, state, and federal laws that promote reforestation and prevent deforestation.**

Wrong Assumptions and the Patterns They Impose
by Wes Jackson

Men are made of what is made,
The meat, the drink, the life, the corn,
Laid up by them, by them reborn.
And self-begotten cycles close
About our way: indigenous art
And simple spells make unafraid
The haunted labyrinths of the heart
And with our wild succession braid
The resurrection of the rose.
　　　　　　　— Edwin Muir

In late June 1989, I watched with dismay as torrents of top soil and water shot through a six foot diameter culvert, like water out of a nozzle, and sprayed into a small creek of southeastern Nebraska. Rills quickly developed on the exposed fields and turned to gullies in a mere half hour, during what turned out to be a heavy overnight rain. Completely stopped or inching along in my pickup, I watched all this loss of soil and thought of the highly paid experts in our state agricultural colleges who are *still* proclaiming American agriculture a success story. I wondered how there can ever be any talk of success in farming so long as such huge amounts of ecological capital erodes seaward.

That loss of topsoil in Nebraska, and ecological degradation across the country, is being caused by some tragically wrong assumptions about agriculture. For example, it takes 500 years to form one inch of topsoil. Yet we're losing one inch of topsoil every 19 years through our misuse of agriculture. Nationally, an estimated 100 million acres of United States cropland already has been abandoned due to topsoil loss. In total, soil erosion and associated water runoff cost the United States an estimated $44 billion annually in direct and indirect effects.

Modern agriculture's destruction of the environment is based on three wrong-headed assumptions: (1) subdue or ignore nature, (2) increase production, and (3) use agriculture as an instrument for the expansion of industry. Not many

Recent research indicates that, for certain crops, fossil fuel energy use could be decreased by 50 percent if soil erosion was reduced, crops rotated, mechanical cultivation substituted for pesticides, and livestock manure substituted for commercial fertilizer.

would agree with these tenets. Yet they form the very foundation of current agriculture production. Few of us saying grace over our food think about this appalling view of agriculture. But far from seeing farming as a nurturing and caring activity, modern agriculture makes it possible to regard food production as a weapon against the natural world.

Taken together, these three assumptions directly threaten Thomas Jefferson's vision of a nation of farmers and free citizens as the best bet for a healthy democracy. Those of us who suggest that we abandon or greatly modify these three assumptions are often accused of nostalgia. But if town meetings were held around the country to address this basic question, "Is the Jeffersonian ideal of the family farm and strong rural community mere nostalgia or a practical necessity in a world of declining energy and material resources?," most would side with Jefferson.

Of course, the three basic assumptions fit modern agriculture's bottom line—short-run profit. As noted by Texas Commissioner of Agriculture Jim Hightower, the major problem today is that American agriculture is geared to benefit the corporate farm at the expense of the family farm. That view stresses cultivation of a single high-yield profit crop over diversified crops. These high-yield type crops are compatible with high volume export needs and have little to do with local needs. Perhaps most problematic for the environment is that these crops require enormous quantities of synthetic chemicals.

Our bottom line must expand past the simple lure of quick profit. Our ultimate goal has to become the assurance of a plentiful and safe food supply for the future. How are we to make this possible? Soil erosion will have to be reduced to natural replacement levels. Our dependency on fossil fuels will have to end. Recent research indicates that, for certain crops, fossil fuel energy use could be decreased by 50 percent if soil erosion was reduced, crops rotated, mechanical cultivation substituted for pesticides, and livestock manure substituted for commercial fertilizer.

Of course, we must limit our use of pesticides. Each year about one billion pounds of pesticides is applied to United States crops at the cost of more than $4 billion. Despite this massive use, about 37 percent of crops are still lost to pests. One major reason for this is that 99.9 percent of applied pesticide never reaches the target pests. Instead, it disperses into the environment and contaminates our water and air. Biological nitrogen fixation will have to replace nitrogen fertilizer. The crumb structure found in healthy soils is enhanced by animal manure. The three billion head of livestock in the United States produce almost two billion tons of manure each year. This amount contains five times

No occupation is so delightful to me as the culture of the earth.

— *Thomas Jefferson*

the fertilizer nutrients contained in all the commercial fertilizer used annually in U.S. agriculture. Getting animals back on the farm and out of commercial feed lots would help our soils and save energy.

In other words, to conserve our agricultural base for the long run, farms must meet certain ecological standards similar to those in natural ecosystems, such as a prairie. The key here is diversity and a manageable scale. To some extent, people power will have to substitute for energy-consuming and polluting machine power. To place agriculture back on its biological feet, millions of people will have to be encouraged to return to the land.

The profit-only corporate farm simply cannot care for the land. Without small farms, no one watches the land under cultivation, especially erosion on land that slopes. Who on the corporate farm takes seriously the slow knowledge and the accumulated mistakes and successes over generations so crucial to sustainable farming? If land is to serve more than as an instrument for yielding a simple cipher in a quarterly report, it will need sympathy and love. In short, a seamless web of people, land, and community are the ecological and cultural requirements for a sustainable agriculture.

To have a sustainable agriculture, rural communities must be large enough to support small family farms and the services and culture that are necessary for them. Without such a community, the income farm families earn immediately goes to outside corporations. We need small businesses to intercept this capital where it can roll over long enough to support the local community, from schools and social services to churches and baseball teams.

This necessary transition cannot begin until we reconsecrate the Jeffersonian idea that the strength of the nation depends on the "free man" on the land. This is not some archaic 200-year-old idea whose utility has vanished. It was an old idea 200 years ago, an idea in Western civilization almost from the beginning. It was there with the Hebrews at Mount Sinai, with the desert and Egypt behind them, as they looked forward to the Promised Land of Canaan where each would sit under his own fig tree, have his own vineyard, and be his own priest. This democratic ideal, thankfully, is also an ecological ideal, for it accommodates the possibility and necessity of people paying close attention to what Thoreau called "meeting the expectations of the land."

THE EMERGENCE OF A BIG IDEA. I think a big idea is emerging in the American mind. It is becoming apparent that our problem with the earth is the result of our "make do and ignore" assumptions, not just about agriculture, but everything else. We have assumed control without an adequate understanding

Modern agriculture's destruction of the environment is based on three wrong headed assumptions: (1) subdue or ignore nature, (2) increase production, and (3) use agriculture as an instrument for the expansion of industry.

of nature's arrangements. Increasingly, we have patterned agricultural production along the same lines as industrial production, ignoring the lessons of nature.

But now many are saying that, since nature had the most sustainable ecosystems and since ultimately agriculture comes out of nature, should not our standard for a sustainable world be based on nature's most sustainable ecosystems? "Nature as the measure." "Nature as an analogy." "Nature as the standard." These ideas are uniting growing numbers of ecologists and agriculturalists.

It won't be the first time, of course, that humans have advocated that we return to nature as our primary teacher. Wendell Berry has traced some of the literary history from Job into the early part of the nineteenth century. It disappears from English literature apparently after Alexander Pope. When it surfaces again, it is among scientists—Liberty Hyde Bailey, J. Russell Smith, and Sir Albert Howard.

In total, soil erosion and associated water runoff cost the United States an estimated $44 billion annually in direct and indirect effects.

This idea of "nature knows" has been linked with the key concept of sustainability. In 1978, I was preparing an article on agriculture policy, titled, "Toward a Sustainable Agriculture." Why I chose that now-celebrated word "sustainable," I don't remember precisely. I do remember thinking about the word "permanent" and rejecting it as not correct for an ever-changing earth. I am sure I am not the first person to use the term in print, though some have credited me for it. Today, the concept and the term have become used in the common culture. Why the term spread so rapidly, beginning about twelve years ago, is a matter of speculation. More importantly, what does sustainable agriculture mean today?

"Sustainable" is fast becoming a highly politicized term. Political terms are especially vulnerable to co-option, even to the point that the term could be used as an instrument of large scale, industrialized agribusiness. Like most political words, it is vulnerable to both history and passion, making it even more important to remember its origins. Remember that the term does not come out of the research plots of the government experiment stations or the private agribusiness companies. We cannot, therefore, allow it to be defined by such people. More accurately, the word comes from those of us in the common culture who are frustrated with the extractive economy and the desecration of the land and water that sustain agriculture. The word will change but retain a core of meanings, a core that will require care and watchfulness. And herein lies the challenge, for only care and practice can keep the ideal healthy. In that sense it is like other words that express our idea, words like justice, truth, beauty, love.

An irate member of an audience at a land grant university once asked me for my definition of "sustainability" and stated that "it had better be in ten words or less or I am not going to listen." I could not accommodate him. Reaching into the core of my understanding, I found myself using such words as diversity, conservation, balance, scale.

So, since it is a political word, political education will be as important as education in proper farming techniques. The proper teachers will be those who start with the assumption that we are mostly ignorant about how to do sustainable agriculture. Since we are basically ignorant about eventual outcomes, it is best to be observant students of the way nature has worked.

Teachers, be they the organic farmer, the environmental activist, or the university professor and researcher, must also be cautious lest they feel inclined toward self-righteousness ("We are farming without chemicals," and "We are farming nature's way") and self-pity ("We do all this extra work so that we don't have to use the chemicals and we are not properly compensated for our labor"). Both will have to be avoided at all costs. We are all in this together, and if we are to be like the best of political educators, our words must reflect the *reality* of our common predicament. This may not be easy, especially when our strongest urges are to remain distant and feel superior. Loving our enemies is not some hollow morality; it is a practical necessity.

GENETIC ENGINEERING. Just as we have attempted to dominate, nature through our use of chemicals, we now tinker with the genes of plants and animals—all in the name of agricultural efficiency. For example, several companies are attempting to market bovine growth hormone (BGH). When injected into cows, this genetically engineered hormone increases milk production up to 30 percent. Studies now predict that this increased milk production, in an already flooded market, could eliminate 30 percent of dairy farmers. Cows will also suffer with increased levels of various diseases. BGH may be efficient for increasing milk. It could spell disaster for the farmer and the cow.

In a another recent application of genetic engineering, United States Department of Agriculture (USDA) scientists spliced a *human* growth hormone gene into swine. Hogs grew faster and leaner, satisfying the commercial grower. Unfortunately, they also were arthritic and cross-eyed. The problems are regarded primarily as a simple matter of fine tuning the hog. Meanwhile, hogs have also been engineered to contain *bovine* growth hormones. They also became leaner, but they experience gastric ulcers, renal disease, dermatitis, an enlarged heart, and arthritis. The justification for these experiments again arises from the assumption that the goal of farming and agricultural research should be to increase the productive capacity of our various crops and livestock. The real

Each year about one billion pounds of pesticides is applied to United States crops at the cost of more than $4 billion.

monsters created by such applications of biotechnology are the humans who see nothing wrong with creating miserable animals.

The biotechnology craze will die down some day, partly because, like other crazes before in biology, payoffs will disappoint the proponents and investors. Furthermore, I think we will see a growing uncertainty about the ecological consequences of altered organisms. Proper assessment will require an understanding of biology at all levels. (Any biologist who has taught general biology will not be encouraged about that possibility.) Moreover, it will soon become apparent that the rewards of biotechnology will run mostly to the suppliers of inputs—the Monsantos—not the farmer and the landscape.

THE LAND INSTITUTE. Our work at The Land Institute in Salina, Kansas, began in 1976. In 1978, I published a paper, mentioned above, in which I suggested that the native prairie be our ecological standard, on the assumption that the best agriculture mimics natural ecosystems. Since then, our small group of researchers has set out to build domestic prairies that would produce perennial grains grown in mixtures as substitutes for annual monocultures on hillsides. Our time frame is in the twenty-five to one hundred year range.

Our work did not come out of a literary and scientific tradition. Instead, it came out of the "familial and communal handing down in the agrarian common culture." We have come to rely on the big idea of "Nature as the measure." In the 1978 paper, which established the paradigm for our research, I also asked, "What will nature require?" Since then we have added a third consideration embedded in the first two, "What will nature help us to do here?" Wendell Berry has pointed out that, as we cut the forests and plowed the great prairies, "we have never known what we were doing because we have never known what we were undoing." A future agriculture will require that we learn as much as possible about what we have undone.

ON NOT BECOMING OPERATIONAL. Edgar Mitchell, the astronaut who has visited the moon, has often been asked what it was like to experience the moon. He has had to reply that he was "too busy being operational to experience the moon." Life on the moon requires the ultimate in instrumentation to keep the little earth environment of the astronaut functioning.

As we employ our knowledge to accommodate our demands and tinker with the earth, we create acid rain, deplete the ozone layer, contaminate groundwater, and maybe cause global warming. Increasingly, we take conscious measures to protect ourselves from the problems we create. We become increasingly busy, *more operational*, with less and less time to *experience* the earth. Such somber thoughts can create somber people. But we have to be careful, for we can become

---

You think farm buildings and broad acres a solid property: but its vaule is flowing like water. It requires as much watching as if you were decanting wine from a cask.

— *R.W. Emerson,*
The Conduct of Life, 1860

so frightened we make it our full-time job to save the earth. Some have done just that, denying themselves the time to enjoy the very earth they are trying to save. In doing so, they lose the sight and feeling for what they are supposedly saving. Edward Abbey said it best a short time before his death in 1989. "Be a half-assed crusader, a part-time fanatic," he said. "Don't worry too much about the fate of the world. Saving the world is only a hobby. Get out there and enjoy the world, your girlfriend, your boyfriend, husbands, wives; climb mountains, run rivers, get drunk, do whatever you want to do while you can, before it's too late."

Tips

- **Diversify crops.** Growing new crops and creating new markets for them is a necessity if we are to create a sustainable agriculture. Government can help. For example, the Texas Department of Agriculture has conducted studies and is opening markets for fourteen new crops, including pinto beans, that can be grown profitably in the Texas bio-region.

- **Try ecological pest management.** A crucial part of sustainable agriculture is the movement away from pesticides. Sustainable pest management strategies include diversification of crops, crop rotation, tillage, improved sanitation, and biological controls including sterile insect releases.

- **Reduce use of chemical fertilizers.** Chemical fertilizers cause water and soil pollution and emit nitrous oxide, a greenhouse gas. Instead of chemical fertilizers, use organic fertilizers and crops that naturally fixate nitrogen.

- **Actively support the sustainable agriculture movement.** Even if you're not a farmer, you can support the sustainable agriculture movement by buying from local growers (preferably organically grown crops) and becoming better informed about the movement.

Sources

The Land Institute, 2440 East Water Well Road, Salina, KS 67401; (913) 823–8967.

The National Coalition Against the Misuse of Pesticides (NCAMP), 530 Seventh Street, SE, Washington, DC 20003; (202) 543–5450.

The International Alliance for Sustainable Agriculture, 1701 University Avenue, SE, Minneapolis, MN 55414; (612) 331–1099.

Saving for the Future
by Martin Teitel

It is becoming increasingly apparent that we are losing our plant genetic diversity. This loss of plant diversity puts our future at risk. Before describing the dangers of diversity loss and how we can begin preventing it, an explanation of biological diversity is in order.

Biological diversity actually describes something each one of us already knows. We live in a world incredibly and beautifully complicated. Those of us lucky enough to have backyards need only glance out the kitchen window to see a tiny corner of that diversity. Looking around, we can see dozens of different tree types and shapes, every possible color of flower, shrubs and bushes of many heights, perhaps a small garden with red, green, purple, orange, and yellow vegetables, and fruits hanging on the bushes and vines.

We might also see dogs, cats, birds, even people who exhibit great variation in size, color, shape, and activity. Unseen from our kitchen window is an even greater diversity in the incredible number of bugs, spiders, and worms creeping and burrowing and flying around our yard, the astounding numbers of microscopic plants and animals and bacteria living in the soil and on the plants. Everywhere in the verdant vista out our window is a rich, multi-layered, complex universe of living things.

We're so used to the diversity that we miss seeing it sometimes. Even though we might not be conscious of the extent of the diversity, it is the most powerful biological fact of our planet. But when you think about it, wouldn't it be simpler to have just one type of tree, one color of cat, even one kind of flu bug? Why is the world around us so elaborate?

Nature needs a large pool of genes to dip into as she reweaves genetic combinations. The more colors on the palette, the better the final picture.

Why is it so important for nature to revise her work? For one thing, it's a rough world out there, especially when one thinks in geologic terms: glaciers

- When the area of a habitat is reduced by 10 percent of its original size, the number of species that can persist in it indefinitely will eventually decline to 50 percent.
- Since 1900, over 86 percent of known apple varieties have become extinct.
- Since 1900, 2,300 pear varieties have become extinct.
- Two-thirds of Japan's rice varieties have been lost in this century.
- About 90 percent of Florida's citrus harvest derives from three varieties.
- Thirty plants contribute 90 percent of all of humanity's caloric intake; four of those plants are responsible for half of our calories.
- Six varieties of corn account for 71 percent of the United States crop.

In 1845, the great Irish Potato Famine was caused by the widespread use in Ireland of a potato that had no resistance to a potato blight. In 1916, over 200 million bushels of wheat were destroyed by red rust. Between 1900 and 1908, over two-thirds of California's Bartlett pear trees were destroyed by fire blight.

come and go; oceans, lakes and rivers appear and disappear; the climate fluctuates. Those who adapt to change, live. Those who do not adapt become extinct.

By definition one can't know what demands the future will make on us. We don't know if we're going to need fur coats or sun block. Nature can best function if the various stresses and strains in the environment can be addressed by a wide selection of adaptive traits that might be possible in various combinations of genetic building blocks. Thus, gradual changes in the environment can be matched by gradual responses in the physical makeup of the beings in that environment.

The gradual nature of genetic change in a species is one of the significant causes for concern that we have heard about recently from scientists and others who are studying global warming or the "greenhouse effect." If the environment changes faster than genetic processes can adapt, the plants and animals that have to live in the new environment risk extinction.

With environmental problems like the greenhouse effect, we see that preserving diversity is not just a question of having a nice view out the kitchen window; it's quite necessary if we and life as we know it on this planet are to thrive and survive.

Thus, we need to value overall diversity, in that a diversity of genetic traits housed in a diversity of species will ensure that some species will manage to survive the environmental changes that occur in the short run. The most simplistic explanation of evolution is based on this premise: those species equipped (genetically speaking) to survive whatever it is that might happen— disease, environmental changes—will then be around to pass those robust genes on to progeny. Those without the robust genes either don't survive, or don't reproduce, or don't reproduce much, thus weighting the future in favor of genetically determined characteristics that further survival.

The greater the number of individuals with divergent characteristics, the greater the chances that the race or species will continue to be around in sufficient numbers as the threats and challenges of the environment wax and wane. If we don't have enough traits among us to address a given environmental threat, then we could *all* be wiped out. The greater the diversity, the greater the chance that a species somewhere will have a trait that keeps them alive long enough to reproduce and pass that survival-oriented trait onto their kids. This same principle of living gene banks is true of course for all living things, not just us.

In biology, rigidity and uniformity work against species survival. The diverse will (and do) inherit the earth. We need to bear in mind that, in that rough world out there, those species that hedge their bets by fielding the most diverse set of individuals who embody the most diverse set of genetic instructions are the most likely to adapt—and survive. Because we're a race of thinking creatures, we can therefore make choices about certain of our actions that can maintain the diversity of the general gene pool around us.

Given the above, the alarming loss of plant genetic diversity around our planet poses a grave threat to the future of humanity, and indeed to all of nature. Modern agricultural history is replete with stories of crop disasters brought on by the use of only a few genetic strains of crops. In 1845, the great Irish Potato Famine was caused by the widespread use in Ireland of a potato that had no resistance to a potato blight. In 1916, over 200 million bushels of wheat were destroyed by red rust. Between 1900 and 1908, over two-thirds of California's Bartlett pear trees were destroyed by fire blight. Other disease disasters brought on by lack of genetic resistance include losses of sorghum, tomatoes, and corn.

And the situation isn't getting any better, primarily because of corporate ownership of seeds. Say "seed source" to most Americans, and I bet they'll say one of two things: "supermarket" or "Burpee." In a nutshell, that's our problem.

The largest seed companies in the United States include Royal Dutch Shell, Ciba-Geigy, and Monsanto. Worldwide, the largest seed company of all is Shell; in fact, of the ten top seed companies in the world, nine are either petrochemical companies like Monsanto or pharmaceutical companies like Ciba-Geigy. Only the tenth largest—Volvo, which alone controls forty-seven seed companies—is not directly in the petrochemical or pharmaceutical business as its prime concern.

What's wrong with big corporations owning seed companies? Don't they just achieve greater economy and wider distribution, especially of the new high-yield or "miracle" varieties? They do that, but it isn't something to celebrate. Here are some of the reasons to be concerned about corporate control of seed companies.

Diminished Diversity. Big corporations tend to offer a limited number of varieties. If Ciba-Geigy dominates the rice seed industry in Indonesia and only offers one or two varieties of rice, then their success in that market will result in genetically uniform crops. If a disease, insect, or weather extreme causes a crop failure of that particular variety, a whole country could starve. Large corporations almost always will do what they can to reduce or eliminate the competition. When the competition is other companies' seeds, since seeds are just containers for transporting genes, the big companies end up with a powerful interest in reducing the diversity of the gene pool, to preserve their market share.

In biology, rigidity and uniformity work against species survival. The diverse will (and do) inherit the earth.

Of the ten top seed companies in the world, nine are either petrochemical companies like Monsanto or pharmaceutical companies like Ciba-Geigy.

Piggybacking. One motivation for large corporations to get into the seed business is that the selling of seeds represents a well-established marketing channel. If you are interested in selling other products to farmers, how will you reach them? You can just piggyback your other products onto the pre-existing transaction of selling seeds. While this may be a brilliant marketing plan, it also has its own set of detriments.

For one thing, the "other products" tend to be noxious pesticides, herbicides, nematocides, and fertilizers. It is from the sale of these chemicals, rather than from the sale of seed, that the great profit is derived. Big corporations have a vested interest in pushing types of seeds that are dependent on the use of large amounts of expensive chemicals. They trumpet the high-yield "miracle" seeds while downplaying or simply not revealing the huge inputs of water and chemicals that are the hidden price of these high yields. If the selection of available seeds is largely limited to those that require pesticides and herbicides for success, it follows that the farmer has virtually no choice but to become "hooked" on chemicals.

Also, the seed companies tend to push hybridized seeds whenever they can. Most hybrids do not occur in nature and will not breed "true" from seed. The seed companies like hybrids because they can actually tailor the seeds to need lots of the chemicals they sell. Further, since hybridized seed can't produce plants that will produce viable seed for self-perpetuation, hybrids automatically create return customers. There is no point in the farmer letting his field go to seed. He must return to the seed store year after year. Thus, for the seed company conglomerates, hybrid seeds are far more profitable than open-pollinated types, both because they must be purchased every year and because they provide a continuous market for agrochemicals.

As farmers grow the hybrids, they usually stop growing the older varieties, sometimes at the strong urging of the big corporations. If the farmer has no stock of the older seed, once he stops growing that older and more diverse plant, it is in danger of becoming extinct. In fact, some important plant varieties have been lost forever in just a few years, just this way.

Flexibility and Flavor. Promotion of genetically uniform, chemical-craving hybrids inevitably results in more and more open-pollinated varieties becoming extinct. Nothing is quite as effective as extinction for narrowing our choices down to whatever seeds the seed companies wish to sell. Much to the frustration of many a gardener, the most readily available seeds (the hybridized, genetically uniform ones) may be poorly suited to local growing conditions.

On the other hand, the less readily available open-pollinated plants—plants that make seeds that make new similar plants—can make use of what scientists call "plastic genes." No, this is not another miracle of modern science. On the contrary, plant genes are naturally quite flexible. Planted in the unique growing conditions of your own backyard, plants from open-pollinated seeds can adapt. If at the end of each growing season you save the seeds from the biggest, hardiest, tastiest, or fastest-growing plants and then the next year plant only those seeds that best represent the characteristics you think are most desirable, you will soon have plants that are ideally suited to your specific growing conditions.

The sub-type that you develop may in a few years be noticeably different from similar plants only half a mile away. But it will be perfectly suited to your yard, your micro-climate, your gardening habits. When you see a neighbor with huge, delicious vegetables and she says that she's been growing them for years, her success is probably due to this kind of selective breeding program.

While generalizations always have exceptions, the most delicious fruits and vegetables do seem to come from non-hybridized seeds. The hybrids were developed to ensure that the particular qualities plant scientists and marketing specialists have decided are important would occur consistently among huge quantities of seeds. The problem lies in the disparity between what plant scientists and marketing specialists regard as important and what the person who grows and eats the food thinks is important. Your local growing conditions and your particular preferences in flavor or texture may not be high on the list of agribusiness' concerns.

Values and History. The matter of locally adapted plants brings us to the least scientific but perhaps most fundamental issue in our discussion of the difficulties posed by the corporate control of seeds.

Plants are the basis of all of our food and much of our clothing and shelter. They help hold the water we drink and manufacture the oxygen we breathe. Human beings have interacted intimately with plants since our earliest beginnings. Even before the advent of modern genetic science, people tinkered with the genetic expression of plants through farming. Though other animals, most notably ants, are farmers, no other creature approaches the depth and breadth of human interaction with the internal and external nature of plants.

Of the many ways we interact with plants, one particular act is crucial to shaping our genetic legacy. First, we prepare the soil. Then a seed is poked into the ground. We provide water, we pull weeds, thin seedlings, and fuss over the tender bright green shoots. Eventually, we have mature plants. We harvest. And then the crucial step is taken.

> The genetic uniformity of a crop amounts to an invitation for an epidemic to destroy that crop. The uniformity itself may result from the inherent pressures of the market place (machine harvesting, processing, etc.), as well as the absence of genetic variety in the crop breeding programme.
>
> — *Pat Roy Mooney,*
> Seeds of the Earth, 1979

The most delicious fruits and vegetables seem to come from non-hybridized seeds.

Faced with a patch of carrots, corn, wheat, or whatever going to seed, we do something that is the crux of agriculture. We manufacture an image, a picture of the future in our minds, of what we want that carrot or wheat to be like. We may not yet see it before us in our garden or field, but we carefully select the plants that most closely approach our mental goal and save only that seed for next year. Every year for countless years, people have taken this crucial step.

We are literally shaping the genetic substance of the world around us *with our minds*. Such is the power of ideas.

Ironically, this process is not unlike the process in which the multinational seed companies engage. They also have an image of their ideal plant. But as we saw in our discussion of flexibility and flavor, their image of the ideal may differ considerably from that of the grower or consumer. In corporate agriculture, an enormous distance separates the person holding the image from the person holding the seeds. The idea for the desired plant exists not in the mind of the Filipino rice farmer or the Ghanaian peanut grower, whose image would produce plants suited to the special requirements of their areas or people, but is instead captured in memos from Basel, or sales presentations in Minneapolis.

The plants are not ours anymore. The ancient and personal interaction between man and plant so integral to the spirit of agriculture is in danger of being lost. Through the development and disbursement of hybrids, agribusiness robs us of innumerable seed varieties, limits our choice of those that are left, and precludes a rare, precious chance for people to interact with nature in a positive, satisfying, and beneficial way.

Yet, it is not too late to reclaim our genetic legacy. The passing down of heirloom seeds through the generations, as so marvelously documented by the Seed Savers Exchange of Decorah, Iowa, can be restarted by any of us, no matter where we live. I have a friend who lives in New York City. In a window box on his fire escape he grows the hot chili peppers that have been passed down to him by his family in Louisiana. Immigrants to this country brought seeds in hat bands and dress hems. The descendants of those seeds still survive in the families that have been their caretakers—and shapers—all these years.

Anyone can play. There are only five steps, one of them optional, to rejoining a wonderful tradition.

Tips

- **Plan and plant a garden.** The trick to planning a garden, if you don't already have one going, is to start with absolutely the smallest garden you can imagine. We amateurs inevitably overextend ourselves, fail, and quit. My own expanded maxi-garden is five feet wide and twenty feet long. Even at this modest scale, I never quite get the whole thing planted. I always tell people I'm letting the South Forty go fallow. In my case, the forty is in inches.

Get an excellent gardening book—it's worth it. Expect to ignore from 50 to 90 percent of what the book says. Your illiterate plants will never know, and at least you'll have a reliable resource.

- **Once you've planned your garden, you're going to need some seeds.** Herein lies a critical test of will power that you should expect to fail, at least in part, for your first few seasons of gardening. Try to avoid the ubiquitous metal spin rack in supermarkets and the plastic trays of already started seedlings outside the hardware store that tempt you on a nice spring Saturday.

Instead, for at least some of your planting, buy open-pollinated seeds. Fortunately, the 1980s have seen a renaissance in small seed companies carrying open-pollinated seeds. Most are mail order, although a few sell in retail stores, too. One store not too far from our house now even sells started seedlings from non-hybrid seeds.

The other source of seed that can be even more fun to explore is other people's gardens. Is Uncle Charlie known for his fabulously tasty tomatoes? Ask him about the seed. They might be from a European-owned conglomerate, but just maybe he has faithfully saved them from his mother or cousin or neighbor. Near neighbors make a particularly good source, since the seeds they have are probably locally adapted and thus much more likely to survive in your garden.

When I planted some of the Louisiana hot peppers that I mentioned had been grown on a fire escape in New York, each one died as soon as it grew far enough above the soil to realize it was in an entirely different zip code. On the other hand, when a friend gave me some amaranth seeds that he had been saving from plants he grew a few miles away, the plants grew huge and strong. At the time I didn't even know what amaranth plants looked like, much less how to care for them. Still they thrived, because they were at home.

- **This is the optional step. If you want, make kids a part of gardening.** Not everyone has kids or wants them messing around in the nice, neat rows of her or his garden. Many people use gardening as a time for solitude, quiet, and reflection. Such time is precious in our loud, hurried world.

But if you don't mind involving kids in a limited way, do so. A feeling of connection with growing plants is as important a value to instill in future custodians of our troubled planet as is teaching young ones about keeping their elbows off the table or sharing toys.

Aside from learning to love dirt and plants, gardening can be an important antidote to "TV time." Too often our kids expect events to be presented and resolved within the span of a twenty-five minute television program. The first time I gave my then three year old daughter some bean seeds to plant, she poked a few into the earth and then stood back, with her hands at her sides, solemnly staring at the depressions her fingers had made. After a few minutes, when I asked her what she was doing, she said she was waiting for her beans because she was hungry. We can get our own sense of time, and that of our kids, back into better harmony with the natural cycles around us simply by planting a small garden.

Involve kids in gardening! Aside from learning to love dirt and plants, gardening can be an important antidote to "TV time."

A good strategy, if you do want to involve kids in gardening, is to give them a special plot of their own, or even just a planter box. This will greatly reduce your heartbreak when the kids thin out every single tomato seedling as happened to me recently. It will also permit you to have neat rows with little label sticks in the ground while the kids use a more casual plan. Anyone with kids under six (ten if they're ball players) should fence their garden.

- **Resist the temptation to rip up all of your plants at the end of the growing season.** It's easy to do, and a packet with enough open-pollinated tomato seeds to fill your backyard with fixings for salads all summer and spaghetti sauce all winter costs only a dollar or two.

  Learn to observe your plants so you will recognize which ones are exhibiting the characteristics you'll want to select when you engage in your own Mendelian experiments. You should be aware that seeds from certain plants, like tomatoes, are harder than others to harvest. Some plants make you labor for the seeds; some practically drop them in your lap. Try it out for yourself. At worst you'll have to invest another dollar in seeds next year. At best you'll have a free, perpetual, custom-tailored source of culinary delight that you can pass along to your children's children.

- After a while, when you've found a plant that you like and that likes you—one that has developed into something you're proud of—**start your own Johnny Appleseed program.**

  Make up little seed packets and give them away to family, friends, neighbors, and co-workers. Though some people will not understand what you're up to, you will invariably run into a dedicated gardener who will reward you with special admiration and appreciation that will add an extra measure of satisfaction to your heritage seed-saving activities.

Grass Roots Organizing
By John O'Connor

Unless we as a global community take dramatic action in this decade, we may irretrievably undermine the sustainability of our planet. There is a growing consensus that we must transform our entire economy—its industry, agriculture, and transportation from a fossil fuel and toxic-based economy to a more sustainable form of human activity.

Simple enough. But how do we move from here to there? What can we do where we live and work to transform our entire way of life to ensure the survival of future generations and the planet itself? What "local actions" will halt global environmental threats such as ozone depletion, global warming, rain forest destruction, and the toxic chemical proliferation that threatens our health?

Environmental Democracy

We must start practicing environmental democracy—each of us taking control of our environmental future. We must organize at the grass roots level to reorient our economy in a just and sustainable direction. While each of us can take individual steps to help save the environment, organizing at the community level is essential to environmental democracy. Whether stopping a local polluter or convincing legislators to pass and enforce legislation, "people power" is required. It works. We've recently seen grass roots organizing result in thousands of people picketing manufacturers of chloroflurocarbons (CFCs), the enactment of local recycling programs, the development of effective carpooling programs, national media exposés of major polluters, and the passage of state legislation limiting the emission of greenhouse gases.

"Home rule" is a key to environmental decisions that affect our health, safety, and the environment. Local communities need to have the ability to decide about the use of dangerous technologies in their areas, especially the existence of facilities that produce or emit poisons. Affected local citizens must have local

History has show us that the only effective way to resolve hazardous waste problems is for citizens to join together.

— *Lois Gibbs,*
Love Canal Organizer

Carcinogenic Air Pollutants: 25 Top Emitters, 1987

Rank: Facility, City, State; Chemical

(1) Eastman Kodak Company, Rochester, NY; Methylene Chloride.

(2) GE Plastics, Mt. Vernon, IN; Methylene Chloride.

(3) The Upjohn Company, Portage, MI; Methylene Chloride.

(4) Eli Lilly and Company, Clinton, IN; Methylene Chloride.

(5) Eli Lilly and Company, Shadeland, IN; Methylene Chloride.

(6) HADCO Corporation, Derry, NH; Methylene Chloride.

(7) AT&T Microelectronics, Richmond, VA; Methylene Chloride.

(8) ALCOA, Riverdale, IA; Perchloroethylene.

(9) Boeing Military Airplanes, Wichita, KS; Trichloroethylene.

(10) Inland Steel Corp., Lake, IN; Benzene.

(11) Dow Chemical Company, Midland, MI; Methylene Chloride.

(12) WESTVACO–Bleached Board Div., Covington, VA; Chloroform.

"participation rights" that guarantee their involvement in establishing pollution prevention agreements between companies and communities.

Organizing efforts have become ever-more important as our ability as individuals to inhibit environmental destruction has been eroded since the advent of the multinational corporation. Years ago, if you poisoned someone's well or cattle, you went to prison. Today, with lax enforcement of environmental laws, the water, air, and land are being poisoned, our wildlife is being killed, we ourselves are victimized—all in the name of corporate profit.

Changing the "power relations" between average Americans and polluting and poisoning corporations is key to transforming our economy. Each of us will have to make our voice heard in the new cry for environmental democracy and a sustainable future.

Our Environmental Legacy

In America, the tradition of environmental concern is a strong and venerable one. From the Native Americans, to Henry David Thoreau and John Muir in the last century, and later Aldo Leopold and a host of others, Americans have always revered the *creation*.

Starting in the late 1950s, however, this American tradition of respect for the earth entered a new, more militant, phase—with the young science of ecology as its partner. As ecology developed, its findings questioned a broad range of industrial and land-use practices. A number of media events brought the ecological concept of the "web of life" into the public mind. This contributed to a growing awareness of the impact of human activity on the delicate balance of biological, geological, and chemical processes in nature. In the late 1950s and early 1960s, for example, extensive media coverage and popular outcry over radioactive fallout, pesticide residues in the food chain, and other problems drove home the issue of environmental quality as a public health concern. As the dangers of carelessly applied technology became increasingly apparent, a new era of environmentalism began. Within a few years, this new environmentalism grew into a groundswell of popular concern and citizen action for the environment.

From the early days of the environmental movement onward, many individuals and citizen groups have participated vigorously in the democratic process—protesting, spreading information, pressuring legislators, intervening in the agency decision-making process, and taking polluters to court. They have made a difference.

In 1958, for example, pioneering activist and biologist Barry Commoner helped form the Greater St. Louis Committee for Nuclear Information to publicize information about the environmental and health effects of fallout from atomic testing in Nevada. The committee later published a news journal, Science and the Citizen, to provide the general public with information the Atomic Energy Commission was reluctant to disseminate. Professor Commoner's committee helped citizens make informed decisions on matters that could affect their health and safety.

Also in the late 1950s, a number of scientists began to suspect that certain new pesticides, especially DDT, harmed wild animals, livestock, and human health. Rachel Carson's 1962 book *Silent Spring*, a detailed account of the effects of chemical pesticides on wildlife, shocked millions of readers into an awareness of the dangers of pesticide use. In the wake of *Silent Spring*, a popular outcry arose in many areas, including Long Island, Michigan, and Wisconsin, where citizens called for restrictions on the use of DDT. Supported by the Audubon Society, a number of scientists, naturalists, and attorneys organized to pursue litigation to prohibit dangerous pesticides and other environmental threats. In 1969, the Environmental Defense Fund petitioned the Department of Agriculture to impose sharp restrictions on the use of DDT. The eventual result of their efforts was a ban on the use of DDT in the United States.

Other conservation and citizen advocacy groups contributed significantly to the development of environmental legislation in the 1960s. The National Wildlife Federation, for example, was the first of the traditional conservation groups to start lobbying Capitol Hill for environmental legislation. Other established groups, including the Audubon Society, the Sierra Club, and the Wilderness Society, gradually attained greater legislative influence. By the early 1970s, a number of new groups appeared as well, including Environmental Action, the Environmental Defense Fund, and the Natural Resources Defense Council. Other parties, ranging from Ralph Nader's coalition to the League of Women Voters, supported clean air and water legislation.

(13) HEATCRAFT INC., Grenada, MS; Trichloroethylene.

(14) Hickory Springs Foam Plant, Conover, NC; Methylene Chloride.

(15) USS Gary Works, Lake, IN; Benzene.

(16) DU PONT, Towanada, PA; Methylene Chloride.

(17) Merck & Co., INC., Albany, GA; Methylene Chloride.

(18) IBM, Endicott, NY; Methylene Chloride.

(19) GE Plastics, Burkville, AL; Methylene Chloride.

(20) Norden Laboratories, INC., Lincoln, NE; Methylene Chloride.

(21) Ford Electronics, Connersville, IN; Trichloroethylene.

(22) SENCO Products, INC., Cincinnati, OH; Methylene Chloride.

(23) Bethlehem Steel Corp., Erie, NY; Benzene.

(24) Wheeling-Pittsburgh Steel, Brooke, WV; Benzene.

(25) Lockheed Aeronautical Systems, Marietta, GA; Trichloroethylene.

Source: United States Environmental Protection Agency, Office of Research and Development, Washington, DC 20460

The Task Ahead

These past successes should inspire us to mobilize as never before to heal the earth. We must decide what to produce and how. We must stop

Superfund Sites, National Priorities List: Nov. 1989.

Rank, City/County, State, Site.

(1) Pitman, NJ: Lipari Landfill.

(2) New Castle County, DE: Tybouts Corner Landfill.

(3) Bruin Borough, PA: Bruin Lagoon.

(4) Mantua Township, NJ: Helen Kramer Landfill.

(5) Woburn, MA: Industri-Plex.

(6) Pleasantville, NJ: Price Landfill.

(7) Oswego, NY: Pollution Abatement Services.

(8) Charles City, IA: La Bounty Site.

(9) New Castle, DE: Army Creek Landfill.

(10) Old Bridge Township, NJ: CPS/Madison Industries.

(11) Ashland, MA: Nyanza Chemical Waste Dump.

(12) Gloucester Township, NJ: GEMS Landfill.

(13) Swartz Creek, MI: Berlin & Farro.

(14) Holbrook, MA: Baird & McGuire.

(15) Freehold Township, NJ: Lone Pine Landfill.

(16) Somersworth, NH: Somersworth Sanitary Landfill.

(17) Fridley, MN: FMC Corp.

(18) Jacksonville, AR: Vertac, Inc.

(19) Epping, NH: Keefe Environmental Services.

(20) Silver Bow/Deer Lodge, MT: Silver Bow Creek/Butte Area.

(21) Whitewood, SD: Whitewood Creek.

(22) Crosby, TX: French, Ltd.

(23) Utica, MI: Liquid Disposal, Inc.

(24) Nashua, NH: Sylvester.

(25) Upper Merion Township, PA: Tysons Dump

(26) McAdoo Borough, PA: McAdoo Associates.

using chemicals and fossil fuels at levels that will kill us all. We cannot continue along our suicidal path.

Practicing environmental democracy in our communities depends on large numbers of people in local organizations being the "eyes on the environment" and "the eyes on the changing technology." Organized citizenry must win a place at the bargaining table to ensure that local corporations stop local poisoning and preserve the planet's limited natural resources. We've got to have more influence over the activities of companies that threaten the environment. Also, we must organize to insure that local, state, and federal legislators pass the necessary laws to help save the planet.

Tips

- **Get relevant information.** Make sure that you have full information about the problem you are organizing around. Whether it's information on polluters or environmental problems that beset your community—get the facts.

  Information might include knowing who owns, or is responsible for dumping in, a hazardous waste site, or which toxics are being emitted by a certain corporation, or which government agency licenses a product.

- **Access all available information sources.** Check local newspapers, city hall, planning boards, local libraries, public records, and all local, state, and federal agencies. Also request information from your local state and federal representatives; they may have quick access to information.

- **Utilize the Freedom of Information Act (FOIA).** If you suspect a federal (or state) agency has the information you want but won't make it public, request the information under federal or state FOIAs. See Model FOIA Letter in chapter 20, "The Environment, the Law, and You" (page 179).

- **If the information gained is complex or scientific, consult experts.** After gaining technical or scientific information, don't attempt to analyze it solely on your own. Whether investigating a nuclear dump, a hazardous chemical, or a genetically engineered organism, try and find experts to help. Contact universities, investigative reporters (who may have contacted experts), local environmental groups, local environmental attorneys, or sympathetic local government scientists.

- **Establish goals.** After obtaining and analyzing information, establish goals. These can include stopping a government project, passing a local zoning ordinance, taking legal action, or simply drawing attention to a local polluter. Remember, in practicing environmental democracy, your group together must: **plan** corrective campaigns; **carry out** or execute the planned actions; and **evaluate** and adjust to take the best next steps. Remember, direct action gets results

- **Name the organization.** Find an appropriate name. Try to make it positive (i.e. not "Citizen's against the Blocker Dam" but rather "Citizen's for the Flowing River").

- **Define organizational structure and responsibilities.** Defined structure and task allocation can keep any one participant from getting "burned out."

- **Build your local organization.** Go door to door to get activists for your local group. (See "Organizing to Win" chapter in Fighting Toxics, Island Press, 1990). Use the media, to publicize your effort. Your core group should build a community group with large numbers of members around an action—first public meeting, demonstration, petition drive, letter writing campaign, etc.

- **Network with other organizations with similar goals.** The more diverse a coalition, the more powerful a constituency. Also experience (and expenditures) can be shared.

- **Write a simple fact sheet.** Have available for organizing and the media a simple fact sheet describing your problem and the sources of your information. This increases credibility with the public, the media and elected officials.

- **Meet with targeted polluter or elected official(s).** Once you have a sizeable following (50–500 members), and some working committees, hold a neighborhood or town meeting, and be sure to invite executives or officials from the offending chemical refinery, military base, supermarket, incinerator, or waste facility. The same applies to elected officials.

- **For corporate targeting, negotiate and implement a "Good Neighbor" agreement.** Having officials at a neighborhood accountability session can get them to begin a course of action resulting in a "Good Neighbor Agreement."

  A "Good Neighbor Agreement," in its simplest form, is a contract between a corporation and a citizen group where the corporation agrees to change a product or process to reduce or eliminate a hazard or practice that threatens the environment. "Good Neighbor Agreements" have been reached between the National Toxics Campaign and corporations in over 1,200 instances. In the vast majority of cases, these agreements resulted in pollution prevention measures more stringent than those required under state or federal law.

  While the substance of the agreement will vary with the types of industry, agriculture, or transportation problems present, at least three guarantees of rights must be present in any enforceable agreement:

  The "Right to Know": citizens must be given information about the types and amounts of chemicals, energy, and materials used in production and emitted as waste.

  The "Right to Inspect": citizens must be given the right to inspect the offending facility in order to see what the problems are and to then monitor process and product changes to prevent pollution.

  The "Right to Negotiate": negotiation is the best tool to reduce local and therefore global environmental poisoning, even where the laws do not yet require it. For instance, several corporations have publicly agreed to eliminate production and use of ozone-destroying CFCs long before current federal and international laws required it. Many firms have reduced fossil fuel use and cut carbon dioxide emissions in half—even though laws do not require it.

(27) La Marque, TX: Motco, Inc.

(28) Darke County, OH: Arcanum Iron & Metal.

(29) East Helena, MT: East Helena.

(30) Crosby, TX: Sikes Disposal Pits.

(31) Limestone/Morgan, AL: Triana/Tennessee River.

(32) Glen Avon Heights, CA: Stringfellow.

(33) Gray, ME: McKin Co.

(34) Houston, TX: Crystal Chemical Co.

(35) Bridgeport, NJ: Bridgeport Rental & Oil Services.

(36) Commerce City, CO: Sand Creek Industrial.

(37) Houston, TX: Geneva Industries/Fuhrmann Energy.

(38) Acton, MA: W.R. Grace & Co. Inc.

(39) St. Louis Park, MN: Reilly Tar.

(40) New Brighton, MN: New Brighton/Arden Hills.

(41) Plant City, FL: Schuykill Metals Corp.

(42) Vineland, NJ: Vineland Chemical Co., Inc.

(43) Marlboro Township, NJ: Burnt Fly Bog.

(44) Philadelphia, PA: Publicker Industries, Inc.

(45) Oyster Bay, NY: Old Bethpage Landfill.

(46) Newfield Borough, NJ: Shieldalloy Corp.

(47) Tampa, FL: Reeves Southeast Galvanizing Corp.

(48) Anaconda, MT: Anaconda Co. Smelter.

(49) Kent, WA: Western Processing Co., Inc.

(50) Germantown, WI: Omega Hills North Landfill.

Source: National Priority List, November, 1989. Available from United States Environmental Protection Agency, Office of Research and Development, Washington, DC 20460.

- **Ascertain if you need an attorney.** For setting up tax exempt status for your organization, or for dealing with environmental law, consult an attorney. (See chapter 20, "The Environment, the Law, and You.")

- **Defend Your Community.** See sidebar for a list of the communities that are the nation's worst Superfund sites, have the most acid rainfall, and experience the worst ozone smog levels.

Boycott: The Activist Consumer's Weapon of Choice
by Carol Grunewald

Commerce is the extraction from, and packaging and selling of, the environment. Whether it be tuna that has been pulled from the sea and packed into cans (whose components are also taken from the earth), or fossil fuels that have been sucked from the earth, converted to (and packaged as) energy and sold to run our factories, delivery trucks, cars, and appliances—all products come from the earth, and to the earth they all return.

Each time we buy something, we do so at a cost to the earth. As consumers, we literally consume our environment.

But, clearly, the pure utilitarian approach to commerce has doomed us. The relentless, rapacious, taking from the earth for the short-term without replenishment, and the disposal of huge amounts of used and unwanted materials, is rapidly destroying our only home in the universe.

Money is the means of purchasing, or bringing about, what we value. Increasingly, people are learning to value their environment. So, too, are they beginning to use their money—their enormous power as consumers—to introduce a new brand of commerce, one that is sustainable and that respects all life.

We can achieve this new economic vision in several ways: by purchasing and using less, by repairing and re-cycling used products, and by purchasing only environmentally-safe and humanely and sustainably-produced products. Just as vitally, we must refuse to purchase products that are harmful to the environment during their production, use, or disposal; and reject all products from companies whose practices and policies are deemed to be harmful and that contravene the new world view.

The 1990s will be the decade of the activist consumer—not only the professional consumer activists who continue to work on our behalf. Activist consumers, conscientious consumers, call them what you will, will participate in the marketplace in a very deliberate way, purchasing—or not purchasing—with a view to saving our earth. The weapon of choice is the consumer boycott.

The 1990s will be the decade of the activist consumer. The weapon of choice is the consumer boycott.

Boycotts are direct— bypassing legislatures, bureaucracies, and the power elite that frequently have a vested interest in maintaining the status quo.

A boycott is a concerted action to isolate, economically or socially, an individual, business, other group, or nation in order to obtain concessions or to express displeasure with certain acts or practices. Until recently, boycotts in the United States were most often used in labor disputes. Businesses also used them to lower prices. To a lesser extent, consumers used them to reduce prices or to protest against a company's or nation's policies.

Boycott is only one form of economic protest along a continuum of related concepts that include divestment (the cessation of financial investment in a targeted company), and embargo (a governmental decree that its citizens must refuse to deal with another party, i.e., another nation).

In addition to the consumer boycott, forms of individual economic protest that are becoming increasingly important are the "buycott," in which consumers are urged to support alternative products to those which are harmful; and personal or family boycotts, those which result not from an organized, large-scale mobilization, but which simply represent the views and values of their owners. When multiplied among families of similar value-orientation, they become effective.

As a tactic, the boycott is advantageous in several ways. Boycotts are direct— bypassing legislatures, bureaucracies, and the power elite that frequently have a vested interest in maintaining the status quo, and that, by their nature, respond slowly and only partially to problems that require immediate and radical solutions. Boycotts also empower people who otherwise may feel overwhelmed and helpless in the face of enormous problems.

Boycotts not only inflict economic pressure on companies, attendant publicity has soiled many a corporate image. Frequently, image damage—or its threat—is enough to force a company to change its policies.

Recent public opinion polls have shown that preservation of the environment is the primary concern of most Americans, and that Americans are willing to pay more for products that are environmentally safe. Recognizing that concern, companies are already becoming sensitive about public perceptions regarding their performance vis-à-vis the environment.

Boycotts have been employed successfully for centuries. However, the term "boycott" was coined after Charles C. Boycott, a late-nineteenth century British land agent, who collected, by force of arms, outrageous rents from laborers in County Mayo, Ireland. Laborers finally took the advice of Charles Parnell, leader of the land agitation movement, and refused to work for Boycott, sell him food, deliver his mail, or provide him with accommodations during his travels.

A popular tactic at various times throughout history, there were 196 recognized boycotts by American labor groups in 1885 alone.

Among the most famous boycotts was the refusal of American colonists to buy British goods after the Stamp Act of 1765, which led to its repeal the following year. Continued British taxation of, and tyranny over, the Americans, however, led up to the Boston Tea Party in 1773 and the American Revolution.

In 1955, a boycott of the city bus system in Montgomery, Alabama, led by the Rev. Dr. Martin Luther King, Jr., forced an end to its segregated seating policy and began the American civil-rights movement.

Recent well-known boycotts include the long battle to force the Nestle Company to abandon its marketing of infant formula as superior to breast-milk in Third World countries. The boycott, which was settled with the company in 1984, was reactivated in 1988 when Nestle failed to comply with updated World Health Assembly codes.

Another famous and effective boycott is still going strong: the United Farm Workers boycott, led by Cesar Chavez, against non-union grapes produced by California growers. Although this boycott began as a labor dispute, it has been expanded to include other complaints, most notably the indiscriminate and irresponsible use of pesticides by growers.

National boycotts usually take considerable time to achieve their goals (although concentrated actions focused on local businesses may succeed quite rapidly). Never become discouraged. While you wait for the combined effect of hundreds of thousands of boycotters on the policies of environmentally-destructive companies, your alternate selections at the market will be life-affirming and life-sustaining.

Below is a partial listing of national environmental and animal-rights boycotts in effect as of January 1990. A fascinating aspect of these boycotts is that few stand alone as purely "environmental" or "animal-rights" boycotts; almost all have implications for global peace, economic justice, human rights, and world health, as well as the environment and the protection of animals. In fact, extraordinarily broad-based coalitions have been formed to win several of these boycotts.

Cesar Chavez, leader of the United Farm Workers (UFW), was perhaps the first truly broad-based organizer. Realizing that UFW members' troubles with California agribusiness had implications far beyond a labor dispute, Chavez, in the late 1970s, formed a coalition of environmental, animal-rights, health, consumer, and labor organizations to win the battle against unfair labor practices, the dangerous use of pesticides, and horrendous conditions for farm animals.

The Latest Boycott Success Story

Pressured by the withdrawal of millions of dollars-worth of contracts to purchase Icelandic fish, Iceland announced in June 1989 that it would not kill whales during 1990. The surrender of Iceland, one of the three remaining whaling nations, is an enormous success for Greenpeace, which in early 1988 had launched a boycott of fish exported from Iceland to force that nation to stop killing whales.

"The boycott demonstrated to the Icelandic government the strength of worldwide public opinion against whaling," said Campbell Plowden, whale campaign coordinator for Greenpeace. "The economic drawbacks caused by major contract cancellations clearly proved to outweigh the benefits of continued whaling."

Greenpeace asked the American public to boycott all fast-food restaurants that purchased large quantities of Icelandic fish. Hundreds of demonstrations were held outside these restaurants, and a massive letter-writing campaign, organized by Greenpeace and other environmental and animal-protection groups, was begun.

Before long, major restaurant and fast-food chains such as Long John Silver's, Red Lobster, and Shoney's Corporation, cancelled major contracts for fish products from Iceland.

In addition, more than 140 schools and school systems, including those in New York City, Boston, and San Diego, pledged not to use Icelandic fish in their cafeterias until Iceland stopped whaling. Internationally, the boycott cost Iceland's fishing industry, which is intimately connected with its whaling industry, over $50 million.

In 1955, a boycott of the city bus system in Montgomery, Alabama, led by the Rev. Dr. Martin Luther King, Jr., forced an end to its segregated seating policy and began the American civil-rights movement.

In the 1990s, such broad-based coalitions will inevitably form as more and more people begin to realize that the environment is not just one area of concern among many. Rather, the environment is the context—the framework—for all other concerns and activities. There can be no global peace, economic justice, or world health on an environmentally devastated planet. Everything is connected. The world view that promotes the ruthless exploitation and destruction of nature and animals, and the mind-set that perpetuates economic injustice and created the instruments of nuclear annihilation, are one and the same.

We can begin to work together to create a new world based not on utility, but on respect for all life. We can start now with our choices at the market.

Note: For those who wish to learn about new boycot and keep up with long-standing ones, the National Boycott News is an excellent source of information; some of the boycotts listed below are analyzed at length (the last issue was 195 pages!) in this periodical. To subscribe, contact founder and editor Todd Putnam at **The Institute for Consumer Responsibility**, 6506 28th Avenue, NE, Seattle, WA 98115; (206) 523–0421. Suggested (four-issue) subscription rates are: $10-individual, $15-organization, $20-corporate. Rates are negotiable for those with low incomes.

Also, Co-op America, Inc., a non-profit organization that promotes an alternative marketplace for socially-responsible businesses, tracks boycotts that it supports in its quarterly magazine. Contact Co-op America at 2100 M Street, NW, Suite 310, Washington, DC 20063; (800) 255–4397 or (202) 872–5307.

Tips

- **Contact boycott sponsors for additional information, updates, and comprehensive product listings on each boycott.** Ascertain the specific demands of each boycott and the conditions under which the sponsors would call it off.

- **Write letters to, and call, the chief executive officers—and board of directors, if you can—of the companies whose products and policies you oppose.** Tell them that you are boycotting their products and why. Tell them that you are working to publicize the boycott among your family, friends, and the general public. Ask them to respond to your complaints in writing.

- **Share the companies' written responses with boycott sponsors.** Be aware that companies sometimes send out misleading, carefully-worded communications that mask the truth. Ask the sponsors how you can best respond to the various points the companies have made in defense of their positions, and write to the companies again. Never take "no" for an answer!

- **Support alternatives to the products and services you are boycotting and the companies whose policies you oppose.** There is always an alternative product and an alternative place to buy it.

- **Shop with conscience to the best of your ability.** You can't boycott everythingm, and sometimes you won't have enough information to make an educated consumer decision. Just do what you can.

The Council on Economic Priorities (CEP) publishes a booklet that, while not exactly comprehensive, will at least guide you in your selections at the supermarket. The guide, *Shopping for a Better World*, rates various brand names vis-à-vis the performance of their parent companies in various areas including the environment, nuclear power, defense contracts, and product-testing on animals. You can get a copy by sending a check for $4.95 to CEP, 30 Irving Place, New York, NY 10003; or call (800) U–CAN–HELP.

Active Boycotts

BOYCOTT: Consumer products of, and investments in, the fifty top nuclear weapons contractors.

Boycott sponsor: Nuclear Free America (NFA), 325 East 25th Street, Baltimore, MD 21218; (301) 235–3575.

Boycott targets: NFA's Top Fifty Nuclear Weapons Contractors (ranked according to total dollar value of prime contract awards for nuclear weapons and nuclear weapons systems from the United States Department of Defense and the United States Department of Energy in Fiscal Year 1988): (1) McDonnell Douglas Corp.; (2) General Electric Corp.; (3) General Dynamics Corp.; (4) Westinghouse Electric Co.; (5) Lockheed Corp.; (6) United Technologies Corp.; (7) University of California; (8) Martin Marietta Corp.; (9) Rockwell International Corp.; (10) E. I. Dupont de Nemours and Co.; (11) AT&T Co.; (12) Boeing Co.; (13) Allied Signal, Inc.; (14) Raytheon Co.; (15) EG&G, Inc.; (16) General Motors Corp.; (17) Grumman Corp.; (18) LTV Corp.; (19) Unisys Corp.; (20) Harsco; (21) Texas Instruments, Inc.; (22) Northrop Corp.; (23) Singer Co.; (24) TRW, Inc.; (25) Loral Corp.; (26) Gencorp, Inc.; (27) Textron, Inc.; (28) ITT Corp.; (29) IBM Corp.; (30) Hercules, Inc.; (31) Rolls Royce PLC; (32) Honeywell, Inc.; (33) Mason & Hanger-Silas Mason; (34) Pan Am; (35) Monsanto Corp.; (36) FMC Corp.; (37) Charles Stark Draper Lab; (38) Litton Industries, Inc.; (39) CAE Industries; (40) Figgie International, Inc.; (41) Control Data Corp.; (42) Thiokol Corp.; (43) Penn Central Corp.; (44) Teledyne, Inc.; (45) North American Philips; (46) Rohr Industries; (47) Williams International Corp.; (48) Sequa Corp.; (49) Sparton Corp.; (50) Emerson Electric Co.

Reason for boycott: NFA is asking individuals and communities not to buy the products of, or invest in, the top fifty United States nuclear weapons contractors as part of a broad campaign against the nuclear weapons industry. The campaign also urges communities to establish Nuclear-Free Zones. Currently, 167 communities—including Chicago and Oakland—sheltering seventeen million people, have declared themselves Nuclear-Free.

In July, 1989, NFA called off its boycott of Morton Salt after Morton Thiokol, which built booster rockets for nuclear weapons and produced Morton Salt, broke off its weapons division from its consumer products business. Thiokol Corp. is now the weapons contractor; Morton, now a separate entity, produces only consumer products. At the height of the boycott, pre-tax profits from Morton Thiokol's salt sales fell by 25 percent.

United States Manufacturers of Ozone-Destroying Chemicals

Facility, Chief Executive Officer, and Address

E.I. Dupont de Numours & Co., Mr. Edgar S. Woolard Jr., President, 1007 Market Street, Wilmington, Delaware 19898; (302) 774–1000.

Allied-Signal Inc., Mr. Alan Belzer, President, Allied-Signal Inc., Columbia Road & Park Avenue, PO Box 3000R, Morristown, New Jersey 07690; (201) 455–2000.

Pennwalt Corp., Mr. Seymour S. Preston, III, President, Three Parkway, Philadelphia, Pennsylvania 19102; (215) 587–7000.

LaRoche Chemical Inc., William LaRoche, President, PO Box 1031, Baton Rouge, Lousiana 70821; (504) 355–3341.

Racon Inc., Mr. Maurice Knopf, President, 6040 Ridge Road, PO Box 198, Wichita, Kansas 67201; (316) 524–3245.

ICI Americas Inc., Mr Harry Coreless, Chairman, Rollins Building, 10th Floor, Wilmington, Delaware 19897; (302) 886–3000.

Great Lakes Chemical Corp., Mr. Emerson Kampen, President, PO Box 2200, West Laffayette, Indiana 47906; (317)497–6100.

Dow Chemical USA, Frank Popoff, President, Corporate Headquarters, Midland, Michigan 48674; (517) 832–1000.

Vulcan Materials, Herbert A. Sklenar, President, PO Box 7689, Birmingham, Alabama 35253; (205) 877–3714.

PPG Industries, Tom Brown, Plant Manager, PO Box 1000, Lake Charles, Lousiana 70602; (318) 491–4500.

Akzo Chemical, Conrad Kent, President, 300 S. Riverside Plaza, Chicago, Illinois 60606; (312) 906–7500.

Products to avoid: Any consumer products made by the top fifty nuclear weapons contractors, especially lightbulbs. Virtually all major manufacturers of lightbulbs are nuclear contractors: General Electric, GTE (Sylvania), and Phillips. NFA, however, is distributing a nuclear-free alternative under the "Ecolites" brand name. Contact NFA to order these bulbs.

BOYCOTT: AT&T, ITT, and MCI long-distance phone services.

Boycott sponsors: Co-op America, 2100 M St., NW, Suite 310, Washington, DC 20063; (202) 872–5307 or (800) 424–2667. Nuclear Free America, 325 East 25th Street, Baltimore, MD 21218; (301) 235–3575.

Boycott target contacts: AT&T, 550 Madison Avenue, New York, NY 10022; (800) 222–0300. ITT, 320 Park Avenue, New York, NY 10022; (800) 526–3000. MCI Communications, 230 Shilling, Hunt Valley, MD 21031; (800) 624–2030.

Reason for boycott: This boycott, related to the boycott targeting the top 50 nuclear weapons contractors, urges people to refrain from using long-distance phone services owned and operated by major nuclear weapons contractors. Themes for the campaign are: "Reach Out and Touch a Nuclear Weapons Contractor," and "AT&T—The Wrong Choice." Contact Co-op America for information on alternative phone services.

BOYCOTT: General Electric Company products.

Boycott sponsor: INFACT, PO Box 3223, South Pasadena, CA 91031; (818) 799–9133, or 256 Hanover Street, Boston, MA 02113; (617) 742–4583.

Boycott target contact: General Electric Co., 3135 Easton Turnpike, Fairfield, CT 06431, John Welch, CEO; (800) 626–2000 or (203) 373–2431.

Reason for boycott: INFACT has singled out General Electric because it produces parts for every major nuclear weapons system and lobbies for the arms buildup, also because GE produces consumer products that can be boycotted until GE stops perpetuating the arms race. INFACT is asking all organizations and individuals to stop purchasing GE lightbulbs and appliances. All products of GE's subsidiary, RCA, are being boycotted, but the NBC communications network, which GE also owns, is not.

A poll commissioned by INFACT revealed that 3.5 million people (more than 1 percent of the United States population) were boycotting GE as of April 1989. The boycott is endorsed by more than 150 organizations and 60 major religious leaders.

Products/services to avoid: GE lightbulbs and lighting accessories; GE Medical Systems equipment; GE and RCA consumer electronics; GE-financed credit cards; Roper lawn equipment; GE and Hotpoint appliances; GE construction materials; GE Capital; Kidder, Peabody and Co.

BOYCOTT: Exxon Corporation products.

Boycott sponsor: Make Exxon Pay (Citizen Action), PO Box 33304, Washington, DC 20033; (202) 857–5153.

Boycott target contact: Exxon Corporation, 1251 Avenue of the Americas, New York, NY 10020–1198, Lawrence Rawl, CEO; (800) 344–4355.

Reason for boycott: Although Citizen Action called this boycott along with a coalition of other environmental and activist groups, thousands of individuals and organizations throughout the country spontaneously began a boycott of Exxon products after that company's blatant irresponsibility in causing—and failing to clean up—the catastrophic oil spill in Valdez, Alaska, in March 1989.

The group is asking consumers to mail Exxon credit cards cut in half, along with pledges to boycott Exxon products and services, to the company chairman. Some consumers have mailed in dead fish. So far, the boycott sponsor reports that 40,000 Exxon credit cards have been mailed back to the company.

BOYCOTT: California table grapes—including "organically-grown" grapes from California.

Boycott sponsor: United Farm Workers (UFW), PO Box 62, Keene, CA 93531; (805) 822–5571, Cesar Chavez, coordinator.

Boycott target contact: Grape Workers and Farmers Coalition, PO Box 64770–757, Los Angeles, CA 90064; (213) 208–0553.

Reason for boycott: Although this boycott was called primarily to win collective-bargaining rights for migrant farm workers in California, there is a major environmental component: to ban the use of the most lethal pesticides and insecticides sprayed on produce. The chemicals have caused several deaths, severe poisonings, illnesses, miscarriages, and birth defects among farm workers and residents of areas adjacent to farm fields—and also threaten the health of consumers.

In 1987 alone, there were nearly 3,000 cases of pesticide-related illness in California. Grapes were targeted for the boycott because they comprise the largest fresh-fruit crop in California, and because most of the pesticide-related and labor-related grievances UFW has are with the grape industry. "Organic" grapes are included in the boycott because organic standards are not well-enforced in California and sometimes bear pesticide residues, according to UFW.

The boycott is endorsed by more than 1,000 organizations and influential individuals including Ralph Nader, the National Council of Churches, the American Public Health Association, and Center for Science in the Public Interest.

BOYCOTT: All polystyrene (including "Styrofoam," a registered brand of Dow, Inc.) products and packaging, with a special focus on McDonald's restaurant fast-food packaging.

Boycott sponsors: Citizen's Clearinghouse for Hazardous Waste, PO Box 926, Arlington, VA 22216; (703) 276–7070. Vermonters Organized for Clean-Up, PO Box 485, Barre, VT 05641; (802) 476–7757.

Boycott target contact: McDonald's Corporation, 1 McDonald's Plaza, Oakbrook, IL 60521, Shelby Yastrow, Vice President for Environmental Affairs.

Reason for boycott: Boycott sponsors are urging people to boycott polystyrene because it increases landfill volume, does not degrade, is toxic when burned, is a wasteful use of fossil fuels, and is sometimes manufactured with chlorofluorocarbons (CFCs) which eat away the ozone layer, causing all living organisms to be exposed to high levels of ultraviolet radiation. In addition, millions of pounds of cancer-causing chemicals are released into the air and water during the production of polystyrene (80 percent of which is manufactured by Mobil and Amoco).

McDonald's and all major users of polystyrene packaging for fast-food products are the targets of this campaign. Boycott sponsors are not happy with McDonald's November, 1989, announcement that it plans to recycle 25 percent of its polystyrene food packaging; they want a ban on polystyrene, period. Some protesters are delivering or mailing McDonald's own used "styrotrash" back to the company.

BOYCOTT: All redwood products.

Boycott sponsor: Earth First!, c/o Darryl Cherney and Greg King, PO Box 34, Garberville, CA 95440; (707) 247–3320 or (707) 923–3097.

Boycott target contacts: MAXXAM Properties, Inc., 5718 Westheimer, Suite 2200, Houston, TX 77057, Charles E. Hurwitz, CEO; (713) 785–6664. Louisiana-Pacific Corp., 111 SW 5th Avenue, Suite 4200, Portland, OR 97204, Harry Merlo, CEO; (503) 221–0800. Georgia-Pacific Corp., PO Box 105605, 133 Peachtree Street, NE, Atlanta, GA 30303, T. Marshall Hahn, Jr., CEO; (404) 521–4000. Simpson Investment Co., 1201 3rd Avenue, Suite 4900, Seattle, WA 98101-3009, Furman Moseley, CEO. Miller and Rellim (Rellim Redwood Co.), 520 SW Yam Hill, 308 Pacific Building, Portland, OR 97204, Dan Dutton, CEO.

Reason for boycott: Earth First! has called this boycott to save the last remaining old-growth stand of coastal redwoods. Decades of logging and development have reduced this stand to only 4 percent of its original size. While all these companies are devastating the redwood forests, MAXXAM, owner of the Pacific Lumber Company, is the worst offender, according to Earth First! MAXXAM plans to level the oldest forest in northern California to repay massive debts incurred during the take-over of Pacific Lumber.

These companies also engage in non-sustainable forestry practices by clear-cutting (as opposed to selective harvesting), burning, and using large amounts of herbicides. Such practices result in massive soil erosion and destruction of wildlife habitat.

Products to avoid: All items made of redwood including: picnic tables, hot tubs, patio furniture, planter boxes, retaining walls, and fencing.

BOYCOTT: All Weyerhaeuser Corporation and Georgia-Pacific Corporation products.

Boycott sponsors: Rainforest Action Network, 301 Broadway, Suite A, San Francisco, CA 94133, Randall Hayes, coordinator; (415) 398–4404. Earth First! Tropical Timber Campaign, PO Box 83, Canyon, CA 94716, Mike Roselle, coordinator; (415) 376–7329.

Boycott target contacts: The Weyerhaeuser Company, Tacoma, WA 98477, George Weyerhaeuser, CEO; (800) 525–5440 or (206) 924–2345. Georgia-Pacific Corp., PO Box 105605, 133 Peachtree Street, NE, Atlanta, GA 30303, T. Marshall Hahn, Jr., CEO; (800) 447–2882.

Reason for boycott: Weyerhaeuser and Georgia-Pacific are primary destroyers of rainforests throughout the world.

Weyerhaeuser is the world's largest private owner of timber, one of North America's largest exporters, and a primary importer of tropical wood. The company imports finished wood products, especially plywood, directly from Indonesia, Malaysia, the Philippines, and Brazil. At least 289 million pounds of rainforest wood were imported between April 1988 and September 1989, according to boycott sponsors. In October 1989, Weyerhaeuser sold much of its wall-panelling business (the largest in the United States) to Chesapeake Hardwood Products, Inc., an affiliate of the Kalimanis Group, one of Indonesia's largest lumber and plywood manufacturers. The raw material for the operation is tropical hardwood plywood from Indonesia. Weyerhaeuser personnel manage the facilities, and the company remains a customer and distributor.

Georgia-Pacific is also a primary importer of tropical hardwood products. Between April 1988 and September 1989, this company imported at least 261 million pounds of rainforest wood, according to boycott sponsors. The company operates a large hardwood veneer plant in Brazil and imports finished wood products, especially plywood, directly from Indonesia, Malaysia, and the Philippines.

The tropical hardwoods industry destroys about 12.5 million acres of rainforest annually and is the major cause of primary rainforest destruction in Africa and Southeast Asia. Not only are these companies destroying precious rainforest, but they are notorious for destructive logging practices all over the world.

Products/services to avoid: Weyerhaeuser products: Disposable diapers. Weyerhaeuser supplies 70 percent of the private-label disposable-diaper market with over 200 brand names sold at the following stores: Toys R Us, Albertson's, Safeway (Truly Fine), K-Mart (Fitt 'Ems), Food Lion, Krogers, Circle Soopers, Dillon, City Markets, and Florida Choice. Weyerhaeuser's own diaper line includes: Diaper Doublers Insert Pads and Smiles Diapers. Ideally, consumers should avoid all disposable diapers. Also, all Weyerhaeuser wood and building products.

Weyerhaeuser services: Weyerhaeuser Real Estate Company, Weyerhaeuser Financial Services, Inc., Weyerhaeuser Mortgage Company, Republic Federal Savings and Loan, GNA Corporation.

Georgia-Pacific products: Angel Soft, Cormatic, and Mr. Big toilet paper; Sparkle, Delta, and Mr. Big paper towels; Coronet, Hudson, and Soft Ply paper napkins; Cardigan and Hopper paper; all Georgia-Pacific wood and building products.

Boycott: Products of additional paper companies engaging in the destruction of rainforests or other irresponsible, unsustainable, forestry practices.

Boycott sponsor: Earth First! Tropical Timber Campaign, PO Box 83, Canyon, CA 94716; (415) 376–7329.

Boycott target contacts: Boise-Cascade Corp., One Jefferson Square, PO Box 50, Boise, ID 83728, John H. Miller, CEO; (208) 384–6161. Champion International, One Champion Plaza, Stamford, CT 06921, Andrew C. Sigler, CEO; (203) 358–7000. Great Nothern Nekoosa Corp., 401 Merrit 7, PO Box 5120, Norwalk, CT 06856, William R. Ladig, CEO; (203) 845–9000. International Paper, Two Manhattanville Rd., Purchase, NY 10577, John A. Georges, CEO; (914) 397–1500. Kimberly-Clark Corp., PO Box 619100, DFW Airport Station, Dallas, TX 75261, Darwin E. Smith, CEO. Scott Paper Co., Scott Plaza, Philadelphia, PA 19113, Philip E. Lippincott, CEO, J. Richard Leaman, Jr., President Scott Worldwide; (800) 835–7268. Westvaco, 299 Park Avenue, New York, NY 10171, John A. Luke, CEO; (212) 688–5000.

Reason for boycott: Boycott sponsors charge the listed companies with engaging in harmful forestry practices, including the destruction of rainforests, clear-cutting, and the use of herbicides and insecticides, among other unsustainable practices.

Products to avoid: Kimberly-Clark products: Hi-Dri paper towels and napkins, Delsey, Huggies diapers, Kotex, Light Days, New Freedom, Depend products.

Scott products: Baby Fresh and Wash-a-Bye Baby Wipes, Baby Scott Diapers, Cashmere Bathroom Tissue, Confidents Maxi Pads, Confidents Sanitary Napkins, Cottonelle Bathroom Tissue, Duvet Bathroom Tissue, Fresh Wipes, Job Squad, Scott Towels, Scott Cut-Rite Wax Paper, Scott Napkins, Scotties Facial Tissues, Soft n' Pretty, Viva Paper Towels, Waldorf.

Boycott: Hawaiian tourism, Hawaiian products.

Boycott sponsor: Rainforest Action Network (RAN), 301 Broadway, Suite A, San Francisco, CA 94133; (415) 398–4404.

Boycott target contacts: Gov. John Waihe'e, Office of the Governor, State Capitol, Honolulu, HI 96813; Hawaii Tourist Bureau, 2270 Kalakaua, Suite 801, Honolulu, HI 96815, Stanley Hong, Director.

Reason for boycott: This boycott has been launched to save the only lowland, tropical rainforest in the United States from development. If current state plans proceed, as many as twelve power plants and connecting roads will dissect thousands of acres of rainforest on the island of Hawaii. More electric power will lead to more development in Hawaii. The forest on the island of Hawaii is unlike any in the world, and scientists predict it will be destroyed if development occurs. Such destruction on United States soil will also undercut efforts by environmental groups to pressure countries such as Brazil, Zaire, Malaysia, and Indonesia to protect their own rainforests.

Products to avoid: Vacations in Hawaii, and all Hawaiian products including: C&H sugar, Dole pineapple, Kona coffee, and macadamia nuts.

Boycott: Mitsubishi Corporation products.

Boycott sponsor: Rainforest Action Network, (RAN), 301 Broadway, Suite A, San Francisco, CA 94133; (415) 398–4404.

Boycott target contact: Mitsubishi Corp., 6–3 Marunouchi 2–Chome, Chiyoda-Ku, Tokyo 100–86, Japan, Shinroku Morohashi, President.

Reason for boycott: Japan is the world's leading importer of tropical wood, and the Mitsubishi Corporation is one of Japan's largest timber-importing companies. Mitsubishi is among the top five Japanese importers of timber from the Malaysian state of Sarawak, on the island of Borneo. At current rates of logging, Borneo will be denuded by the turn of the century, and the traditional lives of thousands of native tribespeople, the Penan, will be destroyed. The Penan, who have been sent to jail for blockading logging roads, are fighting a losing battle. With 80 percent of Sarawak's timber going to Japan, it will not be long before the entire forest is gone.

Boycott: Shrimp.

Boycott sponsor: National Audubon Society, 801 Pennsylvania, Avenue, SE, Washington, DC 20003; (202) 547–9009.

Reason for boycott: National Audubon is urging all Americans to boycott shrimp until Gulf Coast shrimpers obey federal law by using turtle excluder devices (TEDs) on their nets. TEDs, inexpensive, easy-to-use devices, were designed to prevent sea turtles from drowning in shrimpers' nets. However, many shrimpers are refusing to use the devices despite spotty enforcement efforts by the United States Coast Guard. During the summer of 1989, shrimpers blockaded ports and attacked Coast Guard vessels. Some 11,000 endangered sea turtles, including the critically endangered Kemp's ridley sea turtle, three other endangered sea turtle species, and some threatened species, drown in these nets each year.

BOYCOTT: All kinds and all brands of canned tuna fish and pet food containing tuna.

Boycott sponsors: The Humane Society of the United States, 2100 L Street, NW, Washington, DC 20037; (202) 452–1100. Earth Island Institute, 300 Broadway, Suite 28, San Francisco, CA 94133–3312; (415) 788–3666. Greenpeace, 1436 U Street, NW, Washington, DC 20009; (202) 462–1177.

Boycott target contacts: H. J. Heinz Company (Star-Kist brand tuna), PO Box 57, Pittsburgh, PA 15230, Anthony J. F. O'Reilly, CEO. Van Camp Seafood, Inc. (Chicken of the Sea brand tuna), Boatman's Tower, 100 N. Broadway, Suite 900, Street Louis, MO 63102, Jose E. Munoz, Jr., President; (314) 342–9800. Bumble Bee Seafoods, Inc., (Bumble Bee brand tuna), 5775 Roscoe Court, PO Box 23508, San Diego, CA 92123.

Reason for boycott: Some six to ten million dolphins have drowned in tuna fishermen's nets since the early 1960s, when the ultra-profitable purse-seine method of fishing for tuna was widely adopted. More than 125,000 dolphins—sometimes hundreds at a time—continue to drown each year in the Eastern Tropical Pacific Ocean (ETP), which stretches from California to Chile. The ETP is the only ocean in the world where, for unknown reasons, schools of yellowfin tuna swim underneath herds of dolphins.

Knowing that tuna may be swimming below, tuna fishermen in the ETP spot herds of dolphins from helicopters. Crewmen in speedboats herd the dolphins together by tossing explosives in the water, and then encircle them with a mile-long net that is pulled closed to trap both the dolphins and tuna. United States law, requires that crewmen attempt to free dolphins, who are air-breathing mammals. However, this is a tricky procedure that, with unpredictable tides and weather, often turns disastrous. Several species of dolphins are threatened by this destructive method of fishing.

Boycott sponsors demand the United States tuna companies abide by United States law which, since 1981, has required them to develop alternative methods for catching yellowfin tuna that do not involve dolphins. In addition, the sponsors want United States tuna companies to stop buying foreign-caught tuna which ends up on American grocery shelves.

Foreign nations kill approximately four times as many dolphins as American fishermen, yet United States companies continue to buy this tuna and place their brand names on it.

Yellowfin tuna caught "on dolphins" comprises only about 10 percent of the total tuna consumed in the world, however companies continue to catch yellowfin "on dolphins" because it is somewhat more profitable for them to do so.

Although albacore tuna is not caught "on dolphins," boycott sponsors ask that consumers avoid all kinds and brands of canned tuna in order to send the strongest possible economic message to tuna companies; the dolphin slaughter is now in its thirtieth year.

Products to avoid: All canned tuna, especially Star-Kist, Chicken of the Sea, and Bumble Bee brands, and pet food containing tuna. H. J. Heinz Co. owns Heinz Pet Products Co., which makes 9-Lives, Amore, and Kozy Kitten brand pet food.

BOYCOTT: "Milk-fed" veal.

Boycott sponsors: The Humane Society of the United States, 2100 L Street, NW, Washington, DC 20037; (202) 452–1100. Humane Farming Association, 1550 California Street, Suite 6, San Francisco, CA 94109; (415) 485–1495.

Reason for boycott: Boycott sponsors are urging all consumers to boycott "milk-fed" veal because the current practice of raising these animals in intensive confinement is among the most cruel of factory-farming methods, and because of the possible health risks incurred by people who eat these animals.

Calves intended for veal production are removed from their mothers at birth and spend their lives chained at the neck in wooden crates so small that the animals cannot turn around—this on the pretext that it deters bruising and toughening of the animals. Lack of exercise and the administration of a purely liquid diet stops muscle development and ensures tender meat. To keep them alive and to ensure speedy growth, large amounts of antibiotics and hormones are administered, which, in turn, are absorbed by people who consume these animals.

BOYCOTT: All fur coats and items made of animal fur.

Boycott sponsors: Every major animal-rights and animal-protection organization in the United States.

Reason for boycott: Animal-protection organizations throughout the country are urging consumers to participate in a "permanent boycott"— that is, a ban—on all garments and items made of animal fur because fur production causes terrible animal suffering, has an adverse impact on the environment, and because fur garments are unnecessary items that cannot be justified under such conditions.

Approximately seventeen million wild animals are trapped for their fur in the United States each year. An additional five million so-called "trash" or unwanted animals, including many endangered species and domestic animals, are accidentally caught and discarded each year.

Animals caught in leghold traps, Conibear traps, or neck snares often suffer for days—even chewing off limbs to escape—until a trapper arrives to kill them. Trapped animals are killed in a variety of inhumane methods designed to not damage or bloody the pelts.

An additional five million wild animals, including some minks and foxes, are raised in claustrophobic wire cages, on so-called "ranches," until they are killed by anal electrocution, neck breaking, poisoning, or gassing.

BOYCOTT: Ivory and other products made from African elephants.
Boycott sponsors: Every major animal-protection and environmental organization in the United States; also, several major department store chains and well-known clothing designers.
Reason for boycott: Boycott sponsors urge consumers to boycott the purchase or wearing of ivory products because the African elephant is now on the verge of extinction as a direct result of international trade in ivory. At current rates of killing, the African elephant will become extinct within the decade.

Only an estimated 400,000 African elephants remain—down from 1.3 million less than a decade ago. In October 1989, a global conservation convention voted to place the African elephant on its most-protected-animals list, thus banning all international trade in ivory or ivory products. However, at least 80 percent of the ivory produced in the past several years has been from poached (illegally killed) elephants. Because poaching and the illegal sale of ivory is likely to continue, boycott sponsors are trying to de-glamorize ivory and thereby destroy any market for ivory products.

Trade in ivory is still permitted within the United States because the African elephant has not yet been placed on the United States endangered species list, thus making it all the more important to boycott ivory.
Products to avoid: All ivory tusks, jewelry, statues, etc.; elephant-hair jewelry, and elephant-hide products.

BOYCOTT: All milk and dairy products produced by companies using milk from dairy herds treated with bovine somatotropin, also known as bovine growth hormone (BGH).
Boycott sponsor: Foundation on Economic Trends, 1130 17th Street, NW, Suite 630, Washington, DC 20036; (202) 466–2823.

Reason for boycott: BGH is an experimental, genetically-altered hormone, which is being injected into dairy cows to dramatically increase their milk production, and which finds its way into the milk. BGH is the first genetically-altered substance to enter the food supply, and is opposed by a broad coalition of national consumer health, family farm, and animal-protection organizations.

Some scientists have raised questions regarding the safety of BGH, and the United States Food and Drug Administration has not yet approved its use. Nonetheless, BGH has already found its way into the nation's milk supply in various test-markets throughout the country.

Family farmers oppose BGH because the nation already has a surplus of milk, which farmers are paid to produce and then discard. The anticipated 25 percent increase in milk surplus that BGH is expected to create would benefit only corporate factory farms and would wipe out small dairy farmers. Animal-rights groups oppose BGH because it increases the stress of already-overworked dairy cows and predisposes them to illness.

Several supermarkets and dairy processors have so far refused to accept BGH-tainted products; however, this may change if the FDA approves BGH. BGH manufacturers Monsanto, American Cyanamid, Eli Lilly, and Upjohn, who have a multi-billion-dollar stake in BGH, are now pressuring the FDA to approve widespread use of the hormone.

The boycott sponsor, believing that consumers want natural, unadulterated milk products, is urging people to pressure their supermarkets into enacting a permanent ban on BGH products.

Products/companies to support: Stores and processors that do not accept BGH-treated products are: Alta-Dena, American Stores, AMPI in 21 states, Ben & Jerry's Ice Cream, Borden, Cabot Creamery, California Cooperative Creamery, Dairyland Foods, Dannon Yogurt, Dean Foods, Farmland Dairies, First National Supermarkets, Frigo Cheese Corp., Garelick Farms, H.P. Hood Inc., Haagen-Dazs, Kraft General Foods, Kroger markets, Land-O-Sun Dairies, Publix, Safeway, Stop & Shop, Sunnyside Farms, Tillamook County Creamery Association, Vons stores, and Yoplait.

BOYCOTT: John Morrel & Co. meat products.
Boycott Sponsor: United Food and Commerce Workers Local 1142, AFL-CIO, 250 Benson Building, Sioux City, IA 51101; (712) 255–4726.
Boycott target contacts: United Brands/Chiquita Brands, 250 E. Fifth Street, Cincinnati, OH 45202, Keith Lindner, CEO; (513) 784–8000. John Morrell & Co., 250 E. 5th St., PO Box 5703, Cincinnati, OH 45202, Milton Schloss, CEO; (513) 852–3500; FAX: (513) 852–7444. Robert G. Campbell, Senior Vice President, Quality Assurance, John Morrell & Co.; (513) 852–3590 (work); (606) 344–0969 (home).

Reason for boycott: This boycott was called to protest inhumane conditions for both employees and animals at John Morrel and Co. slaughter and meat-packing plants. According to the union, the company has speeded up the assembly-line to increase profits; as a result, employees are having accidents, and animals are needlessly suffering.

For example, at one Iowa plant, pigs are supposed to be rendered unconscious by an electric stunner before being slaughtered. However, because the company fears the pigs' meat will be damaged (and thus cut profits), foremen are ordered to lower the voltage on the stunners. This *routinely* results in fully-conscious pigs being hoisted upside-down, having their throats slit, and then being tossed—often still conscions—into caldrons of scalding water to prepare them for the "de-hairing" machine, according to union representatives. This plant slaughters 15,000 pigs daily (800 an hour).

This giant, national company, is owned by United Brands, which is controlled by millionaire Keith Lindner. Morrell also slaughters pigs, cattle, and lambs at its other plants. This boycott is supported by United Food and Commercial Workers International Union, AFL-CIO.

Products to avoid: Products produced by the Morrell Company include meats sold under the following brands: Hunter, John Morrell, Krey, Nathan's Famous, Partridge, Peyton's, Tobin's First Prize, Rath Blackhawk, Rodeo, Carmel, and Branding Iron. Morrell also supplies ribs to the Carson Rib Co. and hams to the Honeybake Ham Co.

BOYCOTT**:** Cosmetics and household products that have been toxicity-tested on animals.

Boycott sponsor: People for the Ethical Treatment of Animals, PO Box 42516, Washington, DC 20015; (301) 770–7444.

Boycott target contacts: Dial Corporation, (602) 248–2800, call collect; Beecham Products, Division of Beecham Inc., (800) 245–1040; Boyle-Midway, Division of American Home Products, (201) 276–3900, call collect; Bristol-Meyers, (212) 546–4000; Clairol, Inc., (800) 223–5800; The Clorox Company, (800) 227–1860, (800) 772–2469 in California; Colgate-Palmolive, (212) 310–2655, call collect for consumer relations; The Gillette Company, (617) 421–7000; S.C. Johnson & Son, Inc., (800) 558–5252; Lever Brothers, (800) 223–0392; Noxell, (301) 785–7300, call collect; Procter & Gamble, (800) 543–1745, (513) 582–0345 in Ohio.

Reason for boycott: The government does not require toxicity tests on animals for cosmetics or household products, yet most companies test these products anyway on some fourteen million animals annually, causing tremendous pain and suffering. Companies perform these tests because they feel the tests will protect them in case they are sued by a user of their products. There are several non-animal tests now available that provide more reliable results; however, most companies have been slow to adopt them since this would require a complete revamping of their operations. The boycott sponsor says it is unethical to perform these painful tests just so that consumers can have yet another brand of mascara, deodorant, or oven cleaner—especially when alternative testing methods are available.

The most common types of tests are the Draize Acute Eye Irritancy Test and the Lethal Dose 50 (LD-50). In the Draize test, strong chemical substances are placed into the eyes of rabbits—resulting in the destruction of the eyes of these animals. In the LD-50 animals are forced to eat, inhale, or suffer skin exposure to various chemicals and substances until half of them die. Many scientists consider the Draize test, the LD-50, and other tests of similar nature to be both unreliable and unscientific.

There are many brands of cosmetics and household products that do not test on animals, but which have been used safely for years by many people because they contain benign, tried-and-true ingredients. See the "Cruelty-Free Living" chapter for a listing. The use of cruelty-free products is endorsed by every major animal-protection organization in the United States. Contact the boycott sponsor for a complete listing of companies that test on animals.

Products to avoid: Dial Products: Dial Soap, Dial Shampoo, Dial Anti-Perspirant, Tone Soap, Man Power Deodorant and Anti-Perspirant, Liqua 4 Cleansing System, Bruce Floor Care Products, Magic Pre-Wash. **Beecham Products:** Calgonite, Calgon Bubble Bath, Calgon Water Conditioner, Cling-Free Fabric Softener Sheets, Brylcream Hairdressing, Macleans Toothpaste, Rose Milk Moisturizer, Aqua Velva. **Boyle-Midway Products:** Easy-Off, Quick-Dip Silver Cleaner, Sani-Flush Toilet Bowl Cleaner, Black Flag, Wizard Air Freshener and Deodorizer, Aero-Wax, Woolite Cold Water Wash, Woolite Gentle Cycle, Woolite Upholstery & Rug Cleaner, Zud Cleanser, Diaper Pure Laundry Aid. **Bristol Myers Products:** Drano, Windex, Twinkle, Renuzit, Vanish, Endust, Mr. Muscle, Behold, Miracle White Laundry Detergent, Excedrin, Bufferin, Ban, Vitalis, Comtrex, Keri Lotion. **Clairol, Inc. Products:** Herbal Essence Shampoo and Creme Rinse, I Like My Gray Shampoo, Condition Shampoo and Conditioners, Final Net. **Clorox Company Products:** Clorox Liquid Bleach, Clorox II All Fabric Bleach, Formula 409, Liquid-Plummer Drain Opener, Soft Scrub Liquid Cleanser, Twice As Fresh Air Freshener, Tilex Mildew Stain Remover. **Colgate-Palmolive Products:** Cashmere Bouquet Soap, Vel Beauty Bar Soap, Irish Spring Soap, Axion Pre-Soak, Fab Laundry Detergent, Fresh Start Concentrated Laundry Detergent, Dynamo Liquid Laundry Detergent, Cold Power Laundry Detergent, Ajax, Dermassage Dish-washing Liquid, Palmolive Dish-washing Liquid, Rapid Shave, Colgate Toothpaste, Colgate Instant Shave, Fluorigard Anti-Cavity Dental Rinse, Wash 'N Dri Towelettes. **Gillette Company Products:** Right Guard,

Soft & Dri Anti-Perspirant, Dry Idea Anti-Perspirant, Foamy and Trac II Shave Cream, The Hot One Shave Cream, Mink Difference, Silkience, Tame Creme Rinse, Earth Born, Heads Up Hair Groom, Deep Magic Cleansing Lotion, Happy Face Washing Cream, Aapri Facial Scrub, Foot Guard Deodorant. **S. C. Johnson & Son Inc. Products:** Brite, Future, Glo Coat, Klear, Klear Wood, Step Saver, Super Bravo, Beautiful, Johnson's Paste Wax, Super Kleen Floor, Glory Foam, Liquid Glory, Favor, Jubilee, Klean 'N Shine, Pledge, Glade, Big Wally Foam Cleaner, Crew Disinfectant Bathroom Cleaner, Raid Insecticides, Off and Deep Woods Off insect repellent, Agree Shampoo and Conditioner, Edge Protective Shave, Enhance Shampoo and Conditioner, Rain Barrel Fabric Softener, Shout Stain Remover, Shout Liquid Bleach. **Lever Brothers Products:** Liquid ALL Laundry Detergent, Concentrated ALL, Dish-washer ALL, Breeze, Drive, Wisk, Final Touch Fabric Softener, Dove Dish-washing Liquid, Lux Dish-washing Liquid, Caress Soap, Dove Soap, Lifebuoy Soap, Lux Beauty Soap, Phase III Soap, Shield Deodorant Soap, Pepsodent Toothpaste, Close-Up Toothpaste, Aim Toothpaste, Signal Mouthwash. **Noxell Products:** Noxzema, Cover Girl Make-Up. **Procter & Gamble (laundry and cleaning) Products:** Biz, Bounce, Downy, Comet, Comet Liquid, Mr. Clean, Spic 'N Span, Top Job, Camay, Coast, Ivory, Kirk's Castile, Lava, Safeguard, Zest, Bold, Cheer, Tide.

Boycott: McDonald's Restaurants.

Boycott sponsor: Worldwide Boycott McDonald's Coalition/International Animal-Rights Alliance, c/o Heather Schofield, PO Box 1836 GMF, Boston, MA 02205.

Reason for boycott: The boycott sponsor urges consumers to avoid eating at McDonald's until this giant restaurant chain provides an alternative "veggie" burger to its all-meat menu offerings. The sponsor believes that McDonald's has a responsibility to acknowledge the effect meat-eating has on the planet, including its role in world hunger, human health, environmental destruction, and animal suffering.

Boycott: Coca-Cola products and Wrangler jeans.

Boycott sponsor: International Society for Animal Rights, 421 South State Street, Clarks Summit, PA 18411; (717) 586–7603.

Boycott target contacts: The Coca-Cola Company, 1 Coca-Cola Plaza, NW, Atlanta, GA 30301, Robert C. Goizueta, CEO; (404) 676–2121.

Wrangler Corp., PO Box 21488, Greensboro, NC 27420, H. Varnell More, CEO; (919) 373–3580.

Reason for boycott: Both of these companies sponsor and promote national rodeo events in which animals are kicked, hit with electric prods, roped, thrown, and otherwise abused. Rodeos result in high rates of injury for both participants and animals.

Products to avoid: Coca-Cola, Minute Maid, Tab, Sprite, Ramblin' Root Beer, Fanta, Mello Yellow, High C fruit drinks, Five Alive, Belmont Springs bottled water, Taylor wines, Wrangler jeans.

Boycott: Perdue chickens.

Boycott sponsor: Animal Rights International, PO Box 214, Planetarium Station, New York, NY 10024, Henry Spira, Coordinator.

Boycott target contact: Perdue Farms, Inc., PO Box 1537, Salisbury, MD 21801, Frank Perdue, Chairman; (301) 543–3000.

Reason for boycott: Perdue's chickens live lives of misery, treated not as the sentient creatures they are, but as objects. At birth, Perdue's chicks have their beaks burned off with a hot knife. Then they are trucked to "farms" where they are crowded, for reasons of economy, into windowless sheds. There, each bird, which grows to a size of about four pounds, is provided with one square foot—or less—of living space for its entire life. Such stressful overcrowding results in cannibalism, disease, and a high mortality rate. (High losses in corporate factory farming are accepted as an incidental cost of doing business.)

To fight disease, Perdue's chickens receive massive doses of antibiotics and other drugs (which are eventually ingested by people). Perdue chickens are killed on a mechanized assembly line, pinned upside down prior to having their throats slit. The boycott sponsor believes that it is not necessary to treat farm animals inhumanely, and asks that the public boycott Perdue chickens until the following conditions are met: (1) Perdue must provide a complete list of its slaughterhouses and contract farms and allow the media unannounced access to film and report conditions; (2) Perdue must guarantee each bird at least two feet by two feet of living space; (3) Perdue must investigate more investigate more humane methods of raising poultry.

Exercising Citizenship for a Healthy Body Politic
By Claudine Schneider

Over the past several years, we have witnessed record and near record heat waves, droughts, forest fires, hurricanes, floods, and urban pollution. These are all symptoms. Mother Earth is sending us many signals that she is at risk. We ignore her symptoms at our own peril. The gaping hole in the earth's protective ozone shield and the ongoing destruction of vast regions of tropical rainforests threaten humanity's well-being, just as if someone ripped off the skin protecting our bodies.

Each of us can help heal the planet. Choked by the smog of gridlocked autos, we could buy more efficient and less polluting cars, or car pool and remove two or three vehicles from the road; we can take the bus or subway; or even better, we could emulate Dutch and Danish communities, where half the people bicycle to and from work, preventing the release of tons of pollutants.

The food we grow or eat, the homes and appliances we buy, the packaging we avoid, reuse, or recycle, in short, the lifestyles we lead offer endless opportunities for healing the planet by living more ecologically. A healthy future turns on the degree to which we practice a stewardship ethic as if Mother Earth mattered.

Individual changes of habit constitute an essential first step we all must take, but not a sufficient one. In an ideal world, the good stewardship actions willingly undertaken by each person would add up to an ecologically sustained world economy. Unfortunately, we are far from this ideal world. Whether due to ignorance, or slothful indifference, outright greed or callous disregard, the collective actions of humans now wreak havoc on the planet. We need to alter society's habits.

Economic and technological changes have often required changes in social behavior. For example, the advent of the car required individual behavior changes as basic as stopping at intersections to avoid accidents. But not everyone abides by this behavior, so laws are necessary to protect society at large. Thus,

Mother Earth is sending us many signals that she is at risk. We ignore her symptoms at our own peril.

we enforce safe behavior through fines, and in some cases, vehicle impound-ment. The car gives us unbelievable mobility, but it also incurs social obligations and responsibilities.

Greenhouse gases, too, have brought us numerous economic goods and services. But their benefits are now exceeded by their costs and risks. It is time to stop the growth of greenhouse gases and substitute safer alternatives. This will require a broad range of changes at all levels of decision making—at home, at work, through community, state, and federal governments, and by means of international agreements.

Individuals must lobby to change the focus of these various institutions, especially those involved in promulgating legislation. Just as physical exercise maintains a healthy body, so the exercise of citizen advocacy maintains a healthy politic.

> In the struggle for freedom from environmental pollution, the battle is ultimately won not by force but by healing, and within this framework we must all become healers.
> — *Michael Samuels,*
> *(from* Soaring *,1971)*

The healthy body politic is a potent metaphor that emerged in the 1800s. At that time, individuals mobilized to remove the scourge of diseases afflicting society that were spread through contaminated drinking water, due in large part to a lack of sanitary waste disposal options. We need to galvanize public support for sustaining this noble tradition in the face of a new environmental challenge.

Any review of history shows that it takes years, decades, sometimes cen-turies, to effect change on monumental problems. This has been the case with democracies overthrowing dictators, with abolishing slavery, and with protect-ing human rights. These struggles continue in our day, and they all turn on the concern and commitment of individuals working to effect change.

Grappling with global climate change poses a no less daunting task. It is too easy for policymakers elected on two to six year terms to evade action by pushing the problem into the future. Some have referred to this unconscionable behavior as the NIMLT syndrome, "Not in My Life Time."

Without strong, ongoing citizen advocacy for change, most policymakers will continue to support environmental deficit spending, just as they have budget deficit spending. That is to say, current policies encourage squandering the natural endowment of future generations, who will be faced with paying off our environmental debts (pollutants) with fewer capital resources (forests, top soil, watersheds, extinct species, etc.).

I refuse to submit to the gloom and doom future implicit in the policies and practices of our time. Nor should you. Decades of scientific research, technologi-cal advancements, and ecological insights show us that humans can thrive on earth in an ecologically sustainable manner. The key insight of our time is that environmental quality and economic prosperity are compatible. By acting on this insight, we could eliminate the seemingly intractable problems of hunger and poverty and maintain a thriving economy for generations to come.

The major barrier to recognizing this insight is the way policymakers make decisions. Issues get quickly compartmentalized. Transportation, housing, health, security, energy, and environment each get dealt with separately by a specialized bureaucracy, few of whom listen and exchange ideas with their fellow specialists. So we build more highways for polluting cars instead of designing land uses to minimize the need for cars. We operate highly polluting power plants instead of installing lower cost, highly efficient lights, motors, and appliances in homes and businesses. We contaminate soil and groundwater instead of minimizing wastes, or reusing and recycling.

This fragmentary approach must be replaced with an integrated, holistic, legislative framework. This is where citizens can gain considerable leverage from their efforts. There are numerous examples of how cities and states have responded to constituents and established advisory commissions to look at the future shape of their regions and to recommend changes in public policies. In doing so, trends come into sharp relief, problems are more readily identified, and concerned citizens can voice alternative visions that should be further studied and duly incorporated.

Analytic tools have been developed and are available for helping citizens ensure that comprehensive planning is performed. Examples include David Morris's Homegrown Economy, Rodale's Regenerative Economy Project, the Rocky Mountain Institute's Economic Renewal Project, the Earth Day Campus Audit Project. Use of these and other planning methods allow each community and city to inventory resources consumed, pollutants generated, locally available resources that are less costly and polluting, and the employment opportunities to be gained by such changes.

Often, half or more of the food, energy, and water services could be produced locally, saving millions of dollars for the local economy and cutting pollutants and solid wastes by half or more.

With this kind of information base (exchanged between communities in order to refine and improve the information), a powerful tool is available for accelerating public policy change. Public support is more easily generated by using this information to educate voters on how, for example, a lighting retrofit of the entire city is less expensive than simply continuing to operate the utility's dirty coal plants.

A citizens' commission on the future is an excellent vehicle for encompassing the scores, if not hundreds, of actions that need to be carried out by dozens

> Without strong, ongoing citizen advocacy for change, most policymakers will continue to support environmental deficit spending, just as they have budget deficit spending.

Decades of scientific research, technological advancements, and ecological insights show us that humans can thrive on earth in an ecologically sustainable manner.

of diverse agencies in order to displace greenhouse gases (and other pollutants). Many of these actions are readily available for implementation, like energy-saving investments, solar technologies, and waste-reduction efforts. Energy-saving investments alone are *now* capable of cutting the nation's energy bill by $200 billion per year, thereby preventing the release of hundreds of millions of tons of carbon dioxide and other greenhouse gases.

Market imperfections and institutional barriers now block many of these good options, in part because the pace of technological innovation has far outpaced advancements in public policies. The barriers also arise from lack of quality information, shortages of investment capital (especially for the poor, elderly on fixed incomes, and cash-strapped businesses), split incentives between renters and landlords, and vast subsidies for expensive fossil and nuclear fuels. Another serious problem is the failure to have prices reflect the actual costs of pollution, deteriorated health, land abuse, deforestation, and other societal and environmental damages associated with fossil and nuclear energy use.

These manifold problems are being addressed, and solutions are being proposed and tried in different parts of the country and in other countries. Citizen commissions should be set up to network with other communities and resource groups to ensure that no policy option goes unexamined. And the policy options are many.

In 1988, over three thousand legislative bills were introduced at the state level, and an equal number at the federal level, dealing with resource wastes, recycling, ozone-depleting chemicals, and other environmental issues directly or indirectly related to global climate change. There are far too many bills for any individual to monitor. Fortunately, a number of public interest groups now routinely provide detailed analyses of available options, including tax and regulatory incentives and disincentives; carbon fees or levies that reflect environmental and societal costs of using various resources; innovative land, transport, and environmental planning options; budgeting funds for information clearinghouses, research, development, demonstrations, and technology transfer; "least-cost" utility planning and innovative regulatory reforms to promote energy saving investments; changing government procurement practices; banning packaging materials that use ozone-depleting chemicals, or cannot be recycled; and promoting community reforestation.

The end goal of any commission is action. As the Southern California Air Quality Management Board shows in its detailed action report, communities, like individuals, cannot do it alone. Their report details appropriate and necessary state and federal steps. These include improving state building and appliance energy standards, increasing the federal vehicle fuel economy standards, tightening federal pollution standards, and greatly increasing research and development on long-term, non-polluting energy options like energy efficiency and solar and renewable fuels technologies.

A citizens' commission can serve a tremendous education function for voters in helping them to identify similar steps on global climate change that their state and federal officials should be taking. The power of the vote is an often neglected tool. Voter apathy unwittingly encourages the perpetuation of environmental deficit spending by elected officials. Voter involvement can get things changed. At the federal level, this is imperative if citizens are to succeed in getting members of Congress and the president to exemplify the vigorous leadership necessary to pursue international agreements on at least four fronts: (1) phasing out all ozone-depleting chemicals within the next decade; (2) a treaty to halt deforestation and the extinction of biological species and to encourage reforestation; (3) reducing greenhouse gases by 20 percent over the next decade and establishing a long-term goal of phasing out greenhouse gases through greater reliance on efficiency and solar/renewable resources; and (4) achieving population stabilization as rapidly as possible by supporting universal voluntary family planning services—an action that could help achieve a world population level of around ten billion instead of the fourteen billion currently projected for the coming decades.

A healthy ecology is the basis for a healthy economy.

Perhaps never before in history are individual actions so greatly influencing the course of human events. Prevention pays. And it is incumbent upon all of us to capitalize on these opportunities. A healthy ecology is the basis for a healthy economy. In promoting ecologically sound economic practices, we will not only slow global climate change, but greatly alleviate urban smog, acid rain, tropical deforestation, and a host of other social and environmental problems.

Tips

- Become informed about local, state, and federal legislation.

- Write letters and organize letter campaigns in support of environmental legislation. Make sure to include your name and address and the number of the bill that your are writing about.

- Directly lobby your local, state, or federal representatives.

The Environment, The Law, and You

By Andrew C. Kimbrell and Edward Lee Rogers

- The number of leukemia victims in your community has risen tenfold in the past three years, and now more children are becoming ill.

- Your county government has decided to create a three thousand acre solid waste dump adjacent to your property and you can't get information on its potential harm.

- Trucks carrying hazardous wastes pass through your town on a weekly basis, and you are not sure that the necessary precautions have been taken.

- You suspect that a corporation is illegally polluting a nearby river.

- A second airport must be built in your metropolitan area, to handle an ever-increasing flow of air traffic. But if the proposed site for the airport is developed according to plan, it will destroy a major recreational area and an adjacent wetland ecosystem may be adversely affected.

- Local officials lobby for the construction of a low-level nuclear waste underground storage facility in your area.

- The Department of Defense plans to open a biological warfare research laboratory ten miles upwind of your community.

- A private energy consortium wants to build a coal dust fired cogeneration power plant on fifteen acres down the road from your home.

> If we are to save the environment, rather than merely revere it, the citizen can no longer be put off with the easy advice to "go get a statute enacted" or "wait until election day," while the bulldozer or chain saw stands ready to move.
>
> *— Joseph L. Sax*

Problems such as these confront hundreds of thousands of Americans each year. Fortunately, due to several federal and state laws, you may be able to do more than you thought to intervene when you perceive activities by the government or private industry that harm the environment or your health. Today, more opportunities than ever exist for private citizens to defend their environmental interests through the legal process. By intervening in agency decision-making, suing to force agencies to enforce environmental laws, or taking polluters to court, many individuals and citizen groups have made and continue to make a difference all over the United States.

Use of the courts, intervening in agency decision-making, and petitioning for agency rulemaking or other corrective agency actions can be key components

Law is an alliance of those
who have farsight and insight
against the shortsighted.

— Rudolf Von Jhering

in successful environmental action. Such legal actions, even if only partially or temporarily successful, can be a catalyst for developing media coverage and political support and leverage. Remember, however, that lawsuits and other legal remedies are not an environmental panacea. While there is an active and talented pool of public interest environmental lawyers, lawsuits can be time-consuming and expensive. Furthermore, the courts' role in reviewing agencies' actions or polluters' conduct harmful to the environment is, in some instances, limited by the statutory criteria involved. Also, judges may not always be sensitive to the significance of the environmental issues involved or sympathetic to the environmental cause. Therefore, for most environmental problems, using the courts works best in conjunction with a larger strategy of grass roots organizing and continuous pressure on local, state, and federal legislators.

Using FOIA

Effectively pursuing your legal rights often requires obtaining information. Whether it's data on the toxicity of a chemical substance, past records documenting the activity of a major polluter, or environmental assessments of projects being planned by government agencies, chances are you can get this data from the appropriate federal or state government agency. Sometimes a simple request will do. More often you will have to submit a request under the Freedom of Information Act (FOIA).

Americans have a traditional distrust of secretiveness by government agencies. Prior to 1966, however, the view that "people have a right to know" was merely an expression of belief, not law. This changed when Congress enacted the Freedom of Information Act (FOIA) in 1966. This Act gave the citizen a legally enforceable right of access to government documents and data, except for privileged categories. Key FOIA provisions require that agencies make identifiable records available to any person requesting them under the Act. If refused, the person can go to federal district courts and sue the agency to produce the improperly withheld records. If you win, the agency pays all legal costs and attorney fees.

You don't need an attorney to file a FOIA request. A typical FOIA form letter (see model below) is relatively easy to adapt to any circumstances. So if you're wondering about an environmental problem or product, utilize FOIA to become a fully informed citizen. Although FOIA does not apply to state government agencies, virtually all states have similar laws governing disclosure of records.

Sample FOIA Letter

[NAME OF REQUESTER]
[ADDRESS OF REQUESTER]
[DATE OF REQUEST]

[NAME OF DIRECTOR OF AGENCY]
[ADDRESS OF AGENCY]
Dear Director:

In accordance with the Freedom of Information Act (FOIA), 5 U.S.C. 552, and pursuant to the regulations of [NAME OF AGENCY], [NAME OF REQUESTER], [MENTION HERE IF YOU ARE A NON-PROFIT TAX EXEMPT ORGANIZATION] requests a copy of the following documents, or access to them for inspection or duplication, that are in the possession of the [NAME OF AGENCY].

1. The entire file on [LIST HERE HAZARDOUS OR TOXIC SUBSTANCE NAME, OR NAME OF GOVERNMENT OR PRIVATE PROJECT THAT YOU ARE INTERESTED IN].

2. To the extent that the entire file does not include the following documentation, we additionally request documents which refer to, or discuss, or in any way apply to this subject matter, and any other studies, reports, or bibliographies that refer to or discuss the subject matter of the petition.

This request encompasses documents in the broadest sense of the term, as FOIA mandates. This includes all memoranda, notes, records of conversations (phones, person-to person, other), and data. This material is requested regardless of the recording media used, be it manually recorded or mechanical.

If any exemption from FOIA's disclosure requirement is claimed, please describe the general nature of the document and the particular legal basis upon which the exemption is claimed. Please provide any and all non-exempt portions of any document that may be partially exempt due to some privilege.

This request is a matter of great concern to the requester, and your prompt and complete report would be appreciated. If it is not possible to comply with all portions or aspects of this report promptly, please provide a partial response with materials readily available.

(Following paragraph is for tax-exempt organizations) Inasmuch as the [NAME OF ORGANIZATION] is making this inquiry in the course of carrying out its education and other charitable public interest activities, we request that charges for searching and duplicating be waived. Should there be a difficulty with the fee waiver, please contact the [NAME OF REQUESTER] by phone and do not delay processing or answering this request.

Thank you for your attention in this matter.

Sincerely,

[REQUESTER]

cc. relevant local, state, and federal legislators.

By intervening in agency decision-making, suing to force agencies to enforce environmental laws, or taking polluters to court, many individuals and citizen groups have made and continue to make a difference all over the United States.

Using NEPA

Another important, though more complicated, tool for gaining information on the environmental and health impacts of certain government projects is the National Environmental Policy Act (NEPA). Signed into law by President Nixon on New Year's Day 1970, NEPA requires all federal agencies to prepare environmental assessments (EAs) or environmental impacts statements (EISs) on their programs and projects. These agency analyses are required to take a "hard look" at the possible environmental consequences of proposed federal actions and to consider alternative actions where appropriate.

The first United States public law to include the term "biosphere," NEPA effectively required "no less than a revolution in the way we approach problems and make decisions," according to Russell Train, chairman of the first Council on Environmental Quality (CEQ).

Citizens potentially affected by federal projects or other federal actions can usually sue under NEPA to assure that the federal agency involved has adequately assessed *and made public* the potential environmental harm that a project or program can cause *before* those actions can legally begin. Under NEPA, "federal" actions include those projects and programs that will be undertaken by a federal agency itself or for which it will grant a license, approval, or funding to another entity to carry out. Because of this broad concept of federal agency action under NEPA, many private and state projects must comply with NEPA's requirements.

A recent example shows the power of NEPA to address community concerns. In 1987, many citizens in and around Woodbridge, Virginia, expressed concern about the possible environmental and health impacts of a large, sophisticated electronic warfare facility in their neighborhood. The citizens approached the Foundation on Economic Trends, an organization experienced in NEPA law. After ascertaining that the Army had not prepared the required documentation, the Foundation sued the Army under NEPA. After a few months, pursuant to a court order, the Army agreed to prepare the environmental documentation. Ultimately, rather than undergo the full NEPA process and thereby reveal all the problems with the facility, the Army closed the facility down.

The Woodbridge litigation scenario has been repeated in hundreds of NEPA cases around the country. NEPA has stopped or slowed highway construction, clear-cutting of forests, offshore oil leases, destruction of wetlands, building of biological warfare facilities, and a large variety of other federal projects that would have harmed the environment. It is one of the most powerful legal weapons in the environmentalist's arsenal.

Activists should note that NEPA can only force agencies to conduct a detailed environmental study and take environmental impacts into consideration in making its decision on a project. As is often true with FOIA, however, making public the information gained through a NEPA lawsuit is sometimes enough to stop environmentally dangerous projects and programs. As Supreme Count Justice Brandeis stated over a half century ago, "publicity is justly commended as a remedy for social and industrial diseases. Sunlight is said to be the best of disinfectants; electric light the best police man."

But be forewarned; NEPA law can often be complex, so an attorney is very much required.

> The purpose of law is to prevent the strong from always having their way.
> – *Ovid*

Citizen Action Suits

Along with NEPA, many other landmark environmental statutes were enacted into law in the 1970s and 1980s. Congress passed the Clean Air Act in 1970 (replacing prior and ineffectual clean air acts of 1963 and 1967), which was substantially strengthened in subsequent years; the Clean Water Act of 1972 (substantially revised in 1978 and in later years); the Resource Conservation and Recovery Act of 1976, the first comprehensive federal effort to deal with solid waste and hazardous waste; The Federal Insecticide, Fungicide, and Rodenticide Act (FIFRA) passed in 1972 to deal with pesticide distribution, sale and use, and was revised most recently in 1989; and the Toxic Substances Control Act (TSCA) enacted in 1976 and also revised in later years. In 1980, we saw the passage of Superfund—The Comprehensive Environmental Response, Compensation, and Liability Act (CERCLA)—which was substantially revised in 1986.

In many cases, individuals or citizen groups can actually *force* government agencies and private corporations to comply with these various statutory regulations. Through a mechanism referred to as "Citizen Suits," many of these statutes allow the citizen to step in when the agency isn't doing an adequate enforcement job.

If you think that a corporation is polluting a river or stream nearby, or that toxic chemicals are leaking from a container near your home, and no one seems to be doing anything about it, a citizen suit might be the answer. On the following page is a chart of selected citizen suit provisions found in certain environmental statutes.

As with NEPA law suits, citizen suits under these other statutes and any settlement negotiations with polluters will require an experienced lawyer.

Citizen Suit Provisions under Various Statutes

Statute	What It Covers	Who Can Be Sued
Resource Conservation and Recovery Act (RCRA)–7002 (42 USC–6972)	Hazardous and nonhazardous wastes.	Anyone who transports, stores, treats, or disposes of waste and violates a permit condition, order, or regulation under the Act (past violators included). Anyone (including the government) who fails to perform cleanup responsibilities for releases of hazardous substances or pollutants (often from inactive or abandoned waste sites).
Comprehensive Environmental Response, Compensation, and Liability Act (CERCLA, or Superfund)–310 (42 USC–9659)	Hazardous substances or pollutants.	Suppliers or operators of underground injection wells who fail to maintain drinking-water standards or violate orders or regulations under the act.
Safe Drinking Water Act (SDWA)–1449 (42 USC–300j–8)	Public water systems or underground sources of drinking water.	Anyone who violates permits issued for discharge of pollutants into surface waters or any other order or limitation under the act.
Clean Water Act (CWA)–505 (33 USC–1365)	Surface and groundwater.	Anyone who violates a permit condition, order, or regulation under the act, particularly the prohibition against disturbing on- and off-site water quality
Surface Mining Control and Reclamation Act (SMCRA)–520 (30 USC–1270)	Coal mining: during both mining and post mining restoration of sites.	Any one who violates a regulation under the act regarding the safe manufacture, use, disposal, and processing of chemicals, including PCBs.

SOURCE: Adapted from *The Poisoned Well*, (Sierra Club Legal Defense Fund, 1989).

Consult national environmental organizations for advice. Local law schools and bar associations might also be helpful.

Action against Agencies

Whether enforcing NEPA or the other environmental statutes, remember to try and stay aware of what local, state, and federal governments are doing. Though it may often seem difficult and complex, carefully read any proposed actions, permits, approvals, or rulemaking by agencies on environmental issues that affect your community or that you are interested in. Keep abreast of notices of proposed zoning variances and building permits in your area and investigate them.

The following are two stories of how citizens became involved in agency action and won:

When a number of concerned Kentuckians discovered that the Left Beaver Coal Company had contaminated their groundwater by pouring coal sludge into an abandoned mineshaft, they petitioned the state mining authority for a formal hearing to have the company's permit denied. Assisted by the Appalachian Regional Defense Fund, they negotiated a settlement by which the coal company agreed to drill deeper wells and install water purification equipment in the affected homes.

When residents of Chickasaw, Alabama, learned that Waste Management, Inc., planned to transport toxic wastes through their town, they organized the Chickasaw Community Affairs Group (CCAG) and pressured the town council to pass ordinances placing restrictions on such transport including:

- prior notification of the police as to truck routes and times of travel, to allow for escorts;
- maintenance of 150 feet of distance between any truck and the nearest vehicle;
- bans on travel during bad weather; and
- lowered weight limits on some roads and bridges.

The CCAG also succeeded in convincing authorities in the nearby city of Mobile, Alabama, to implement further restrictions on hazardous waste transportation and storage.

If you think that a corporation is polluting a river or stream nearby, or that toxic chemicals are leaking from a container near your home, and no one seems to be doing anything about it, a citizen suit might be the answer.

Consumers are
generally among
the best vindicators
of the public interest.

— *Warren E. Burger,
Chief Justice*

Personal Injury Suits

Besides securing information and enforcing environmental statutes, you can also directly sue polluters for damages they have caused to you and/or your property. These lawsuits are sometimes based on specific statutory provisions or on certain common law concepts or combinations of both. Under these laws, one may sue under nuisance, trespass, negligence, strict liability, or product liability concepts or statutory provisions. Most often these personal injury lawsuits involve use of state courts and law. However, under certain circumstances, federal courts can also be available.

Courts have compensated injury in a wide variety of circumstances. These have included paying compensation for injuries and other damages when several people became ill from consuming water contaminated from chemicals dumped into a nearby waste dump. Plaintiffs have also been paid compensation for injuries caused by asbestos in buildings.

In another well-publicized case, residents of a small community in upstate New York began to wonder why their children were always getting sick. A number of residents started asking the right questions. To their horror, they discovered that what looked like a harmless open field in their neighborhood had once been a dumping ground for a nearby chemical company—they were living atop *20,000 tons* of highly toxic chemical wastes. What did they do?

Led by Lois Gibbs, a concerned mother, a number of citizens contacted local and state government offices, discovering that the Hooker Chemical Corporation was the previous owner of their "harmless open field." At their city hall they discovered numerous past complaints on file from residents, and they found out that an environmental assessment had been conducted in 1976 by local health officials and the EPA. A look in the library showed them that the local newspaper had run stories on the problems at Love Canal. They also discovered that the local school board, which had bought the field from Hooker, had encountered significant difficulties in building the local school due to the presence of the hazardous materials.

Their discoveries confirmed the suspicions of parents with sick children and gave the members of the newly formed Love Canal Homeowners Association the evidence they needed to take on Hooker Chemical, city hall, the state, and the White House in what turned out to be a long, hard-fought, legal and political battle. When the smoke finally cleared, Lois Gibbs and the small, blue-collar community of Love Canal had achieved their main goals—evacuation and full compensation of the five hundred affected families, and the creation of nation-wide concern over the issue of improper toxic waste disposal.

Personal injury law suits can be very effective, but they can also be expensive and lengthy. Often illnesses and property damage occur only after a long period of time has passed since an area was polluted. States often impose time limits on how long after an act of pollution you can sue, thereby effectively preventing polluters from being sued. Once again, good legal advice is essential, so utilize law schools and bar associations for referrals.

Finding a Knowledgeable Lawyer

Finding a knowledgeable and experienced environmental or toxic tort attorney willing to undertake your particular case is a formidable but readily achievable task. As with many areas of law, it is usually helpful if the lawyer is knowledgeable about the particular area of environmental or toxic tort law relevant to your particular case. Many different sources can help you find a suitable lawyer. Check with your local and state bar association, lawyer referral services, and your local law schools. Another good source are national, state, or local environmental organizations and the Environmental Law Institute of Washington, D.C., and its directory of Environmental Law Associates, a list of environmental lawyers, many of whom are in private practice, who are located in almost every state in the country. You may also wish to confer with your own attorney or with other attorneys located in your area. While they may not be knowledgeable about the area of law in question, they may be able to refer you to an appropriate attorney. Once you have a list of suitable candidates, interview each one of them carefully and ask for references and evidence of their track records in the area of law of concern to you.

In you win in federal court, under federal "fee-shifting" statutes, you are usually entitled to recover most, if not all, of the attorney's fees and expenses you incurred in the litigation. Because of such statutes, public-spirited attorneys are often willing to take sound environmental cases on a reduced or no-fee basis, hoping to recover such statutory fees upon winning the case for their clients.

In you win in federal court, under federal "fee-shifting" statutes, you are usually entitled to recover most, if not all, of the attorney's fees and expenses you incurred in the litigation.

Tips

- **Know what is going on in your community.** Stay abreast of re-zoning proposals, funding requests, and other matters being considered by your town or city council and by federal, state, and local agencies in your area. Consider the possible social and environmental effects of the decisions to be made, and ask yourself what price your community can afford to pay for "progress." Remember that the future of your children is too important to leave to the "experts" and the "specialists."

- **Know what is going on in your own backyard.** Be suspicious of, for example, rusty fifty-gallon drums dumped in the woods or pipes spewing waste water into your creek. And make sure that your house does not have asbestos insulation and is not built on a radioactive landfill.

- **Get involved *before* problems arise—before disaster strikes.** Join or support a citizens' action group in your area. Don't take statements from public officials at face value. Get promises in writing, and if an official says he or she is not responsible for something, find out who is responsible.

- **Get full information!** Effective action is impossible without information and hard evidence. Depending on the issue at hand, you may need to know things like the possible sources of pollutants or the potential social, economic, and environmental consequences of a proposed action.

  In many cases, the information you need is available through state and federal agencies, and a simple request will give you access to it. However, to protect their plans from disruption, agencies are often very reluctant to share information with potential adversaries. In these cases, you will need to use the Freedom of Information Act or its state equivalent. With a few limited exceptions, FOIA gives you the right to request and receive any document, file, or other record in possession of any federal agency. All states have similar laws covering state and local agencies.

- **Monitor and contribute to the decision-making process of federal, state, and local agencies.** Have a clear goal in mind when approaching an agency. Try to ask for things you know are within the agency's powers.

  Remember to first identify which particular person within the agency is responsible for your area of concern. Then write to that specific person. If, however, that person is unresponsive, go "up the ladder" in the agency.

  If possible provide any request with statements from experts and others whom the agency will recognize. Evidence is generally more convincing to an agency than passion.

- **When required, hire a lawyer.** When involved in NEPA law, agency intervention, or toxic tort suits, hiring a lawyer with relevant experience is recommended.

  You may also need a lawyer's help to file for tax-exempt status as a non-profit corporation. The decision to incorporate, however, should not be taken lightly. If you do incorporate, it is important that your attorney know the tax laws as they apply to your type of organization, lest you get into deep trouble with the IRS.

  An attorney can also advise on a variety of direct action question including picketing, boycotts, leafletting, and other first amendment-related matters, including the dangers of defamation, libel, and slander.

Bibliography

Getting Information

Freedom of Information Act Clearinghouse. *The Freedom of Information Act: A User's Guide.* Washington, DC: June 1987. To order, contact the Freedom of Information Clearinghouse, PO Box 19367, Washington, DC 20036; (202) 785–3704. The Clearinghouse is an excellent source of information for FOIA-related questions and information and provides legal representation for FOIA challenges.

Washington Researchers. *How to Find Information about Companies.* Washington, DC: 1979. To order, contact Washington Researchers, 918 16th Street, NW, Washington, DC 20006; (202) 828–4800.

The Administrative Process

Belfiglio, Jeff, Thomas Lippe, and Steve Franklin. *Hazardous Waste Disposal Sites: A Handbook for Public Input and Review.* Palo Alto, CA: Stanford Environmental Law Society, 1981.

Citizen's Clearinghouse for Hazardous Wastes. *Leadership Handbook on Hazardous Waste.* Arlington, VA: CCHW, 1983. To order, contact CCHW, PO Box 926, Arlington, VA 22216; (703) 276–7070.

East Michigan Environmental Action Council. *Community Care: A Guide to Local Environmental Action.* Birmingham, MI: 1982. To order, write East Michigan Environmental Action Council, 21220 W. Fourteen Mile Road, Birmingham, MI 48010; (313) 258–5188.

Environmental Action (magazine). To order, contact the Environmental Action Foundation, 1525 New Hampshire Avenue, NW, Washington, DC 20036; (202) 745–4870.

Environmental Defense Fund. *Dumpsite Cleanups: A Citizen's Guide to the Superfund Program.* Washington, DC: 1984.

Epstein, Samuel S., Lester O. Brown, and Carl Pope. *Hazardous Waste in America.* San Francisco, CA: Sierra Club Books, 1982.

Gordon, Wendy. *A Citizen's Handbook on Groundwater Protection.* New York, NY: Natural Resources Defense Council, 1984.

Izaak Walton League of America. *Guide to Conservation Action.* Arlington, VA: 1983. To order, contact the Izaak Walton League of America, 1401 Wilson Boulevard., Level B, Arlington, VA 22209; (703) 528–1818.

Loveland, David Gray, and Diane Greer. *Groundwater: A Citizen's Guide.* Washington, DC: League of Women Voters Education Fund, 1986. To order, contact the League of Women Voters of the United States, 1730 M Street, NW, Washington, DC 20036; (202) 429–1965.

National Campaign against Toxic Hazards (NCATH). *The Citizens' Toxics Protection Manual.* Boston, MA: 1987.

National Wildlife Federation. *The Toxic Substances Dilemma: A Plan for Citizen Action.* Washington, DC, 1980.

Sierra Club Legal Defense Fund. *The Poisoned Well: New Strategies for Groundwater Protection*. Washington, DC: Island Press, 1989.

Going to Court

American Civil Liberties Union Foundation. *Litigation under the Federal Freedom of Information Act and Privacy Act*, 14th edition, June 1989, Washington, DC. Available from the ACLU Foundation Publications Department, 122 Maryland Avenue, NE, Washington, DC 20002. The regular price is $40, but tax-exempt organizations, law students, and faculty may receive copies for $12.50. This book is a complete guide, highly useful to lawyers and non-lawyers, on how to use the FOIA effectively before the federal agency and in the courts.

Citizen's Clearinghouse for Hazardous Wastes. *User's Guide to Lawyers*. Arlington, VA: 1985. To order, send $5.75 to CCHW, PO Box 926, Arlington, VA 22216; (703) 276–7070.

Environmental Law Institute. *Citizen Suits: An Analysis of Citizen Enforcement Action under EPA-Administered Statutes*. Washington, DC: 1984.

Jorgensen, Lisa, and Jeffrey Kimmel. *Environmental Citizen Suits: Confronting the Corporation*. Washington, DC: Bureau of National Affairs, 1988. To order BNA publications, call the BNA Response Center at (800) 372–1033, or write BNA's Customer Service Center, 9435 Key West Avenue, Rockville, MD 20850.

Moore, Andrew Owens. *Making Polluters Pay: A Citizens' Guide to Legal Action and Organizing*. Washington, DC: Environmental Action Foundation, 1987. To order, contact the Environmental Action Foundation, 1525 New Hampshire Avenue, NW, Washington, DC, 20036; (202) 745–4870.

Sierra Club Legal Defense Fund. *The Poisoned Well: New Strategies for Groundwater Protection*. Washington, DC: Island Press, 1989.

General Background

Caldwell, Lynton K. *Citizens and the Environment: Case Studies in Popular Action*. Bloomington: University of Indiana Press, 1978.

Carson, Rachel L. *Silent Spring*. New York: Fawcett, 1978.

Hays, Samuel P. *Beauty, Health, and Permanence: Environmental Politics in the United States, 1955–1985*. New York: Cambridge University Press, 1987.

Hoban, Thomas More, and Richard Oliver Brooks. *Green Justice: The Environment and the Courts*. Boulder: Westview Press, 1987.

Nash, Roderick. *Wilderness and the American Mind*. New Haven, CT: Yale University Press, 1973.

A Bibliography for Community Organizers
By Donald E. Davis

The following bibliography is a resource directory for community organizers. The purpose of the directory is to inform organizers and activists about community organizing literature and other related information sources. The bibliography consists of (1) an annotated bibliography; (2) a "comprehensive" bibliography; and (3) a listing of journals, periodicals, and resource centers.

The annotated bibliography is arranged alphabetically by author or editor and consists of titles ranging from Saul Alinsky's *Rules For Radicals* to Paul Wellstone's *How The Poor Got Power*. The annotated bibliography focuses on texts published since 1980; however, standards such as Piven and Cloward's *Poor People's Movements* (1977) were also included.

The comprehensive bibliography is arranged according to the following subheadings: "Community Organizing," "Environment; Green Politics," "Labor/Union Organizing," and "Civil Rights."

It is hoped that this guide will aid organizers in their ongoing efforts and struggles. By learning about the successes and failures of others, community groups can eliminate many of the mistakes due to simple inexperience or political naiveté. However, because the goal of the community organization is also permanent empowerment for its members, there are clearly paths that they should take or avoid when such groups are mobilizing their resources and energy. Ideally, this bibliography will assist the community organizer in finding those paths, so that she or he can effectively empower the community organization.

Annotated Bibliography

Alinsky, Saul. *Rules for Radicals: A Pragmatic Primer for Realistic Radicals*. New York: Vintage Books, 1972. 196 pages.

Since the early 1970s, *Rules for Radicals* has been one of the most widely used manuals for social change activists. The book features Alinsky's own personal organizing philosophy, as well as discussions of direct action, styles of organizing, organizer education, and the proper use of tactics. Five essential elements make up the organizing approach outlined in the book: (1) The Professional Organizer is the Catalyst for Social Change; (2) The Task Is to Build a Democratic Community-Based Organization; (3) The Goal Is to Win Power; (4) Use Any Tactics Necessary; (5) A People's Organization Must Be Pragmatic and Nonideological. Many activists consider Alinsky's organizing methods to be universally applicable. However, it should be pointed out that Alinsky's style of organizing is not suitable for all community organizations. The approach is primarily an urban one, which grew out of Alinsky's experiences in Chicago in the 1930s and 1940s. Organizing in rural areas often requires methods and tactics not mentioned in this volume. *Rules for Radicals*, nevertheless, remains one of the best organizing primers and should be read by all would-be activists and organizers.

Boyte, Harry C., Heather Booth, Steve Max. *Citizen Action and the New American Populism*. Philadelphia, PA: Temple University Press, 1986. 215 pages.

According to the three authors, this work is "a beginning statement about the new progressive populism." Populism, which has traditionally fought for more economic and political power for all citizens, is said to be returning to American politics by way of new grass roots or "citizen action" organizations. These organizations represent a variety of constituencies, cutting across racial, class, and geographical boundaries. Activities of these groups range from the stopping of farm foreclosures to assisting the senior citizen unable to pay heating or cooling bills. The text draws from interviews with organizers, citizens, and community leaders, and is told primary from the vantage point of Citizen Action, a national coalition of progressive citizen groups. Contents include: chapter 1, "Thunder on the Right," a discussion of the rise of Reagan conservatism in the 1980s; chapter 2, "Progressive Populism," a survey of the political and economic conditions of the 1970s and 1980s; chapter 3, "Organizers and Activists," a brief history of the formation of the Citizen Action Coalition; chapter 4, "Carrying a Message," an introduction to canvassing techniques used by the new citizen's organizations; chapter 5, "Energy Politics," a summary of populist efforts to limit the monopolizing powers of the petroleum industry; chapter 6, "Plagues on the Land," documents the campaigns against dumping toxic and hazardous wastes in local communities; chapter 7, "Hard Times on the Farm," surveys the upsurge of farm and rural activism in the Midwest; chapter 8, "Populist Politics," documents the return of the populist philosophy and political platform to municipal and national levels; and chapter 9, "Democratic Visions," discusses the religious and moral roots of citizen organizing as well as the possibility of developing a truly working democracy. Notes. Numerous photographs.

Boyte, Harry C., and Frank Riessman (Eds.). *The New Populism: The Politics of Empowerment.* Philadelphia, PA: Temple University Press, 1986. 323 pages.

"Populism," in the words of co-editor Harry Boyte, "calls for the return of power to ordinary people." Traditionally, populism has empowered grass roots individuals by giving them a voice in established political processes. The new populism, according to the various contributors, requires not only creating space for the grass roots in mainstream politics, but also the empowerment of individuals through the development of voluntary, or noninstitutional, political organizations. The book traces the history and development of populism from its origins in the late 1800s to its reemergence in the American political campaigns of the 1980s. The question of "right" individual and community empowerment remains a central theme of the book and is discussed on a number of conceptual levels. Part two, entitled "The Politics of Empowerment," consists of two chapters that directly address the empowerment issue: Frank Riessman's "The New Populism and the Empowerment Ethos"; and Julian Rappaport's essay "Collaborating for Empowerment: Creating the Language of Mutual Help." Both Riessman and Rappaport see many positive qualities in mutual aid or "self-help" organizations and see their emergence as a sign of a new populist spirit or "ethos" in American society. Other important essays include Lawrence Goodwyn's "Populism and Powerlessness", Cora Tucker's "Born a Rebel", Mike Miller's slightly critical "Populist Promises and Problems", and Harry Boyte's "Populism and Free Spaces." The book contains an excellent annotated bibliography, subdivided into the following categories: "Key Historical Works," "Manifestos and Statements of the New Populism," "Right-Wing Populist Statements and Manifestos," "New Populism," "Descriptive and Journalistic Treatments," and "Theoretical Treatments of Modern Populism."

Coover, Virginia, Ellen Deacon, Charles Esser, and Christopher Moore. *Resource Manual For A Living Revolution.* Philadelphia, PA: 1985. 330 pages.

This comprehensive, nine-part manual is an excellent resource tool for individuals and community organizers working for nonviolent social change. The book offers ideas on improving the group process of meetings, suggestions for developing workshops and educational seminars, and a number of community-building exercises. Case histories of both successful and unsuccessful organizing activities are presented throughout the text. Theoretical concerns are adequately dealt with as a considerable portion of the book (pages 7–43) discusses the basic tenets of various "social change" theories—Marxism, Anarchism, Feminism, Fascism, Gandhian Nonviolence (satyagraha), Liberal Reform, and Libertarianism. Select bibliographies on related subject areas are also provided. An appended index lists all bibliographies, exercises, and tools described in the manual. An invaluable resource guide for the community organizer/activist.

Delgado, Gary. *Organizing the Movement: The Roots and Growth of ACORN*. Philadelphia, PA: Temple University Press, 1986. 269 pages.

This book presents a detailed history of one of the most successful poor people's organizations in recent American history—ACORN (Association of Community Organizations for Reform Now). The author, a founding member and former organizer for the group, provides a detailed narrative account of the organization's development from the early 1970s to the mid-1980s. Delgado is familiar with a number of community organizing models (for example, resource mobilization) and discusses each of these in terms of what he perceives as their strengths and weaknesses. He argues that organizations like ACORN must join to form coalitions and larger organizational networks so that they might influence national politics and effect systemic social reform. However, he also believes that an organization's participation in electoral politics is not sufficient. Without the involvement of the group in more militant, disruptive activities, the community's more immediate social needs cannot be met. Finally, Delgado observes that a great deal of the value of community organizations lies in the process of organizing itself. In his words, "[C]ommunity organizations help people get a sense of the way the world works, open a path for them to think about how it could be, and provide them with an opportunity to change at least a small part of it." Bibliography.

Fisher, Robert. *Let the People Decide: Neighborhood Organizing in America*. Boston, MA: Twayne Publishers, 1984. 197 pages.

Covering almost a century of neighborhood organizing in America, Fisher's book provides a thorough analysis of community grass roots activism as well as the social and political conditions that have spawned and sustained it. The material is arranged chronologically, in six self-contained chapters. Contents include: chapter 1, "Social Welfare Neighborhood Organizing, 1886–1929"; chapter 2, "Radical Neighborhood Organizing, 1929–1946"; chapter 3, "Conservative Neighborhood Organizing, 1946–1960"; chapter 4, "The Neighborhood Organizing 'Revolution' of the 1960s"; chapter 5, "The New Populism of the 1970s"; and chapter 6, "Conclusion: The Nature and Potential of Neighborhood Organizing." What is perhaps unique about this book is the author's informed understanding of the changes not only in community organizing styles, but also in the community itself: the "neighborhood" of the 1920s and 1930s is not the same as the "neighborhood" of the 1970s. Over the years, changing demographics, mass industrialization, and the transition from rural to suburban political economies has created new and ever more challenging problems for 1980s neighborhood organizing. The contemporary political landscape, as Fisher himself notes in the conclusion to this well-documented work, requires that "neighborhood organizing movements develop in an historical context that includes but transcends local community boarders" (p. 159). The characterization of the neighborhood as one that extends beyond geographical boundaries is an extremely important one, especially as the reader is made aware of the critical interaction between neighborhood organizing projects and broader social movements. In sum, Fisher's book is an important one for neighborhood or community organizing: his analysis of groups like SDS, ACORN, and SNCC provides invaluable background information upon which to build a truly "people owned" organization. Annotated notes and index. A "Bibliographic essay" provides additional references and sources.

Hall, Bob (Ed.). *Environmental Politics: Lessons from the Grassroots*. Durham, NC: Institute for Southern Studies, 1989. 122 pages.

This collection of short essays provides an important introduction to environmental organizing at the grass roots level. The essays, written by the organizers and activists themselves, show how successful organizing campaigns must connect "environmental" concerns to broader public health and economic concerns. The case studies take place in North Carolina, a state whose economy is linked directly to the quality, productivity, and attractiveness of the living environment. Select essays include Mark Hellman's "Durhams Progressive Coalition," a look at coalition building among blacks and progressive white's in Durham (pp. 31–47); Edgar Miller's "Too Hot To Handle: Where to Put Radioactive Waste," a report of the siting of a low-level radioactive waste incinerator in northwest Bladen County (pp. 48–55); and Millie Buchanan's "No Safe Haven for Mr. Foushee's Incinerator," a documentation of the fight to keep an incineration facility out of Caldwell, North Carolina (pp. 85–91). Appendix 1, "Who Owns North Carolina," by Bob Hall, is a summary report of the largest single land ownership investigation ever undertaken for a particular state or region in the United States (pp. 106–121). Photographs, maps.

Hess, Karl. *Community Technology*. New York, NY: Harper & Row, 1979. 107 pages.

The technology question, in the compiler's opinion, is discussed far too little in community organization and development circles. The author of *Community Technology* makes a good argument for bringing the technology issue to the forefront of all community organization agendas. In this book, Hess has documented the organizing work in Adams-Morgan— a seventy-block neighborhood in Washington, D.C.—where thousands of individuals in the 1970s collectively participated in creating an "alternative" community technology program. The Adams-Morgan project was organized locally, within the political structures of neighborhood and municipal assemblies. According to Hess, the larger goal of community organization should be political and economic self-sufficiency: communities should use local resources and produce as much of their own food and energy as technologically possible. The

alternative technology mandate restructures not only the local community organization but also the larger institutions. For example, the large corporations and state and federal government, which have traditionally controlled the economic and political realities of local communities and townships, have their roles redefined through this process.

Kahn, Si. *Organizing: A Guide for Grassroots Leaders*. New York, NY: McGraw-Hill, 1982. 387 pages.

Written in a clear, readable style, Kahn's manual remains one of the best introductions to grass roots organizing. Fundamental concerns such as leadership development (chapter 2), issues (chapter 5), strategy (chapter 8), tactics (chapter 10), and communication (chapter 12) are discussed in detail, using examples from numerous case studies. As in his earlier book, Kahn is concerned with how people get power—both from and within institutions. For the author, organizing "means building permanent organizations" (p. 55), so the manual is concerned primarily with developing institutions capable of sustaining themselves "over a long period of time" (p. 58). This organizing "bias" has implications for the author's promotion of certain organizing techniques and strategies, including the selection of issues and the recruitment and training of members. Although the "organizational" model is unapologetically embraced by Kahn, his discussions of member ownership (chapter 3) and the preservation of cultural values (chapter 18) demonstrate that he is aware that organizational models may create, within some community groups, unwanted bureaucracy and elitist professionalism. Other important topics covered in the book include the proper use of media (chapter 13), the building of coalitions (chapter 15), and the relationship of people's organizations to local and national politics (chapter 17). Index.

Pierce, Gregory F. *Activism that Makes Sense: Congregations and Community Organization*. New York: Paulist Press, 1984. 148 pages.

This small book, by a former organizer with the Industrial Areas Foundation (founded by Saul Alinsky), is a basic handbook for community organizers and/or church activists. According to the author, participation in community organizations is a way for congregations to fulfill a "biblical mandate" consistent with their own religious and civic heritage. In the opening two chapters, the relationship between congregational responsibility and effective community activism is discussed. The question of obtaining power through organization is addressed in chapters three and four and is depicted as a necessary part of the ongoing organizing process. Chapter 5 concerns the role of allies in coalition building; chapter six, the group dynamics of political controversy and organization tactics. The concluding chapter instructs organizers on finding and training leaders. Basic rules to follow and considerations to keep in mind when organizing are scattered throughout the text. The book concludes with an excellent discussion of professional organizers who, Pierce argues, must avoid creating bonds of dependency between organization members and themselves. Notes.

Piven, Frances Fox, and Richard A. Cloward. *Poor People's Movements: Why They Succeed, How They Fail.* New York: Pantheon Books, 1977. 381 pages.

This important study examines the role of organizations and organizers in controlling or limiting poor people's movements. The authors suggest that organizers often disrupt or curtail "lower-class" mobilization by focusing too heavily on traditional organization-building activities (for example, fundraising, drafting constitutions, leadership development). Moreover, they argue that leaders and organizers of the poor often channel insurgency and dissent into "normal" politics: the activities of most poor people's organizations lead only to social and political reforms favoring those in power. Fox and Cloward support their position by looking at the development of the unemployed worker's movements of the 1930s (chapter 2), the industrial worker's movements of the post-World War II era (chapter 3), the Civil Rights movement of the 1950s and 1960s (chapter 4), and the welfare rights movement of the 1960s and 1970s (chapter 5). Suspicious of traditional political institutions and structures, the authors make a good case in

this book for "de-institutionalizing" organizational practices. Only then, argue the authors, will the poor be fully empowered.

Staples, Lee. *Roots to Power: A Manual for Grassroots Organizing.* New York: Praeger Publishers, 1984. 234 pages.

One of the better manuals on community organizing from a grass roots perspective. Staples, a former organizer and trainer with FAIR SHARE, WAGE, and ACORN, presents in five chapters knowledge and information about his own organizing experiences. In the author's own words, the book "examines strategies and tactics, methods and techniques that people can use to deal with basic problems and concerns that flow from everyday situations. It presents some of the root philosophy and goals of grass roots organizing and discusses social conflict, self-interest, and the role of the organizer. It lays out a model for building a new organization, offers guidelines for choosing issues, and examines the elements of a successful issue campaign. . . . [It]focuses on ongoing activities such as recruitment, meetings and actions, leadership development, negotiations, press relations, and working with other groups" (p. ix). The sixth and final chapter, "Nuts and Bolts, Some Do's and Don'ts" is a look at specific concerns of grassroots organizers, offering helpful advice on such topics as research strategy, direct action, successful negotiation, lobbying, fundraising, organizational development, coalition building, and public relations. A brief introduction by Richard Cloward and France Fox Piven, authors of *Poor People's Movements*, puts Staples' book within the context of community organizing history and philosophy. An appendix gives examples of actual materials used by ACORN in a number of organizing campaigns.

Wellstone, David. *How the Rural Poor Got Power: Narrative of a Grassroots Organizer.* Amherst, MA: University of Massachusetts Press, 1978. 227 pages.

This book is a study of rural poverty and politics. The focus is on the development of the Organization for a Better Rice County (ORBC), a poor people's organization located in a rural, small-town community of south-eastern Minnesota. The author, a college professor, was a volunteer member of the

ORBC organization for several years and critically discusses the group's political successes and organizational defeats. The group's initial organizing activities centered around welfare rights, although later ORCB activities included lobbying for better daycare and transportation facilities. Emphasis is placed on the thoughts and actions of individual ORBC members, the development of indigenous leadership, and problems associated with maintaining a poor people's organization. A postscript discusses the proper function of organizers and leaders, as well as the necessity of building, within community organizations, collective grass roots leadership. Preface by Robert Coles.

Comprehensive Bibliography

Alinsky, Saul D. *Reveille for Radicals.* New York: Vintage Books, 1946, 1969.

—————. *The Professional Radical.* New York: Harper & Row, 1970.

—————. *Rules For Radicals: A Realistic Primer for Realistic Radicals.* New York: Vintage Books, 1972.

Alperowitz, Gar, and Jeff Faux. *Rebuilding America.* New York: Pantheon, 1984.

Bennis, Warren G., Kenneth D. Benne, and Robert Chin. *The Planning of Change, fourth edition.* New York: Holt, Rhinehart, Winston, 1985.

Bilken, Douglas P. *Community Organizing: Theory and Practice.* New York: 1985.

Boyte, Harry. T*he Backyard Revolution: Understanding The Citizens Movement.* Philadelphia, PA: Temple University Press, 1980.

—————. *Community Is Possible: Repairing America's Roots.* New York: Harper & Row, 1984.

Community Services Administration. *Citizen Participation.* Washington, DC: United States Government Printing Office, 1978.

Cooney, R., and H. Michalowski. *The Power of the People. Revised Edition.* Philadelphia, PA: Temple University Press, 1985.

Coover, Virginia, et al. *Resource Manual for a Living Revolution: A Handbook of Skills and Tools for Social Change Activists.* Philadelphia, PA: New Society Publishers, 1985.

Cox, Fred M., John L. Erlich, Jack Rothman, and John E. Tropman (Eds.). *Strategies of Community Organizing, third edition.* Itasca, IL: F. E. Peacock Publishers, 1979.

Delgado, Gary. *Organizing The Movement: The Roots and Growth of ACORN.* Philadelphia, PA: Temple University Press, 1986.

Evans, Sarah. *Personal Politics: The Roots of Women's Liberation in the Civil Rights Movement and the New Left.* New York: Vintage Books, 1980.

Fink, P. David. *The Radical Vision of Saul Alinsky.* Mahwah, NJ: Paulist Press, 1984.

Fisher, Robert. *Let the People Decide: Neighborhood Organizing in America.* Boston, MA: Twayne Publishers, 1984.

Gitlin, Todd. *The Whole World Is Watching: Mass Media and the Making of the New Left.* Berkeley, CA: University of California Press, 1980.

Gittell, Marilyn. *Limits to Citizen Participation.* Beverly Hills, CA: Sage Publications, 1980.

Green, Gerson. *Who's Organizing the Neighborhood?* Washington, DC: Community Anti-Crime Program, United States Department of Justice, September 1978.

Hess, Karl. *Community Technology.* New York: Harper & Row. 1980.

Jones, W. Ron. *Finding Community: A Guide to Community Research and Action.* Palo Alto, CA: James E. Frel & Associates, 1971.

Kahn, Si. *How People Get Power: Organizing Oppressed Communities for Action.* New York: McGraw-Hill, 1970.

Kahn, Si. *Organizing: A Guide for Grassroots Leaders.* New York: McGraw-Hill, 1982.

Katz, Alfred H., and Eugene I. Bender. *The Strength in Us: Self Help Groups In the Modern World*. New York: New Viewpoints (Franklin Watts), 1976.

Morris, David, and Karl Hess. *Neighborhood Power: The New Localism*. Boston, MA: Beacon Press, 1975.

Pierce, Gregory F. *Activism that Makes Sense: Congregations and Community Organization*. New York: Paulist Press, 1984.

Piven, Frances Fox, and Richard Cloward. *Poor People's Movements: Why They Succeed, How They Fail*. New York: Vintage Books, 1979.

Staples, Lee. *Roots to Power: A Manual for Grassroots Organizing*. New York: Praeger Publishers, 1984.

Tjerandsen, Carl. *Education for Citizenship*. San Francisco, CA: Emil Schwarzhaupt Foundation, 1980.

Warren, Rachelle B., and Donald I. Warren. *The Neighborhood Organizer's Handbook*. Notre Dame, IN: University of Notre Dame Press, 1977.

Wellstone, Paul. *How the Rural Poor Got Power: Narrative of a Grass Roots Organizer*. Amherst, MA: University of Massachusetts Press, 1978.

Environment; "Green" Politics

Bookchin, Murray. *The Rise of Urbanization and the Decline of Citizenship*. San Francisco, CA: Sierra Club Books, 1987.

Brown, Michael H. *The Toxic Cloud: The Poisoning of America's Air*. New York: Harper & Row, 1988.

Gibbs, Lois Marie. *Love Canal: My Story*. Albany, NY: State University of New York Press, 1982.

Hall, Bob (Ed.). *Environmental Politics: Lessons from the Grassroots*. Durham, NC: Institute for Southern Studies, 1988.

Kazis, Richard, and Richard Grossman. *Fear at Work: Job Blackmail, Labor, and the Environment*. New York: The Pilgrim Press, 1982.

Lash, Jonathan, Katherine Gillman, and David Sheridan. *A Season of Spoils: The Reagen Administration's Attack on the Environment*. New York: Pantheon Books, 1984.

Sale, Kirpatrick. *Dwellers in the Land: The Bioregional Vision*. San Francisco, CA: Sierra Club Books, 1985.

Tokar, Brian. *The Green Alternative*. San Pedro, CA: R & E Miles, 1987.

Vietor, Richard H. *Environmental Politics and the Coal Coalition*. College Station, TX: Texas A&M University Press, 1987.

Labor/Union Organizing

Botsch, Robert B. *We Shall Not Overcome: Populism and Southern Blue Collar Workers*. Chapel Hill, NC: University of North Carolina Press, 1980.

Brody, David. *Industrial America: Essays on the Twentieth Century Struggle*. New York: Oxford University Press, 1980.

Bernstein, Irving. *Turbulent Years: A History of the American Worker, 1933–1941*. Boston, MA: Houghton Mifflin, 1971.

Galenson, Walter. *The CIO Challenge to the AFL: A History of the American Labor Movement, 1935–1941*. Cambridge, MA: Harvard University Press, 1960.

Gutman, Herbert G. *Power and Culture: Essays On The American Working Class*. New York: Pantheon Books, 1987.

Hevener, John W. *Which Side Are You on?: The Harlan County Coal Miners, 1931–39*. Urbana, IL: University of Illinois Press, 1978.

Mann, Eric. *Taking On General Motors: A Case Study of the UAW Campaign to Keep GM Van Nuys Open*. Berkeley, CA: Center For Labor and Education, Institute For Industrial Relations, University of California, 1977.

Rowan, Richard L. *Employee Relations, Trends and Practices in the Textile Industry*. Philadelphia, PA: Industrial Research Unit, The Wharton School, University of Pennsylvania, 1987.

Truchil, Barzy E. *Capital-Labor Relations in the United States Textile Industry*. New York: Praeger, 1988.

Civil Rights

Adamson, Madeline, and Seth Borgos. *The Mighty Dream*. Boston, MA: Routledge & Kegan Paul, 1984.

Andolsen, Barbara Hilkert. *Daughters of Jefferson, Daughters of Bootblacks: Racism and American Feminism*. Macon, GA: Mercer University Press, 1986.

Fairclough, Adam. *To Redeem the Soul of America: The Southern Christian Leadership Conference and Martin Luther King, Jr.* Athens, GA: The University of Georgia Press, 1987.

Frye, Hardy T. *Black Parties and Political Power*. Boston, MA: G. K. Hall, 1980.

Garrow, David J. *Protest at Selma: Martin Luther King, Jr., and the Voting Rights Act of 1965*. New Haven, CT: 1978.

Garrow, David J. (Ed.) *The Montgomery Bus Boycott and the Women Who Started It: The Memoir of Jo Ann Gibson Robinson*. Knoxville, TN: The University of Tennessee Press, 1987.

Grant, Nancy L. *TVA and Black Americans: Planning for the Status Quo*. Philadelphia, PA: Temple University Press, 1989.

Lewis, Ronald L. *Black Coal Miners in America: Race, Class, and Conflict, 1780–1980*. Lexington, KY: The University Press of Kentucky, 1987.

McAdam, Doulas. *Political Processes and the Development of Black Insurgency, 1930–1970*. Chicago, IL: The University of Chicago Press, 1982.

Morris, Aldon D. *The Origins of the Civil Rights Movement: Black Communities Organizing for Change*. New York: Free Press, 1984.

Sitkoff, Harvard. *The Struggle for Black Equality, 1954–1980*. New York: Hill and Wang, 1981.

Williams, Juan. *Eyes on the Prize: America's Civil Rights Years, 1954–1965*. New York: Viking Press, 1987.

Journals and Periodicals

Community Jobs, Anne Martin, editor, 1516 P Street, NW, Washington, DC 20005; (202) 667–0661. Publishes monthly listings for available community organizing jobs and internships. Job descriptions are listed regionally (East, Midwest, South, Washington, DC), with salary information and application deadlines.

Earth First! The Radical Environmental Journal, Dave Forman, editor, PO Box 5871, Tucson, AZ 85703. Published eight times a year by Earth First!, a "no-compromise environmental movement/organization." Provides a variety of articles on "monkeywrenching" (ecological sabotage) and direct action wilderness preservation.

Environmental Action, 1525 New Hampshire Avenue, NW, Washington, DC 20036; (202) 745–4870. Published monthly by Environmental Action, Inc., a national political lobbying and educational organization devoted to environmental issue organizing.

Foxfire, Rabun Gap, GA 30568. Published quarterly by the students of Rabun County High School in Clayton, Georgia. Features folklore, north Georgia oral history, and crafts. Occasional articles on organizing or political themes.

Grassroots, PO Box 9586, Charlotte, NC 28299. *Grassroots* is the newsletter of Grassroots Leadership, a training and resource center for grass roots activists and organizations. Published four times a year.

Mother Jones, Douglas Foster, editor, 1663 Mission Street, Second Floor, San Francisco, CA 94103. A monthly magazine devoted to labor and social justice issues, "left" politics, and progressive organizing activities.

Radical America, 1 Summer Street, Somerville, MA 02143. Published five times a year. Features articles on American organizing activities past and present.

Sojourners, 1321 Otis Street, NE, Box 29272, Washington, DC 27702. An ecumenical Christian magazine devoted to progressive ideas and causes.

Southern Exposure, Eric Bates, editor, PO Box 531, Durham, NC 27702. Published quarterly by the Institute for Southern Studies. The only journal devoted specifically to Southern organizing history. Full length articles, book reviews, and news from across the region.

United Mine Workers Journal, John Duray, editor, 1525 New Hampshire Avenue, NW, Washington, DC 20036; (202) 745–4870. Official publication of the United Mine Workers Union. News updates on union activities, as well as local and federal mining legislation.

Utne Reader, Eric Utne, editor, 2732 West 43rd Street, Minneapolis, MN 55410. "The best of the alternative press"—a bimonthly digest of articles and magazine reviews from alternative sources. Frequent articles on progressive community organizing and grassroots movements.

Organizations and Centers

Association of Community Organizations for Reform Now (ACORN), 410 South Michigan Avenue, Fourth Floor Annex, Chicago, IL 60605; (312) 939–7488. A national network of multi-issue organizations representing low and moderate-income people. ACORN is involved in direct action neighborhood organizing, political education, and indigenous leadership development. Membership totals more 50,000 with neighborhood organizations in some twenty-six states.

Citizens Clearinghouse for Hazardous Wastes, PO Box 926, Arlington, VA.

Commission on Religion in Appalachia (CORA), 864 Weisgarber Road, NW, Knoxville, TN 37919; (615) 584–6133. CORA, an ecumenical organization, was formed in 1965 in order to "build community and combat poverty" in the Appalachian region. Funds grass roots projects, designs educational programs, and conducts studies and surveys on the social and economic conditions of the area.

Envirosouth, Inc., PO Box 11468, Montgomery, AL 36111; (205) 277–7050. A private, nonprofit, environmental public information service organization working in Alabama to create an environmentally literate citizenry within the state and to tailor a balanced growth through practical application of the region's resources.

Family Farm Organization Resource Center, 2595 University Avenue, Suite 202, Saint Paul, MN 55114; (612) 645–1231.

An information clearinghouse for rural grass roots organizations working to save the family farm.

Grassroots Leadership, 2300 East Seventh Street, PO Box 9586, Charlotte, NC 28299; (704) 332–3090. A training and resource center for grass roots activists and community leaders. Founded and co-directed by organizer/musician Si Kahn.

Highlander Education and Research Center, RFD 3, Box 370, New Market, TN 37820; (615) 933–3443. Promotes social change through its educational workshops and community empowerment programs. Maintains an extensive library, containing archival materials, videos and audiotapes, and special collections files. An invaluable resource institution for the community organizer.

Institute for Local Self Reliance, 2425 18th Street, NW, Washington, DC 20009. A Washington-based organization involved with promoting recycling alternatives, small scale technology, and sustainable community development. A clearinghouse for information on waste incinerators and their harmful environmental effects.

Media Network, 121 Fulton Street, New York, NY 10038.

National Toxics Campaign, 29 Temple Place, Boston, MA 02111.

Piedmont Peace Project, 500 Archdale Drive, Concord, NC 28025. The Piedmont Peace Project is an organization that addresses the social and economic impact of uncontrolled military spending. Membership includes farmers, mill workers, ministers, teachers, and parents.

Southern Empowerment Project, 323 Ellis Avenue, Maryville, TN 37801; (615) 984–6500. The Southern Empowerment Project (SEP) recruits and trains community organizers in the southern United States. It represents an association of member organizations who want to develop capable organizers who understand Southern traditions, institutions, and belief systems. Also publishes a newsletter and maintains a job bank for organizers in the southern region.

The North Carolina A. Philip Randolph Institute, 3923 Homestead Lane, Winston-Salem, NC 27106; (919) 924–8588. The A. Philip Randolph Institute strives to increase the participa-

tion of blacks in the skilled trades and in the labor move-
ment. The institute's membership includes not only black trade unionists but also other union and community members who work on voter registration and political education.

The Environmental Crisis

WHAT IS GLOBAL WARMING? The year—2035. Phoenix is baking in its third week of temperatures of over 115° F. Coastal cities such as New York and Miami are threatened by rising sea levels. Decades of drought have laid waste to the once fertile Midwest farm belt. Hurricanes batter the East and Gulf Coasts, and forest fires continue to blacken thousands of acres across the country.

During the torrid summer months, large sections of the Mississippi turn into mud flats, closing the river to commercial traffic. In other parts of the globe, millions perish in the wake of prolonged droughts and devastating floods.

Science fiction? Hardly. These are some of the sobering scenarios that many scientists believe may happen if we continue to pollute the planet as we have in the past. While scientists debate whether current heat waves are linked to the "greenhouse effect," most climatologists now believe we are on the threshold of a fundamental global warming capable of severely disrupting ecosystems and social systems around the world.

Throughout much of the earth's history, there has been a natural greenhouse effect. Certain gases have formed a blanket around the earth. This greenhouse blanket allows the sun's rays to pass through to the surface of the earth, while absorbing some of the reflected heat energy. This trapped heat insulates the earth, making life possible. Without the natural greenhouse effect, our planet would be frigid and lifeless. Unfortunately, this stabilizing, beneficial phenomenon is now becoming a life-threatening process of global change as various industrial gases are thickening the greenhouse blanket, which is trapping more and more heat around the planet.

Over the last fifteen years, scientists have closely monitored this increased level of air pollution in the earth's atmosphere. Their objective: to determine whether industrial pollution will affect the world's temperature. Their conclusion: the planet is moving into the early stages of an unprecedented shift in climate—a global warming trend of alarming proportions. If left unchecked, this global warming trend will adversely affect all life on earth. This global warming is called the "greenhouse effect."

Many scientists are now predicting that if current trends in greenhouse pollution continue, industrial activities will subject the globe to a temperature rise of 4° to 9° F in the next seven decades. By comparison, the average global temperature has not varied more than 3.6° F in the 18,000 years during which human civilization has emerged. A temperature climb of 4° to 9° F would exceed the entire increase in global temperatures since the end of the last Ice Age. By continuing our excessive and irresponsible energy policies, and by encouraging uncontrolled industrial growth, we are subjecting the earth to changes that may be second only to nuclear destruction in their potential harm to the planet. The buildup of greenhouse gases will radically affect temperatures, rainfall patterns, agricultural productivity, and natural ecosystems throughout the world. "We may be moving through an entire geological epoch in a single century . . . changing the entire fabric of nature," states John Hoffman, director of the global atmosphere program at the Environmental Protection Agency (EPA).

The potential consequences of global warming are far reaching and devastating. For example, global warming could lead to the thermal expansion of seawater and melting of land ice in the polar regions. Climatologists are predicting a dramatic rise of up to five feet (1.5 meters) in sea level by the year 2050. A one to five foot rise in water level in less than sixty-five years could flood coastal areas where half of the world's population resides, resulting in massive loss of lives and property. The cost of protecting the shore areas of the East Coast of the United States could be between $10 billion and $100 billion in the wake of a three-foot rise in the ocean level.

The rise in sea level could also destroy major port facilities, disrupting drainage systems, locks, and canals. Many nations are already concerned over the possibility of salt water contamination of freshwater rivers and groundwater, essential sources of drinking water of millions of people.

Sea level rise could also significantly damage the remaining coastal wetlands, salt marshes, swamps, and bayous—most of which lie in the southeastern region off the Gulf of Mexico and Atlantic seaboard. An EPA study predicts that a five-foot rise in sea level will destroy upward of 90 percent of America's wetlands, a rich and diverse complex of unique eco-systems that have flourished unmolested since well before the dawn of recorded history.

The rise in sea temperature and sea level could also increase both the number and intensity of hurricanes worldwide. Hurricane intensity is directly linked to the temperature of the water surface. According to meteorologists, the increase in global warming and sea warming could increase the intensity of hurricanes by 40 to 50 percent.

Global warming may also fundamentally alter precipitation patterns in every region of the globe. In some areas, lakes, rivers, and aquifers may dry up altogether. In other regions, new lakes and streams will appear for the first time in human history, radically changing the topography and environment.

Global warming could also lead to mass extinction of tree species and the loss of millions of acres of forest, especially in the middle latitudes of the planet. According to the Bellagio Report, a detailed study conducted in 1988 by some of the world's leading climatologists and environmental activists, the greenhouse phenomenon is likely to have major effects on forests by the year 2000. The authors of the report predict a large-scale forest dieback before 2100 A.D.

The rapid destruction of forest habitats will also accelerate the loss of animal life and could lead to the mass extinction of many remaining species. We are already losing one species to extinction every sixty minutes. It is estimated that even without the global warming phenomenon, we might lose up to 17 percent of all the remaining species of life over the next few decades as a result of the ravaging of tropical rain forests for development purposes—timbering, grazing, and cropping.

Forests will not be able to migrate as fast as the climate changes accelerate. Writing in the journal *Science*, Richard A. Kerr points out that "each degree centigrade of warming pushes climatic zones 100 to 150 kilometers [60 to 95 miles] northward."

The global greenhouse warming is the first truly universal crisis that our species has ever faced. The altered climate of the globe affects every aspect of existence, from the reproductive success of the lowliest plankton on the ocean surface to the survival of the great urban cultures that occupy the coastal land mass of the planet. Its impact will be felt across all geopolitical, ethnic, and class boundaries. The global warming is the first human crisis in which the context is the entire planet.

In order to address this unprecedented global environmental crisis, we will have to check the emission of greenhouse gases. These include:

Carbon Dioxide—About 50 percent of the greenhouse effect is caused by atmospheric increases in carbon dioxide (CO_2). Since the advent of the industrial revolution, manmade CO_2 emissions have increased by 5,300 percent. Every year 5.5 billion tons of CO_2 are added to the earth's atmosphere. In the United States, we generate about six tons of CO_2 a year per person. This results primarily when fossil fuels such as coal, oil, and natural gas are burned to run our power plants, homes, automobiles, and factories. Deforestation and the resulting clearing and burning of trees is also a significant cause of CO_2 pollution. Trees absorb vast amounts of CO_2. Currently, the worldwide rate of deforestation—27 million acres per year—is ten times the rate of reforestation. Much of the deforestation takes place in Brazil, Indonesia, and Zaire, which contain nearly half of the forests in the tropics.

Chlorofluorocarbons—Approximately 15 to 20 percent of the greenhouse effect is caused by chlorofluorocarbons (CFCs). CFCs are industrial chemicals widely used in air conditioners, refrigerators, solvents, plastic packaging, and foam insulation. CFCs are a persistent greenhouse gas. Many CFCs hold several thousand times as much heat in the atmosphere as CO_2 particles and remain in the atmosphere for over 100 years. (See also Ozone Depletion section *infra*.)

Methane—Accounts for approximately 18 percent of the greenhouse effect. Methane is produced by cattle and rice fields and is also emitted by landfills when organic waste breaks down.

Nitrous Oxides—Account for approximately 10 percent of the greenhouse effect. They are formed by the burning of fossil fuels, natural microbial activity in the soil, and the breakdown of chemical fertilizers.

Ozone—Is a vital component of the upper atmosphere. But at ground level, ozone is a dangerous pollutant and accounts for about 5 percent of the greenhouse effect. Motor vehicles, power plants, and oil refineries generate ground-level ozone.

The United States bears a primary responsibility in the production of greenhouse gases. Though America has only 5 percent of the world's population, we contribute 26 percent of the world's CO_2 and 27 percent of the world's CFCs.

WHAT IS OZONE DEPLETION? Ozone, a dangerous air pollutant at ground level, is an essential element of the earth's upper atmosphere. The ozone layer, part of the stratosphere (seven to fifteen miles above the earth's surface), shields life on earth from the sun's harmful ultraviolet rays.

As life evolved during the last billion years, the ozone layer protected the surface of the earth from much of the sun's ultraviolet radiation. Since ultraviolet light damages the DNA building blocks of life, evolution has been dependent upon the ozone layer shielding life from harmful solar radiation. At the same time, ozone helped life on earth develop as part of the earth's natural greenhouse effect—warming the planet so life could survive.

Now, however, worldwide emissions of CFCs are destroying this fragile and essential ozone shield. CFCs migrate to the upper atmosphere where they are broken down by the sun's rays, releasing atoms of chlorine, which in turn destroy ozone. A chlorine atom is capable of destroying as many as 100,000 ozone molecules before is becomes inactive. CFCs can stay active in the atmosphere for over a century.

The main ozone depleting chemicals and their approximate percentage contribution to ozone depletion are: CFC–12 (45 percent), used in automobile, commercial, and industrial air conditioning, home and retail refrigeration, and in packaging and insulation; CFC–11 (26 percent), used in insulation packaging, cushioning material in car seats, furniture, and commercial air conditioning; CFC–113 (12 percent), used in solvents for computers and electronic equipment, as well as in dry cleaning; carbon tetrachloride (8 percent), used in petroleum refining, pharmaceutical manufacturing; methyl chloroform (5 percent), used as a solvent in aerospace industries, electronics, and chemical manufacturing; and halon 1301 (4 percent), used in fire extinguishers.

Concern over CFCs has heightened over the past few years with the startling discovery in 1985 of a hole in the ozone layer above Antarctica.

The depletion of Antarctic ozone increases each year. Researchers recorded a 50 percent loss in 1985 and a 60 percent loss in 1987 and reported a gaping hole in the ozone layer the size of the continental United States. More recently, 100 leading atmospheric scientists reported a second tear in the ozone shield over the mid-Northern Hemisphere. Now there are indications that a third tear has opened up in the Arctic, with scientists reporting a hole in the stratosphere the size of Greenland. The United States National Aeronautics and Space Administration (NASA) projects that a 3 percent increase in CFC emissions will cause a 10 percent depletion of the ozone layer around the earth by the year 2050.

Ozone depletion and the resulting increase in radiation will have significant impacts on human health. The EPA predicts that a dramatic reduction in ozone protection will result in two million additional skin cancer cases annually. Additionally, the agency estimates that in the United States, a "no action" policy on CFC production will result in an increase of up to 178 million cases of non-melanoma skin cancer by the year 2075. According to John Hoffman, Director of the Office of Global Change at the EPA, people who work outside, such as farmers and construction workers, are especially susceptible to such a health risk: "You can say with certainty that people with outdoor occupations will be subject to larger increases in fatalities" from non-melanoma skin cancers due to ozone destruction.

Cataract occurrence is another health problem that would increase significantly should the United States fail to curtail CFC production. A 1 percent increase in ultraviolet radiation from ozone depletion will result in a 0.5 percent increase in cataract occurrence. If no action is taken, the number of cases of cataracts could reach twenty million by the year 2075. This includes individuals who would not otherwise develop cataracts as well as those who would contract the disease prematurely. Cataracts are the third leading cause of legal blindness in the United States.

Outdoor workers are also particularly susceptible to yet another danger to the eye, a condition called acute photokeratosis. The effect of this condition is like that of a sunburn on the cornea caused by increased exposure of UV-B radiation. Severe cases result in the death of corneal cells and a scratching sensation in the eyes.

Additionally, increases in ultraviolet radiation caused by ozone depletion will significantly weaken human immune systems, thus increasing our susceptibility to infectious diseases. Studies indicate that as ultraviolet exposure increases, human beings would become increasingly defenseless against micro-organisms that enter through the skin, such as bacteria and viruses.

Plant and animal species are also vulnerable to the increase in ultraviolet radiation. Researchers at the University of Maryland found that ultraviolet radiation results in tissue and cell damage in two-thirds of the 200 species tested. For example, ozone depletion has been shown to be damaging to soybean crop yields. Soybeans, which comprise the fifth largest crop in the world and the third largest United States crop, are essential to the world economy.

A one quarter decline in the ozone layer would reduce soybean crop yield by one quarter. Moreover, the effects of ozone depletion are less harmful to weeds than to crops and cause the crops to be more susceptible to disease and destruction by insects. All these factors combined could reduce soybean crop yield by half. This result would be similar for many crops and, according to Richard Adams of Oregon University, a 15 percent reduction in stratospheric ozone by the year 2050 could cause crop losses of $2.6 billion a year in the United States.

Perhaps the most dangerous finding to date is the effect of ultraviolet radiation on the photosynthesis and metabolism of plankton, the microscopic marine organisms that are the base of the ocean food chain. A recent study has reported serious effects on plankton in Antarctica in 1987, raising questions about the very survivability of aquatic life in the wake of increased ultraviolet radiation exposure.

In 1987, thirty-four nations signed the Montreal Protocol on CFCs, which calls for a 35 to 50 percent reduction in CFC emissions by the year 2000. While the press and industry made much of the document, many environmental scientists contend that the agreement falls short of the steps required to address the growing problems of CFC emissions effectively. They point out that ozone depletion has been occurring at a far faster rate since 1987 then was predicted. Additionally, the Montreal Protocol does not cover several chemicals that contribute to ozone depletion. There is also concern that many nations will simply disregard both the spirit and the letter of the agreement and will continue to allow CFC emissions within their national boundaries.

Furthermore, a number of estimates have suggested that we need at least a 90 percent ban—a percentage originally proposed by United States environmentalists and rejected by the United States delegation as too radical—if we are to prevent the ozone hole from expanding further.

WHAT IS ACID RAIN? Throughout human history, rain has been regarded as a nurturing phenomenon. It is the basic supplier of water for all living things. Ironically, during the last several years, rain has become an acute threat to the environment and human health.

The reason—pollution is entering the atmosphere and causing rain to become acidified. "Acid rain" is the term used to describe rain, sleet, snow, mist, fog, and clouds containing sulfuric acid and nitric acid. In some areas, rain approaches the acidic level of vinegar. This acidification is caused by the burning of coal, oil, and gasoline. When this acidified rain falls to the earth, it destroys fish life in lakes and streams, poses a short and long term threat to the world's forests, and can cause a wide variety of human diseases.

Over one hundred and fifty years ago, scientists observed that rain falling in heavily industrialized cities, such as Manchester, England, had a much higher sulfuric acid content then normal rain. Now, pollution produced by coal burning plants, automobiles, and a variety of industrial activities has turned acid rain from a local urban concern to a global environmental crisis.

Acid rain decimates aquatic life around the world. In the United States, many lakes in the Northeast have experienced devastating reductions in fish life because of increased acidity. Now acid rain poses an increasing risk to our Western and Southern lakes and streams.

Acid rain also kills forests. It destroys trees in two ways. For trees growing at high altitudes—bathed in acidified fog and clouds—acid rain damages needles and leaves essential to the tree's ability to survive. In one federally funded experiment, acid rain was shown to kill, outright, the needles of Red Spruce trees—a major tree variety of Northeast forests that has suffered a steep decline since 1960. Acid rain also presents a long term threat to forests by depleting the soil of two nutrients vital to trees—magnesium and calcium. The effects of acid rain on soil result in the stunting of the growth of trees and the destruction of root systems. Of course, acid rain does not just destroy American forests. In 1984, the German government reported that 50 percent of German forests were damaged by acid rain. In many other European countries, 25 to 50 percent of forests have been severely damaged by acid rain.

Remarkably, the significant impacts of acid rain on human health have received less public notice than its impacts on lakes and forests. It has been estimated that acid rain is probably the third largest contributor to lung disease in the United States. Additionally, scientists have found that acid rain can increase the health risks produced by metals such as aluminum, cadmium, mercury, and lead in drinking water. One aspect of this is the tendency of acid rain to leach aluminum from soils. This aluminum not only destroys fish and trees but has been linked to human disease, including Alzheimer's disease. Acid rain also causes a break down of metals in municipal and home water pipes, leading to high concentrations of lead in drinking water. Lead poisoning has been linked to several human diseases including brain and neurological disorders in children.

Acid rain also contributes to the greenhouse effect. Recent research indicates that acid rain prevents soil microbes from consuming methane, a leading greenhouse gas.

The total financial losses each year to acid rain are staggering. The yearly worldwide damage to human health, crops, forests, lakes, and buildings is in the tens of billions of dollars.

Appendix Two/Chapter 23

Quick Fixes

The False Promise of Nuclear Energy

By Alex Antypas and Jeanne Lawson

Nuclear energy...must be revitalized in order to alleviate the greenhouse effect.
> — Edward M. Davis,
> *President of the American Nuclear*
> *Energy Council*

The nuclear industry is now trying to revive itself by selling the public and decision makers on the belief that nuclear power can significantly help to alleviate the global warming trend. However, nuclear power faces serious obstacles, including prohibitive costs, long construction lead times, dwindling public support, and inherent environmental problems.

In fact, a close examination of the nuclear industry's claims reveals that:

- Nuclear power can have virtually no effect on the global warming trend.

- A second generation of so-called advanced reactors is likely to be plagued by problems similar to those experienced by the current generation.

- Immediate energy efficiency improvements and renewable energy sources in the near term are our best defence against global warming.

Nuclear Economics. The experience of the recent past can be used as an indicator of nuclear power costs in the future. In 1987 and 1988, thirteen nuclear power plants were completed in the United States at an average cost of $4,049 per kilowatt, or more than four billion dollars for a 1,000 megawatt (MW) plant in 1987 dollars. When operating and construction costs are combined, nuclear power costs almost three times as much as natural gas. In addition, nuclear power necessitates additional expenses for decommissioning, waste disposal, major repairs, and the cost of possible accidents.

Theoretically, if nuclear power were to entirely replace fossil fuels as the source of the nation's electricity at current costs, an initial investment of $1.6 trillion would be required to finance the construction of 400 new 1,000 MW reactors at $4,000 per kilowatt. In comparison, the total gross private domestic investment in all sectors of the U.S. economy was only $712.9 billion in 1987. Therefore, the simple economics of nuclear power eliminate it as a realistic consideration for a meaningful role in solving the greenhouse crisis.

Lead Time. In addition to nuclear power's prohibitive costs, reactors cannot be built quickly enough to significantly avert the global warming process. While the nuclear industry claims it can build plants in five to six years, it currently takes about eight to twelve years to bring a plant on line. Simultaneous construction of even half of the 400 reactors discussed above is financially and physically impossible. Therefore, the building of the plants would have to be staggered over time as fossil-fuel plants were phased out or came to the end of their lifespans. This reality virtually eliminates any potential immediate impact on the global warming trend by nuclear power.

To reduce fossil fuel use for electric generation by even half, the world's nuclear plant completion rate between 1995 and 2020 would need to grow forty-fold from the 1975-1985 rate of one every three weeks to two every day, assuming no increase in energy efficiency.

Even assuming the same worldwide growth rate in energy efficiency as that which occurred in the U.S. between 1978 and 1986, the international nuclear plant completion rate would have to increase nine-fold to three each week to reduce fossil fuel use by half.

Social Acceptability. Public support for new nuclear power plants has evaporated. Any attempt to revive the nuclear option would run afoul of strong popular opposition, according to every independent national energy survey taken during the 1980s. Further polling data indicate that opposition to building new reactors increased from roughly 20 percent in 1975 to more than 60 percent in 1988. Only 30 percent considered themselves advocates of nuclear power growth. A solid majority of Americans don't believe the industry's claim that a new generation of reactors would be safer or cheaper.

Environmental Safety. Unlike energy efficiency and renewable energy technologies, nuclear power poses serious threats to the environment as well as to human and animal health. For example, by 1985, nuclear power plants had generated a total of 12,400 metric tons of highly radioactive waste in the form of irradiated fuel. Even assuming no nuclear plants are ordered by the year 2000, an estimated 41,000 metric tons of high level waste will await permanent storage at the turn of the century. The amount of irradiated fuel will escalate thereafter to more than 1,900 metric tons each year.

Increased use of nuclear power, in an attempt to reduce carbon dioxide emissions, would produce a corresponding increase in radioactive waste. If 400 nuclear power plants were built, each producing approximately 25 metric tons of high level waste every year, the combined waste production from 400 plants would be about 300,000 metric tons during the reactor's thirty years of operation. Combined with the waste from the 112 licensed reactors, the approximate 383,250 metric tons of radioactive waste would require siting in six permanent repositories.

Moreover, there is no indication that current technology can safely dispose of nuclear waste. Even "low-level" nuclear waste dumps have had to close down due to radioactive contamination of communities. In its 1983 report on radioactive waste disposal, the National Academy of Sciences determined that it would take three million years for spent fuel to decay to the point of posing the same level of risk as the uranium ore from which it came. During that time, radioactive material can be significantly carcinogenic. Recent studies indicate that there is no threshold below which radiation does not negatively impact human health. In other words, any amount of radiation, no matter how small, may cause serious health problems.

Accidents also pose a significant environmental and health threat. The Nuclear Regulatory Commission (NRC) has documented more than 30,000 mishaps and unplanned "events" at nuclear power plants in the United States since the 1979 Three Mile Island accident. Furthermore, the NRC has concluded that the chances of a severe core meltdown occurring at one of the 112 licensed U.S. power plants by the year 2005 is as high as 45 percent. West German and Swedish scientists have predicted a 70 percent chance of a Chernobyl-scale accident occurring at one of the world's nuclear plants every five to six years.

Nuclear accidents can also happen on the road. Studies indicate that by the year 2000, 120 trucks per day will be carrying nuclear waste on the nation's highways. Each shipment will contain many times the radioactivity released by the atomic bomb at Hiroshima. NRC calculations show that a relatively small radioactive release in a major metropolitan area could cause up to $4 billion in damages. But many experts have criticized the Commission's estimates as unrealistically low. Most communities are not prepared to handle a nuclear transport accident.

A New Generation. Responding to fears about nuclear power's impact on the environment, the nuclear industry now suggests that second generation nuclear plants will be safer and cheaper than current models. Both claims by the industry are dubious, no demonstration reactors have yet been built, and the history of the current generation of nuclear power plants indicates otherwise.

It has been estimated that it will take about ten years to construct a single demonstration plant, and another two or more decades to bring significant numbers of these plants on line. In short, a second generation of nuclear power plants will be beset by unresolved economic and safety problems.

(Adapted from *Mythbuster* numbers 2 and 3 of The Safe Energy Communication Council.)

Playing God with the Genetic Code

By Jeremy Rifkin and Andrew C. Kimbrell

Introduction. With recombinant DNA technology, it is now possible to snip, insert, recombine, rearrange, edit, program, and produce genetic material. We are now creating new combinations of living things. Just as our ancestors were able to heat, burn, melt, and solder together various inert materials, creating new materials like steel, glass, shapes, combinations, and forms of inanimate matter. With this newfound ability to manipulate the blueprint of living organisms, we assume a new role in the natural scheme of things. For the first time in history, we become the architects of life itself. We become the creator and designer. We begin to reprogram the genetic codes of living things to suit our own cultural and economic needs. We take on the task of creating a second genesis, this time a synthetic one geared to the requisites of efficiency and productivity.

Some in the scientific community are now suggesting that genetic engineering might be a panacea for global warming, ozone depletion, and acid rain. They suggest that soon scientists may be able to genetically engineer plants and animals to withstand higher temperatures, grow in drought conditions, withstand greater ultraviolet exposure, or survive in highly acidic waters. Yet, if history has taught us anything, it is that every new technological revolution brings with it both benefits and costs; that short term gains often lead to long term harm. Indeed, the more powerful the technology is at expropriating and controlling the forces of nature, the more exacting the price we are forced to pay in terms of disruption and destruction wreaked on the ecosystems that sustain life. Certainly our recent experience with both the nuclear and petro-chemical revolutions bears out this truth.

The question of whether we should embark on a long journey in which we become the architects of life is, along with the nuclear issue, the most important ever to face the human family. Though the benefits of biotechnology are heavily advertised, we are long past due for a discussion of the costs. In fact, the full-scale use of biotechnology in agriculture and industry, and in human reproduction and health, raises environmental, economic, and ethical concerns that are without parallel.

Environmental Risks. The biotechnology industry is preparing to release scores of genetically engineered viruses, bacteria, plant strains, and transgenic animals into the environment in the next few years. In coming decades, hundreds, even thousands, of genetically engineered life forms may enter the world's ecosystems in massive commercial volumes. A central question we must answer prior to releasing any large quantities of genetically engineered organisms into the environment is what risks such products pose to human health and the earth's ecology.

Because they are alive, genetically engineered products are inherently more unpredictable than chemical products. Genetically engineered products can reproduce, mutate, and migrate. Once released, it is virtually impossible to recall these living products back to the laboratory. A survey of one hundred top scientists in the United States acknowledged the potential benefits of genetic engineering but warned that "its imprudent or careless use . . . could lead to irreversible, devastating damage to the ecology."

Moreover, environmental scientists have compared the risk of releasing biotechnology products to those we have encountered in introducing exotic organisms to North American habitats. While most of these organisms have adapted to our ecosystems, several such as chestnut blight, kudzu vine, dutch elm disease, and the gypsy moth, have wreaked havoc on the environment.

The long term cumulative environmental impact of the deliberate release of thousands of genetically engineered organisms could be devastating. The sensible approach now being undertaken in Japan and several European countries is to have a moratorium on the deliberate release of any and all genetically engineered organisms until such time as a "predictive ecology" can be developed that will be capable of adequately assessing the effect that these organisms will have on the environment.

Socio-Economic Dislocation. The use of biotechnology creates the potential for considerable social and economic dislocation, especially in the American and international farming communities. Even a single biotechnological product can have significant adverse impacts. A timely illustration is the recent research and development of bovine growth hormone (BGH). When injected into cattle on a daily basis, this hormone, cloned through genetic engineering, can increase milk production by at least 30 percent per dairy cow. Because of the already flooded milk market, BGH poses a serious threat to dairy farmers. It has been estimated that milk prices may fall 10 to 15 percent within the first three years of the introduction of BGH. It has been further estimated that the number of dairy farmers may have to be reduced 25 to 30 percent to restore market equilibrium.

Additionally, a congressional report concluded that the use of BGH could cause an historic shift in American milk production from the traditional, smaller dairy farms in the Northeast to larger dairy farms in the West. These dislocations, and problems resulting from similar biotechnology products, will have dramatic social, economic, and cultural effects unless the dissemination of genetically engineered products is strictly controlled both national and internationally.

Ethical Considerations. The use of biotechnology creates profound and difficult ethical questions. Its use in reproduction and genetic screening bring unique questions of discrimination, exploitation of women, and the prospect of a commercial eugenics. Moreover, genetic engineering is being used to revolutionize biological warfare through the creation of "novel" viruses and bacteria that could have catastrophic effects and initiate a genetic arms race.

Most worrisome is that scientists are crossing species boundaries at an ever increasing rate, inserting human genes into animals, and animal genes into other animals and plants. Many recent achievements sound more like science fiction than science fact. For example, scientists have taken the gene that makes the firefly emit light and inserted it into the permanent genetic makeup of a tobacco plant; the altered tobacco leaves actually glow in the dark. Researchers have inserted human growth hormone genes into the genetic code of rats and pigs; the rats grow twice as fast and twice as big as normal. Scientists have fused sheep and goat cells, creating the geep—a half sheep, half goat chimera.

Should biotechnology be allowed to use the environmental crisis as an excuse to play God, crossing human genes into animals, and animal genes into plants? These techniques go far beyond any traditional breeding of animal or plant species. Cross-species genetic transfers may be the ultimate offense to the dignity and integrity of the biotic community. Prolonged and expanded use of these cross-species engineering feats could mean the end of the natural world as we currently know it.

Recently, the Patent and Trademark Office of the United States granted the first patent on a genetically engineered animal. This regulatory edict, the first ever commercial patent on animals, reduced genetically engineered animals to the status of manufactured products. This decision bodes ill for the future. Will succeeding generations of children grow up in a world where the genetic codes of plants, animals, and humans are interchangeable, and living things are programmed as engineered products with no greater intrinsic value than automobiles or toasters?

Conclusion. Before we allow the biotechnology industry and the scientific community to push society headlong into the biotechnology revolution, the American and international communities need to give thorough scrutiny to the long-term environmental, economic, and ethical issues raised by this powerful new technology. It is now clear that, when society commercialized the nuclear and petrochemical revolutions, it did so without first resolving the "hard" questions about the ultimate impacts of those technologies. As a result, we are now confronted with a huge environmental and societal bill including undisposable nuclear waste, toxic waste dumps, acid rain, the greenhouse effect, and ozone depletion.

Let us hope that the world's scientists and leaders have learned from these mistakes and that this time, with biotechnology, they will raise the important questions before rather than after the damage is done. Only through this kind of foresight can we assure that human choices will dictate the growth of technology rather than allow technology to control the future of humanity.

Appendix Three/Chapter 24

Books to Read for the Global Future
by Donald E. Davis

We have built a greenhouse, a human greenhouse, where once there bloomed a sweet and wild garden.
— Bill McKibben, *The End Of Nature*

A new environmental ethic is emerging. This new ethic will require a radical shift in the way humans think about, and relate to, the natural world. Fortunately, we are not without guidance. A generation of thinkers in a variety of fields have described cultural paths less destructive to the environment. The following is an annotated list of some of these books. These works discuss a wide variety of disciplines from history, economics, politics, and philosophy to architecture, urban planning, agriculture, and wilderness management. The suggested titles are designed to help the reader to gain a broader and deeper understanding of the ideas and trends shaping the coming ecological age. Armed with this kind of knowledge, we will be better able to begin the crucial task of healing the earth.

For a more thorough survey of the available literature, see my recent book, Ecophilosophy: A Field Guide to the Literature (San Pedro, CA: R. & E. Miles, 1989). The following are environmentally related bibliographies: Mary Anglemyer, et al., *The Natural Environment: An Annotated Bibliography on Attitudes and Values* (Washington, DC: Smithsonian Institution Press, 1984); Charles Magel, *A Bibliography Of Animal Rights and Related Matters* (Lanham, MD: University Press of America, 1981); Loren C. Owings, *Environmental Values, 1860-1972: A Guide to Information Sources* (Detroit: 1976); Mary Vance, *Human Ecology: Monographs Published in the 1980s* (Monticello, IL: Vance Bibliographies, 1988).

Reading List

Abbey, Edward. *Desert Solitaire*. New York: Touchstone Books, 1970.

———. *The Journey Home*. New York: E. P. Dutton, 1977. A writer and part-time park ranger's words in defense of his beloved canyonlands.

———. *One Life at a Time, Please*. New York: Henry Holt, 1988. 225 pages. An Abbey anthology including an interview with Joseph Wood Krutch, an essay about San Francisco, a diatribe against cowboys, a study of Ralph Waldo Emerson, and a television script written for an NBC program entitled "Almanac."

———. *The Monkey Wrench Gang*. Salt Lake City: Dream Garden Press, 1985 (tenth anniversary edition). 356 pages. A tale of four defenders of the canyon country of the American Southwest, *The Monkey Wrench Gang* has inspired a new breed of outlaw environmentalists— monkeywrenchers—who commit ecotage on corporate and state development projects.

Arrandale, Thomas. "The Battle for Natural Resources." Washington, DC: *Congressional Quarterly*, 1983.

Ashby, Eric. *Reconciling Man with the Environment*. Stanford, CA: Stanford University Press, 1978. 104 pages. Ashby, a biologist at Cambridge University, examines the social and political dimensions of the environmental crisis, concluding that reconciliation with the environment can only take place if the public is willing to bring about a radical changes in society.

Attfield, Robin. *The Ethics of Environmental Concern*. New York: Columbia Press, 1983. 220 pages. This work has two parts: "Problems And Traditions," a survey of Judaeo-Christian attitudes toward nature; and "Applied Ethics," a discussion of utilitarian moral theory as it relates to environmental concerns.

Bahro, Rudolph. *Building the Green Movement*. Philadelphia: New Society Publishers, 1986. 219 pages. In this study of the social, philosophical, and religious aspects of the Green political movement, Bahro advocates the decentralization of society, the transformation of work, a new spiritual awareness, and a communal order that rejects what he calls our "exterminous" society.

Bakeless, John. *Eyes of Discovery: America as Seen by the First Explorers (1953)*. New York: Dover, 1961. A survey of the major explorations of North America.

Barfield, Owen. *Saving the Appearances: A Study in Idolatry*. New York: Harcourt Brace Jovanovich, 1965. 190 pages. A critique of the modern worldview, providing the basis for a challenging reinterpretation of our relationship to science, religion, and nature.

Bates, Marston. *The Forest and the Sea: A Look at the Economy Of Nature and the Ecology of Man*. New York: Random House, 1960. 278 pages. A narrative on the relationships between ecosystems and human society.

Bateson, Gregory. *Mind and Nature: A Necessary Unity*. New York: E. P. Dutton, 1979. 238 pages. A renowned psychologist and anthropologist discusses the relationship between human thought and natural, living systems.

Bergon, Frank (Ed.). *The Wilderness Reader*. New York: New American Library, 1980. 372 pages. An anthology on the relationship between man and wilderness. Includes essays by a number of historical figures, including William Byrd, Meriwether Lewis, George Catlin, John James Audubon, Francis Parkman, and John Muir.

Berman, Morris. *The Reenchantment of the World*. New York: Bantam Books, 1984. 357 pages. In this critique of the modern mechanistic worldview. Berman argues that nature must be resacralized if we are to overcome the environmental crisis.

Berry, Thomas. *The Dream of the Earth*. San Francisco: Sierra Club Books, 1988. 256 pages. An important thinker in the environmental movement, Father Thomas Berry discusses a number of topics, including "bioregionalism," American Indian culture, and American higher education in the ecological age.

Berry, Wendell. *The Unsettling of America: Culture and Agriculture*. San Francisco: Sierra Club Books, 1977. 228 pages. A poet and farmer from Port Royal, Kentucky, Berry advocates a return to traditional farming methods in response to the destructive effects of "agribusiness" on the environment, rural communities, and social life in general. He argues that the environmental crisis is ultimately a crisis of morality.

———. *Home Economics*. San Francisco: North Point Press, 1987. 192 pages. Fourteen of Berry's finest essays covering topics such as wilderness preservation, the family farm, and rural culture.

Birch, Charles, and John Cobb. *The Liberation of Life from the Cell to the Community*. Cambridge, MA: Cambridge University Press, 1983. 353 pages. In this book, the authors, a theologian and a biologist, argue that the liberation of humanity presupposes the liberation of nature from the molecular to the community levels.

Bookchin, Murray. *The Ecology of Freedom*. Palo Alto, CA: Cheshire Books, 1982. 385 pages. A critique of hierarchical institutions in modern society. Bookchin argues that the domination of nature results from the domination of some humans over others.

———. *The Modern Crisis*. Philadelphia: New Society Publishers, 1985. 167 pages. Five essays representing the author's views on social ecology, moral economics, ecological and social reconstruction, and the relationship between nature and society.

————. *The Rise Of Urbanization and the Decline of Citizenship.* San Francisco: Sierra Club Books, 1987. Bookchin maintains that cities, originally havens of democratic ideas and principles, have become primary sources of environmental degradation and human despair. In this book, he argues that we need to bring human ecological principles back into the urban landscape.

Botkin, Daniel B., et al. *Managing the Global Environment: Perspectives on Human Involvement.* New York: Harcourt Brace Jovanovich, 1989. 459 pages. Botkin surveys the field of environmental management, calling for a new approach to understanding the global ecosystem.

Bradford, Sue. *The Last Frontier: Fighting over Land in the Amazon.* London: Ned Books, 1985. 330 pages. An examination of the political, economic, historical, and environmental factors contributing to the rainforest crisis.

Brinton, Daniel G. *The Myths of the New World: A Treatise on the Symbolism and Mythology of the Red Face of America (1986).* St. Clair Shores, MI: Scholarly Press, 1972. A discussion of the religions of the North American Indians.

Brooks, Paul. *Speaking for Nature: How Literary Naturalists, from Henry Thoreau to Rachel Carson, Have Shaped America.* Boston: Houghton Mifflin, 1980. 304 pages. A study of how the literary naturalists influenced the political, social, and ecological heritage of America.

Callicott, J. Baird (Ed.). *Companion to a Sand County Almanac.* Madison: University Of Wisconsin Press, 1987. 308 pages. This collection of essays focuses on Aldo Leopold's classic *A Sand County Almanac.* The authors include Susan Flader, Holmes Rolston, III, Roderick Nash, and Peter Fritzell.

Carson, Rachel. *Silent Spring.* Boston: Houghton Mifflin, 1962. 368 pages. After more than twenty-five years in print, *Silent Spring* remains an inspiration to environmentalists everywhere. A jeremiad against carelessness, greed, and irresponsibility, this environmental classic documents the ecological consequences of pollution, pesticides, and overpopulation.

————. *The Sea around Us.* New York: Oxford University Press, 1951. Like other Carson titles, including *Under the Sea Wind* and *The Edge of the Sea*, this book combines literature and oceanography. "For all at last return to the sea—to Oceanus, the ocean river, like the everflowing stream of time, the beginning and the end."

Catton, William R., Jr. *Overshoot: The Ecological Basis of Revolutionary Change.* Urbana: University of Illinois Press, 1980. 298 pages. Our society, according to the author, ignores the basic principles of ecology, stealing from the future in order to maintain an overproductive present. In order to make the basic necessities of life accessible to all peoples, Catton argues that we must recognize nature's "carrying capacity."

Caufield, Catherine. *In the Rainforest.* New York: Random House, 1985. 304 pages. A history of the Amazonian rainforest and its indigenous peoples, examining the destructive effects of colonization, industrialization, and other factors.

Chase, Alston. *Playing God in Yellowstone: The Destruction of America's First National Park.* New York: Atlantic Monthly, 1986. 446 pages. Chase, a wilderness preservation advocate, argues that our national parks are being destroyed by the same people who try to protect and enjoy them.

Clark, Stephen. *The Moral Status of Animals.* Oxford: Clarendon Press, 1977. 221 pages. Chase discusses several viewpoints on the animal-rights issue. He concludes that the eating of animals and most biomedical research on animals should be discontinued.

Clawson, Marion. *Forests for Whom and for What? Baltimore: Resources for the Future, 1975.*

Coggins, George Cameron, and Charles F. Wilkinson. *Federal Public Land and Resource Law.* (University Casebook Law Series. Mineola, NY: Foundation Press, 1981.

Cohen, Michael. *The Pathless Way: John Muir and the American Wilderness*. Madison: University of Wisconsin Press, 1984. 408 pages. A biographical account of John Muir's personal and political struggle to promote harmony between society and wilderness. This work puts particular emphasis on Muir's conflict with forester Gifford Pinchot.

Corbett, Michael. *A Better Place to Live: New Designs For Tomorrow's Communities*. Emmanus, PA: Rodale Press, 1982. Corbett advocates constructing smaller communities that facilitate human growth and freedom while preserving the integrity of the environment.

Cronon, William. *Changes in the Land: Indians, Colonists, and the Ecology of New England*. New York: Hill and Wang, 1983. 241 pages. Cronon's book shows how the transition from Indian to English ways of life dramatically transformed the ecology of colonial New England. He deals with changes in attitudes towards agriculture, animals, and property.

Crosby, Alfred W. *Ecological Imperialism: The Biological Expansions of Europe 900–1900*. New York: Cambridge University Press, 1987. 400 pages. The author links the success of European colonial expansion with the successful introduction of European plant and animal species into newly colonized areas.

Darling, F. Frazer, and Noel D. Eichhorn. *Man and Nature in the National Parks*. Washington, DC: The Conservation Foundation, 1971.

Day, David. *The Doomsday Book of Animals: A Natural History of Vanished Species*. New York: Viking Press, 1981. 287 pages. A comprehensive reference work on the natural history of extinct plant and animal species.

Devall, Bill. *Simple in Means, Rich in Ends: Practicing Deep Ecology*. Layton, UT: Gibbs M. Smith, 1988. A statement on the practice of deep ecology by one of the principle philosophers of the deep ecology movement.

Devall, Bill, and George Sessions. *Deep Ecology: Living As If Nature Mattered*. Salt Lake City: Peregrine Smith Books, 1985. 266 pages. Deep ecology, a term coined by Norwegian philosopher Arne Naess, is the study of the relationships between nature, consciousness, and culture. The book explores the anthropological and sociological roots of our industrial civilization, addresses the moral problems of a society living out of sync with nature, and criticizes the "anthropocentism" of contemporary environmental policy.

Doyle, Jack. *Altered Harvest: Agriculture, Genetics, and the Fate of the World's Food Supply*. New York: Viking Press, 1985. 502 pages. In this critique of the centralizing tendencies of "agribusiness," Doyle narrates the history of the seed business in the United States and discusses the evolving role of genetic engineering in agriculture.

Drengson, Alan R. *Beyond Environmental Crisis: From Technocrat To Planetary Person*. New York: Peter Lang, 1989. A revised edition of the author's earlier work, *Shifting Paradigms* (1983), this book focuses on creating an environmental ethic for the West. With new materials, Drengson attempts "to clarify the ecological sense and dimensions of the relationships between community, self, and nature." Includes tips for individuals.

Ehrlich, Paul, and Anne Ehrlich. *Extinction: The Causes and Consequences of the Disappearance of Species*. New York: Ballantine, 1981. 384 pages. The authors examine the political, aesthetic, ethical, and ecological aspects of the species extinction problem.

Engel, J. Ronald. *Sacred Sand: The Struggle for Community in the Indiana Dunes*. Middletown, CT: Wesleyan University Press, 1983. 352 pages. Engel describes the social, cultural, and religious forces that came together to save this region and establish the Indiana Dunes National Seashore in 1966.

Everndon, Neil. *The Natural Alien: Humankind and Environment*. Toronto: University of Toronto Press, 1985. 160 pages. Evernden argues that the human species is presently "rootless" and needs to regain its natural attitude by rediscovering the natural world.

Farallones Institute. *The Integral Urban House*. San Francisco: Sierra Club Books, 1979. With sections on recycling, energy conservation, and safe disposal of wastes, this book describes how we can transform our urban households into self-sufficient "ecosystems."

Farb, Peter. *Man's Rise to Civilization*. Revised edition. New York: E. P. Dutton, 1978. A comprehensive survey of North American Indians from their origins to the twentieth century.

Flader, Susan L. *Thinking Like a Mountain: Aldo Leopold and the Evolution of an Ecological Attitude toward Deer, Wolves, and Forests*. Columbia, MO: The University of Missouri Press, 1974. 284 pages. Flader examines the formation of Aldo Leopold's attitudes towards wildlife, wilderness, and land use. Leopold wrote *A Sand County Almanac* (1949), a classic in environmental thought.

Fox, Stephen. *John Muir and His Legacy: The American Conservation Movement*. Boston: Little, Brown & Co., 1981. This book is especially valuable for its tracing of conflict between the preservationist ethic of Muir and conservation-for-use doctrine advocated by Gifford Pinchot.

Freeman, David, and Dave Haywood. *Ecodefense: A Field Guide to Monkeywrenching, 2nd ed*. Tucson, AZ: Earth First! Books, 1987. 312 pages. A handbook on the controversial (and generally illegal) practice of "monkeywrenching" or "ecotage" tactics. This expanded edition gives advice on "tree-spiking," removing billboards, fence cut-ting, etc. The editors are founding members of Earth First!, whose motto is: "No compromise in the defense of mother earth!"

Fritsch, Albert J. *Renew the Face of the Earth*. Chicago: Loyola University Press, 1987. 280 pages. Author of several books on environmental issues, Jesuit Father Al Fritsch currently directs Appalachia—Science in the Public Interest. In this book, he presents a completely Christianized philosophy of nature, using a creative and ecumenical blend of scriptural, liturgical, and theological sources.

Gorz, Andre. *Ecology as Politics*. Boston: South End Press, 1980. 215 pages. A study of ecological social movements by a French Marxist theorist. Gorz analyzes environmental movements in mostly economic and political terms.

Graber, Linda H. *Wilderness as Sacred Space*. Washington, DC: Association of American Geographers, 1976. 124 pages. The author contends that wilderness preservation is ultimately motivated by the understanding of wilderness as sacred space.

Granberg-Michaelson, Wesley. *A Worldly Spirituality: The Call to Redeem Life on Earth*. New York: Harper & Row, 1984. 210 pages. This work critically integrates sociological, political, and economic thought with biblical, theological, and ethical teachings. It concludes with an informed critique of biotechnology.

Grant, George. *Technology and Justice*. Notre Dame, IN: University Of Notre Dame Press, 1986. 133 pages. Grant, Canada's leading political philosopher, and author of *Technology and Empire* (1969), presents six new essays on the impact of technology on modern life and the environment. Essays cover topics such as technology, computers, and euthanasia.

Hall, Bob (Ed.). *Environmental Politics: Lessons from the Grassroots*. Durham, NC: Institute For Southern Studies, 1989. 122 pages. This work is a collection of essays by successful environmental organizers and activists.

Halpern, Daniel (Ed.). *On Nature: Nature, Landscape, and Natural History*. San Francisco: North Point Press, 1987. 319 pages. This anthology features essays by a number of prominent nature writers, including Annie Dillard, Noel Perrin, Edward O. Wilson, and John Rodman. Includes an extensive bibliography.

Hanson, Philip P. (Ed.). *Environmental Ethics: Philosophical And Policy Perspectives*. Burnaby, BC: Simon Fraser University Press, 1986. 199 pages. A collection of seventeen essays on topics ranging from animal rights to environmental management and public policy.

Hardin, Garrett. *Filter against Folly: How to Survive Despite Economists, Ecologists, and the Merely Eloquent*. New York: Viking, 1985. 240 pages. Hardin suggests that there are basically three ways of examining the world: the "literate," the "numerate," and the "ecolate." Unless economists, businessmen, journalists, and scientists begin to utilize all three views, he argues, the results will be ecologically disastrous.

Hargrove, Eugene C. *Foundations of Environmental Ethics*. Englewood Cliffs, NJ: Prentice-Hall, 1989. 229 pages. Arguing that Western philosophy confers too little value on the natural world, Hargrove builds his ethical foundation on the aesthetic value of nature.

Hart, John. *The Spirit of The Earth: A Theology of the Land*. Ramsey, NJ: Paulist Press, 1984. 165 pages. Hart, a theologian, argues that we are more fully human to the extent that we recognize and respect our ecological limitations. Topics discussed include land abuse, the ecological consciousness of the American Indians, Christian stewardship, and the American political tradition.

Hays, Samuel P. *Beauty, Health, and Permanence: Environmental Politics in the United States, 1950-1985*. New York: Cambridge University Press, 1987. An historical account of the transition from the traditional conservation ethic to current environmentalism. Includes a chapter on the Reagan "anti-environmental revolution."

————. *Conservation and the Gospel of Efficiency: The Progressive Conservation Movement, 1890-1920*. Cambridge: Harvard University Press, 1959. A history and discussion of the American conservation movement.

Hearne, Vicki. *Adam's Task: Calling Animals by Name*. New York: Alfred Knopf, 1986. 274 pages. The author, a professional horse and dog trainer, argues that animals have capacities for understanding and commitment and should be treated accordingly.

Henderson, Hazel. *Politics of the Solar Age: The Alternatives to Economics*. New York: Doubleday, 1981. 433 pages. An ecological critique of neoconservative and supply-side economics. Futurist Hazel Henderson draws from the works of Barry Commoner, E. F. Schumacher, and many others, calling for the transformation to a more ecologically sustainable economic system based on barter, decentralized production, and solar energy.

Howard, Ted, and Jeremy Rifkin. *Who Should Play God?* New York: Dell Publishing Co., 1977. 272 pages. A prophetic statement on the potential dangers of genetic engineering. The authors argue that we need to expand the ethical debate surrounding the uses and abuses of biotechnological research before continuing such research.

Hubble, Sue. *A Country Year: Living the Questions*. New York: Harper & Row, 1987. 221 pages. This book celebrates the natural and human elements of day to day life in the Missouri Ozarks.

Huth, Hans. *Nature and the American (1957)*. Lincoln: University of Nebraska Press, 1972. A lavishly illustrated account of three centuries of changing attitudes toward nature, both in literature and in painting.

Jackson, Wes. *Altars of Unhewn Stone: Science and the Earth*. San Francisco: North Point Press, 1987. 158 pages. In this volume of essays, Jackson questions many technological developments in agriculture, including recent efforts in genetic engineering. The future task of the environmentally conscious farmer, according to Jackson, is to "simulate" the natural environment as closely as possible by relying more on perennial crops.

Johnson, Warren. *Muddling toward Frugality*. Boulder: Shambala, 1979. 189 pages. Johnson offers a prudent prescription for making our society more ecologically sound.

Jonas, Hans. *The Imperative of Responsibility: In Search of an Ethics for the Technological Age*. Chicago: University of Chicago Press, 1984. 255 pages. This book discusses the search for an "ethics of responsibility" in the modern technological age." Jonas, the author of *The Phenomenon of Life* (1966), updates his earlier critique of technology to include recent advances in genetic engineering.

Joranson, Phillip N., and Ken Butigan (Eds.). *Cry of the Environment: Rebuilding the Christian Creation Tradition.* Santa Fe, NM: Bear & Company, 1984. 476 pages. A study of the historical relationship between the Judeo-Christian tradition and our present environmental crisis. This volumes rejects the belief that Christianity has been responsible for environmental degradation.

Kaufman, Les and Mallory (Eds.). *The Last Extinction.* Cambridge: The MIT Press, 1986. 208 pages. A critical discussion of current methods of endangered species preservation and of the general problem of biological diversity losses. It includes a list of organizations involved in species preservation.

Kelly, Petra. *Fighting for Hope.* West Germany: South End Press, 1984. 121 pages. Kelly, a founding member of West Germany's Green Party, describes the political past, present, and future of the environmental and peace movements in Germany. There is a special emphasis on the role of women.

Kimes, Maymie and William F. (Eds.). *The Complete John Muir: A Reading Bibliography.* Fresno, CA: Panorama West, 1986. 208 pages. This bibliography represents over thirty years of research into the life and writings of John Muir.

Kohák, Erazim. *The Embers and the Stars: A Philosophical Inquiry into the Moral Sense of Nature.* Chicago: The University of Chicago Press, 1984. 269 pages. The author, a professor of philosophy at Boston College, discusses the moral dimensions of nature.

Leopold, Aldo. *Sand County Almanac: And Sketches Here and There.* New York: Oxford University Press, 1987. Special Commemorative Edition. 228 pages. First published in 1949, this environmental classic outlines Leopold's influential concept of a "land ethic."

Linberg, David C., and L. Ronald Numbers. *God and Nature: Historical Essays on the Encounter Between Christianity and Science.* Berkeley: University of California Press, 1986. 516 pages. An outgrowth of an international conference on the historical relations of Christianity and science, this anthology covers the historical relationship between faith, science, nature, and reason.

Linzey, Andrew. *Christianity and the Rights of Animals.* New York: Crossroads Publishing, 1987. 197 pages. In this study of the place of animals in the Christian theological tradition, the author argues that animals are subjects of inherent value to God and ought to be treated as such.

Livingston, John A. The Fallacy of Wildlife Conservation. Toronto: McClelland and Stewart, 1981. 126 pages. Livingston, a Canadian poet and naturalist, takes a hard look at conventional approaches to wildlife conservation, arguing that bureaucracies tend to subordinate ecological integrity to economic expansion.

Lovelock, J. E. *Gaia: A New Look at Life on Earth.* New York: Oxford University Press, 1979. 157 pages. Lovelock sets forth the Gaia hypothesis, suggesting that the earth is itself a living, self-regulating organism—Gaia—that maintains optimal conditions for animal and plant life.

Magel, Charles R. *A Bibliography of Animal Rights and Related Matters.* Lanham, MD: University Press of America, 1981. 622 pages. This bibliography lists 3,210 sources on animal-rights and animal rights theory. The literature on animals is arranged historically, beginning with ancient Greek materials. This work includes a comprehensive list of magazines and journals that regularly cover animal concerns.

Marsh, George Perkins. *Man and Nature (1864).* Cambridge: Harvard University Press, 1965. A book long considered "the fountainhead of the conservation movement."

Marx, Leo. *Machine in the Garden: Technology and the Pastoral Ideal in America (1924).* New York: Oxford University Press, 1967. An analysis of the enduring conflict in our society between the desire for a rural paradise and an industrialized nation.

Matthiessen, Peter. *Wildlife in America (1956)*. New York: Penguin, 1978. A close look at our wildlife, both past and present, by the well-known novelist and naturalist.

McKibben, Bill. *The End of Nature*. New York: Random House, 1989. 226 pages. Global warming, the destruction of the rainforest, and environmental pollution, McKibben argues, are symptomatic of our intellectual and physical disregard for the natural world. He concludes that we must resurrect the idea of nature if we are to save the planet and ourselves from ecological destruction.

McLuban, Teri. *Touch the Earth (1971)*. New York: Touchstone Books, 1976. A selection of writings by North American Indians that reveals their earth sustaining values.

McPhee, John. *Encounters with the Archdruid*. New York: Farrar, Straus and Giroux, 1971. 245 pages. McPhee addresses the question of wilderness preservation, focussing on three wilderness areas—the Sea Islands of south Georgia, the Glacier Peak Wilderness in the Cascades, and the Colorado River.

————. *The Control of Nature*. New York: Farrar, Straus and Giroux, 1989. 272 pages. McPhee discusses the economic and environmental costs involved in efforts to control natural areas. He focusses on the transformation of the Mississippi Delta, the Los Angeles area, and Iceland.

Meeker, Lowry. *Economics As If Earth Really Mattered: A Catalyst Guide to Socially Conscious Investing*. Santa Cruz, CA: New Society Publishers, 1988. 260 pages. Topics include boycotts, shareholder action, socially responsible investment funds, small-scale investing, "new community economics," and alternative exchange systems. The book concludes with a list of sources and contacts.

Merchant, Carolyn. *The Death of Nature: Women, Ecology, and the Scientific Revolution*. San Francisco: Harper & Row, 1980. 348 pages. A historian of science explores the historical and cultural connections between women's issues and ecology, science, and environmental degradation. A powerful critique of the age of Enlightenment.

Midgley, Mary. *Beast and Man: The Roots of Human Nature*. Ithaca, NY: Cornell University Press, 1978. 377 pages. This book argues that, in order for us fully to understand ourselves as human beings, we must recognize our status as true members of the animal kingdom.

————. *Animals and Why They Matter: A Journey around the Species Barrier*. Athens, GA: University of Georgia Press, 1984. 158 pages. A philosophical journey through the history of our relationship to animals, focussing on relevant texts from the last two centuries.

Miller, Harlan B., and William H. Willam. *Ethics and Animals*. Clifton, NJ: Humanities Press, 1983. 416 pages. A collection of essays presenting a wide range of views on the treatment of animals. Includes contributions by Tom Regan, Bernard Rollin, Stephen Clark, and others.

Muir, John. *Wilderness Essays*. Salt Lake City: Peregrine Smith Books, 1980. 288 pages. Ten essays on wilderness.

Naess, Arne. *Ecology, Community, and Life Style*. Cambridge: Cambridge University Press, 1988. The founder of the deep ecology movement discusses the relationships between environmental decay and the evolution of communities and life styles.

Nash, Roderick. *The Rights of Nature: A History of Environmental Ethics*. Madison: The University of Wisconsin Press, 1989. 290 pages. Roderick Nash traces environmental thinking from the 1700s to the present. Topics discussed range from deep ecology and ecophilosophy to "monkeywrenching" and civil disobedience.

————. *Wilderness and the American Mind*. New Haven, CT: Yale University Press, 1982. 256 pages. A history of American attitudes towards wilderness, covering the Puritans, transcendentalists, early conservationists, contemporary environmentalists, and others.

Norton, Bryan G. *The Preservation of Species: The Value Of Biological Diversity*. Princeton: Princeton University Press, 1986. 272 pages. Norton, a professor of philosophy at the

Georgia Institute of Technology, presents eleven essays on the value of preserving biological diversity.

Passmore, John. *Man's Responsibility toward Nature: Ecological Problems and Western Traditions.* New York: Scribner's, 1974. 213 pages. In this study of environmental concepts such as pollution, conservation, preservation, and population growth, Passmore concludes that the history of Western thought and practice is not intrinsically unecological and should not be stereotyped as such.

Petulla, Joseph M. *American Environmentalism: Values, Tactics, Priorities.* College Station, TX: Texas University Press, 1980. 239 pages. An historical survey of environmentalism in the United States.

Raphael, Ray. *Edges: Human Ecology of the Backcountry.* Lincoln, NE: University of Nebraska Press, 1986. 233 pages. Concentrating on rural and small town life in northwestern California, Raphael argues for the preservation of the sustainable, dignified ways of those who live on the "edges."

Regan, Tom. *The Case for Animal Rights.* Berkeley: University of California Press, 1983. 425 pages. An argument for the humane treatment of animals.

————. *The Struggle for Animal Rights.* Clarks Summit, PA: International Society for Animal Rights, 1987. 197 pages. Regan, an animal-rights activist, recounts his efforts in the animal-rights movement.

Richardson, Robert D. *Henry Thoreau: A Life of the Mind.* Berkeley: University of California Press, 1986. 455 pages. A study of Thoreau's intellectual formation, emphasizing the relationship between Thoreau's literary and naturalistic pursuits.

Rifkin, Jeremy. *Time Wars: The Primary Conflict in Human History.* New York: Simon and Schuster, 1989. 302 pages. A look at the temporal dimensions of human experience—past, present, and future—and their relations to human society and the environment. Topics discussed include the history of human conceptions of time, biological clocks, and computer simulation.

Rifkin, Jeremy, with Ted Howard. *Entropy: Into the Greenhouse World.* New York: Bantam Books, 1989. Revised edition. 355 pages. In the original edition of this book, Rifkin and Howard explained the universal tendency of economic, social, and environmental systems to move from an ordered to a disordered state—the entropy principle. The current edition has been updated to include the greenhouse effect and other global environmental issues.

Rolston, Holmes, III. *Environmental Ethics: Duties to and Values in the Natural World.* Philadelphia: Temple University Press, 1988. 391 pages.

Rozak, Theodore. *Person/Planet: The Creative Disintegration of Industrial Society.* Garden City, NY: Anchor/Doubleday, 1978. 347 pages. According to the author, "This book concerns itself with the point at which human psychology and natural ecology meet. The needs of the planet and the needs of the person have become one . . . ."

Sale, Kirpatrick. *Dwellers in the Land: The Bioregional Vision.* San Francisco: Sierra Club Books, 1985. 217 pages. The author outlines the concept of bioregionalism—a view of world order based on natural geographic regions, defined by differences in flora, fauna, landforms, and watersheds, rather than on arbitrary political divisions.

Satin, Mark. *New Age Politics: Healing Self and Society.* New York: Delta Books, 1979. 349 pages. A survey of "New Age" political ideas and activities. Topics include the human potential, feminist, environmental, and appropriate technology movements. Included are an extensive bibliography and a list of "New Age" organizations.

Sax, Joseph L. *Mountains without Handrails: Reflections on the National Parks.* Ann Arbor: University of Michigan Press, 1981.

Schumacher, E. F. *A Guide for the Perplexed.* New York: Harper & Row, 1977. A philosophical guidebook for personal and spiritual survival in the modern world. The author repudiates scientism, hierarchical modes of thinking, and the "cult of the self."

Serpell, James. *In the Company of Animals: A Study of Human-Animal Relationships.* New York: Basil Blackwell, 1986. 215 pages. Serpell, a research associate in animal behavior, discusses the role of pets and other animals in human history.

Shepard, Paul. *The Tender Carnivore and the Sacred Game.* New York: Scribner's, 1973. 302 pages. This work represents the author's ecotopian vision that generally seeks the return of man the hunter/gatherer.

————. *Thinking Animals: Animals and the Development of Human Intelligence.* New York: Viking Press, 1978. 274 pages. Drawing from the fields of literature, anthropology, and psychology, the author makes the case that the proper development of human consciousness depends on the physical and conceptual presence of animals.

Shi, David E. *In Search of the Simple Life.* Salt Lake City: Gibbs M. Smith, 1986. 345 pages. Presents the tradition of simple living as an ecological ideal. Includes references to the thoughts of John Winthrop, Thomas Jefferson, Ralph Waldo Emerson, Henry David Thoreau, and John Burroughs.

————. *Plain Living and High Thinking in American Culture.* New York: Oxford University Press, 1985. 322 pages. This book examines the complex relationship between concepts of virtue and practical, self-sufficient lifestyles. Chapters on the Puritans, Quakers, and early Republicans, as well as on the role of simple living ideas in our time.

Skolimowski, Henry. *Eco-Philosophy: Designing New Tactics for Living.* London and New Hampshire: Marion Boyars, 1981. 117 pages. The author advocates the restoration of an ecological humanism.

Spretnak, Charlene. *The Spiritual Dimension of Green Politics.* Santa Fe, NM: Bear & Company, 1986. 95 pages. Spretnak defends the place of religious values in the green movement.

Spretnak, Charlene, and Fritjof Capra. *Green Politics: The Global Promise.* New York: E.P. Dutton, 1984. 254 pages. A discussion of the worldwide impact of the German Green movement, including the potential for the development of a Green party in the United States.

Stokes, Samuel, and Elizabeth Watson. *Saving America's Countryside: A Guide to Rural Conservation.* Baltimore: John Hopkins University Press, 1989. 306 pages. Published for the National Trust of Historic Places, this book provides excellent information on rural, small town, and historic landmark preservation. Sections on preparing documentation for historic preservation sites, acquiring land for land trusts, and organizing citizen opposition to changes of zoning laws and ordinances. Case studies from across the United States included.

Stone, Christopher. *Earth and other Ethics: The Case for Moral Pluralism.* New York: Harper & Row, 1987. 280 pages. This book is an expansion of the author's earlier work *Should Trees Have Standing?* (1974). Stone expands the question of "tree rights" to the entire biotic community, arguing that there can be no single ethical system for preserving the natural world.

————. *Should Trees Have Standing?: Toward Legal Rights for Natural Objects.* Los Altos, CA: William Kaufmann, Inc., 1974. 102 pages. A professor of law, Stone proposes that trees, forests, rivers, beaches, and all other natural entities have legal "rights."

Taylor, Paul W. *Respect for Nature: A Theory of Environmental Ethics.* Princeton: Princeton University Press, 1986. 329 pages. Outlining a "non-anthropocentric" environmental ethic, Taylor emphasizes man's dependent status as part of the biosphere.

Thompson, William Irvin (Ed.). *Gaia: A New Way of Knowing.* New York: The Lindisfarne Press, 1988. 217 pages. The Gaia hypothesis deals with the self-regulating effects of organic life on earth's atmosphere. The editor of this book extends the Gaia principle to the political sphere, where he and others use this metaphor to advance a critique of our modern perception of life. Selections are by Gregory

Bateson, James Lovelock, Lynn Margulis, John Todd, and Hazel Henderson.

Thoreau, Henry David. *The Selected Works of Thoreau.* Boston: Houghton Mifflin, 1975. 851 pages. A reprinted version of the original Cambridge edition of *The Works of Thoreau.* Include's Thoreau's most influential writings, including "The Maine Woods," "Walden," and "A Week on the Concord and Merrimack Rivers."

Tobias, Michael. *Deep Ecology.* San Diego: Avant Books, 1985. 296 pages. A collection of essays concerning the deep ecology philosophy. The essays are by some of the noted ecological philosophers in the field: Arne Naess, Murray Bookchin, Gary Snyder, Paul Shepard, Herman Daly, William Catton, and Roderick Nash.

Todd, Nancy, and John Todd. *Bioshelters, Ocean Arks, City Farming: Ecology as the Basis of Design.* San Francisco: Sierra Club Books, 1984. 210 pages. This book explains how architecture can learn from natural processes instead of working against them. Includes design plans and illustrations.

Tokar, Brain. *The Green Alternative: Creating an Ecological Future.* San Pedro, CA: R. & E. Miles, 1987. 174 pages. A study of grass roots environmental activism in North America.

Trimble, Stephen (Ed.). *Words from the Land: Encounters with Natural History Writing.* Salt Lake City: Peregrine Smith Books, 1988. 303 pages. A collection of essays by philosophers, biologists, naturalists, and journalists all recognized for their natural history writings. Includes pieces by John McPhee, Annie Dillard, Edward Abbey, Gretel Ehrlich, Sue Hubbell, Barry Lopez, and Wendell Berry.

Tuan, Yi-Fu. *Segmented Worlds and Self: Group Life and Individual Consciousness.* Minneapolis: University Of Minnesota Press, 1982. 222 pages. In this work, Tuan explores the psychological aspects of the relationship between man and nature.

Turner, Fredrick Jackson. "The Significance of the Frontier in American History." New York: Henry Holt and Co., 1983. Reprint Edition. Report of the American Historical Association 1893.

Walker, Stephen. *Animal Thought.* London: Routledge & Kegan Paul, 1983. 437 pages. A scholarly survey of past and present theories of animal thought, perception, and intelligence.

Wallace, David Rains. *Idle Weeds: The Klamath Knot: Explorations of Myth and Evolution.* San Francisco: Sierra Club Books, 1983. 149 pages. The Klamath Mountains of Oregon and northern California are the setting for this natural history account of evolution and ecological change.

Waterman, Laura, and Guy Waterman. Backwoods Ethics: Environmental Concerns for Hikers and Campers. Boston: Stone Wall Press, 1979.

Winner, Langdon. *The Whale and the Reactor: A Search for Limits in an Age of High Technology.* Chicago: The University of Chicago Press, 1986. 200 pages. Winner examines the effects of technology on social life, arguing that technology not only transforms human experience, but actually creates the cultural conditions of society.

Woodhouse, Tom (Ed.). *People and Planet.* Devon, England: Green Books, 1987. 220 pages. An anthology of speeches by Alternative Nobel Prize recipients. The awards, which go to individuals who have worked on developing new approaches to problems in the areas of human rights, people's economics, ecological conservation, and appropriate technology, are given annually by the Right Livelihood Foundation of Great Britain. Essays by Petra Kelly, Amory and Hunter Lovins, Pat Mooney, Patrick van Rensburg, and Leif Sandholt.

Woodring, Carl. *Nature into Art.* Cambridge: Harvard University Press, 1989. 360 pages. In this study of aesthetic trends in eighteenth century America, the author argues that, when our predecessors stopped imitating nature in art, they lost their reverence for the natural world.

Worster, Donald. *Nature's Economy: The Roots of Ecology*. San Francisco: Sierra Club Books, 1977. 404 pages. An historical study of the development of ecological thought in relation to changes in science and culture.

Environmental Periodicals

This section lists journals, magazines, newsletters, and other periodicals which deal with environmental issues.

Alternatives, Faculty of Environmental Studies, The University of Waterloo, Waterloo, Ontario, Canada N2L 3G1. An environmental quarterly that tries to "blend and balance the care and precision of scholarship with the timeliness and concern of citizen environmental activism." Features in-depth articles on land use, alternative energy strategies, pollution, and environmental health. 40 to 60 pages; book reviews.

The Amicus Journal, Peter Borrelli, Editor, Clarkson University, Potsdam, NY 13676. Published quarterly by the National Defense Council. Feature length articles and reports on environmental activities throughout North America. Well illustrated.

Creation, Matthew Fox, Editor, 40 Maria Way, Orina, CA 94563. Published six times a year by Friends of Creation Spirituality, this journal celebrates the "sacred of the earth and all its creatures." according to the editorial note, the goal of Creation is to "bring out the wisdom and mystery of the cosmos . . . as celebrated by today's sciences and the wisdom of Western mystics, primal peoples, and artists." Book reviews and other resources.

The Deep Ecologist, John Martin, Editor, 10 Alamein Avenue, Warraknabeal, Victoria, Australia. Australia provides some of the most progressive environmentalist literature available. The Deep Ecologist is a newsletter published in Australia by John Martin and is dedicated to preserving a deep ecology perspective and practice.

Earth First! The Radical Environmental Journal, Dave Foreman, Editor, PO Box 5871, Tucson, AZ 85703. Published eight times a year by the Earth First! organization, a "no-compromise environmental movement." Provides a variety of articles on "monkeywrenching," direct action organizing, and wilderness preservation. Book reviews, illustrations, 30 to 50 pages.

Earth Island Journal, Gar Smith, Editor, 300 Broadway, Suite 28, San Francisco, CA 94133. An international environmental news magazine published by the Earth Island Institute. Features local news stories from around the globe. Book reviews, letters, photography.

The Ecologist, Worthyvale Manor Farm Camelford, Cornwall, England PL32 9TT. Published six times a year, *The Ecologist* "is one of the few journals still prepared to give its authors the space to consider, in-depth, the environmental and social issues facing the world today—and their philosophical implication." Recommended.

Ecophilosophy, George Sessions, Editor, Sierra College, Rockland, CA 95677. The editor, a professor of philosophy and co-author of *Deep Ecology* (1985), provides a "state-of-the art" newsletter and literature review of environmental texts.

The EGG: A Journal of Eco-Justice, William Gibson, Editor, Anabel Hall, Cornell University, Ithaca, NY 14853. "Quarterly of the Eco-Justice Project and Network Center for Religion, Ethics and Social Policy." Contains well-edited essays on the relationship of ecology to social responsibility, economic development, and ethics.

Environmental Review, William G. Robbins, Editor, Department of History, Oregon State University, Corvallis, OR 97331. Published by the American Society for Environmental History, this quarterly "seeks understanding of human ecology through the perspectives of history and the humanities." Feature articles and book reviews.

Environmental Ethics, Eugene Hargrove, Editor, Department of Philosophy, University of Georgia, Athens, GA 30602. An interdisciplinary journal, published quarterly, "dedicated to the philosophical aspects of environmental problems." One of the leading, if not the leading, environmental philosophy publications. Provides feature articles, discussion papers, and book reviews.

Environmental Action, 1525 New Hampshire Avenue, NW, Washington, DC 20036. Published bimonthly by Environmental Action, Inc., a national political lobbying and education organization devoted to environmental protection. Book reviews and feature length articles on a variety of topics related to environmental hazards and direct action environmental organizing.

Ethics and Animals, Harlan B. Miller, Editor, Department of Philosophy, Virginia Polytechnic Institute, Blacksburg, VA 24061. The quarterly journal of the Society for the Study of Ethics and Animals. Offers in-depth discussions on animal rights and welfare. Feature length articles, reviews.

The Eleventh Commandment Newsletter, Vincent Rossi, Editor, PO Box 14727, San Francisco, CA 94114. A newsletter published by the Eleventh Commandment Fellowship, which believes that "the Earth is the Lord's and the fullness thereof; thou shalt not despoil the Earth nor destroy the life thereon." Articles, poetry, illustrations.

Firmament, NACCE Quarterly, 309 Front Street, Traverse City, MI 49684. A quarterly devoted to expressing the ecological dimensions of Christianity and Christian thought. The journal is the product of the North American Conference on Christianity and Ecology, a nonprofit organization that has recently formed to "elucidate the ecological dimension inherent in Christianity, and to help churches and organizations with their ecological work." Book reviews, book lists. Calendar and announcements.

Journal of Environmental Education, 4000 Albemarle Street, NW, Washington, DC 20016. Published four times a year by the Helen Dwight Reid Educational Foundation, in association with the North American Association for Environmental Education. Assists educators at all levels in selecting appropriate information from the available environmental education curricula.

Journal of Forest History, Harold Steen, Editor, 701 Vickers Avenue, Durham, NC 27701. Published four times a year by the Forest History Society in association with Duke University Press. The journal features articles on environmental history, book reviews, and current news in the field. The "Biblioscope" section lists new books and articles on topics ranging from human ecology to wilderness preservation.

National Parks, Michele Strutin, Editor, 1015 thirty-first Street, NW, Washington, DC 20007. This magazine is published bimonthly by the National Parks and Conservation Association, a national, nonprofit organization that focuses on defending, promoting, and improving the National Park system.

New Options, Mark Satin, Editor, PO Box 19324, Washington, DC 20036. A small but informative newsletter summarizing political events, conferences, and other happenings related to ecological awareness. Timely letters and book reviews in this newsletter.

Not Man Apart, Friends of the Earth, 1045 Sansome Street, San Francisco, CA 94111. The bimonthly publication of the Friends of the Earth. The authors tend to stress the use of alternative energy sources and focus primarily on issues related directly to FOE activities.

The Newsletter for the International Network for Religion and Animals, PO Box 33061, Washington, DC 20033. Provides information and other materials related to religious appreciation and respect for animals as well as networking for animal-rights activists.

Pan Ecology, Marshfield Institute, PO Box 1, Viola, ID 83872. An irregular journal of nature and human nature published by the Marshfield Institute of Idaho. Recent articles on sustainable land use and environmental ethics.

Raise the Stakes, Planet Drum Foundation, Box 31251, San Francisco, CA 94131. Published bi-annually by the Planet

Drum Foundation, an organization devoted to developing and communicating the concept of bioregionalism. Contains information about local bioregional activities and happenings, feature length articles, reviews, and maps.

Resurgence, Satish Kumar, Editor, Worthyvale Manor Farm, Camelford, Cornwall, England PL32 9TT. A bi-monthly British magazine featuring articles, book reviews, and poetry on eco-political themes. International in scope, this publication has offerings for readers on both sides of the Atlantic.

Sierra: The Sierra Club Bulletin, The Sierra Club, 730 Polk Street, San Francisco, CA 94109. The official magazine of the Sierra Club. Publishes articles, news items, reports, and reviews. Considers impact on the environment of political and social issues, as well as providing information on camping, hiking, etc.

The Trumpeter, Alan Drengson, Editor, Lightstar, PO Box 5853, Victoria, British Columbia, Canada V8R 6S8. "Voices from the Canadian Ecophilosophy Network." An excellent journal, published four times a year, that aims to provide a diversity of perspectives on the human-nature relationship.

Utne Reader, Eric Utne, Editor, PO Box 1974, Marion, Ohio 43305. "The best of the alternative press"—a bimonthly digest of articles and magazine reviews from alternative sources. Frequently contains articles on bioregionalism, deep ecology, environmental ethics, and alternative agriculture.

Contributing Authors

THOMAS BERRY is an historian of cultures, a professor of theology at Fordham University, and Director of the Riverdale Center of Religious Research. He is also author of The Dream of the Earth (1988).

DONALD E. DAVIS is an adjunct researcher and consultant to the Foundation on Economic Trends in Washington, D.C. In this capacity he collaborated with Jeremy Rifkin on the recently published book *Time Wars: The Primary Conflict in Human History*. An occasional contributor to the *Utne Reader*, *Environmental Ethics*, and *The Trumpeter*, Mr. Davis compiled and edited *Ecophilosophy: A Field Guide to the Literature* (1989), an extensive bibliography of sources on environmental thought.

LARRY DOSSEY, M.D., is a co-founder and staff member of the Dallas Diagnostic Association, the largest association of internal medicine practitioners in the United States. A Vietnam veteran and former Chief of Staff of the Medical City Hospital in Dallas, Dr. Dossey is also a former president of the Isthmus Institute of Dallas, an organization dedicated to exploring the relationships between science and religion. Dr. Dossey is author of *Space, Time, and Medicine* (1982), *Beyond Illness* (1984), and *Recovering the Soul: A Scientific and Spiritual Search* (1989). His goal has been to anchor the so-called holistic health movement in respectable science, while still preserving its spiritual emphasis.

DR. MICHAEL W. FOX is Vice President for Bioethics and Farm Animals for the Humane Society of the United States. Dr. Fox is author of over thirty books, contributing editor to *McCall's* magazine, and syndicated columnist ("Ask Your Animal Doctor"). A consulting veterinarian, he gives lectures and seminars around the world on animal welfare, behavior, and conservation. In 1987, Dr. Fox was appointed Director the Humane Society's new established Center for Respect of Life and Environment.

CAROL GRUNEWALD is an animal rights/environmental activist and journalist currently working with The Humane Society of the United States in Washington, D.C.

WES JACKSON, a geneticist of international stature, is founder and director of the Land Institute in Salina, Kansas, a non-profit education and research organization devoted to finding sustainable alternatives in agriculture. Also founder and former director of the Environmental Studies Program at California State University in Sacramento, Professor Jackson has written numerous papers and book chapters on agriculture and genetics. His books include *Man and the Environment* (1971), an environmental studies anthology; *New Roots for Agriculture* (1985); *Meeting the Expectations of the Land* with Wendell Berry and Bruce Colman (1985); and *Altars of Unhewn Stone* (1987).

GENE KARPINSKI is Executive Director of the U.S. Public Interest Research Group (U.S. PIRG), the national lobbying office for state PIRGs across the country. PIRGs are non-profit, non-partisan consumer and environmental advocacy groups. Before joining U.S. PIRG in 1984, Mr. Karpinski was field director for People for the American Way, a civil liberties group; and field director for Congress Watch, a Ralph Nader lobbying organization.

ANDREW C. KIMBRELL is an attorney, author, and longtime environmental activist. He has written and lectured on a variety of environmental issues. In recent years, Mr. Kimbrell has devoted his litigation and lobbying efforts to environmental problems and control of genetic engineering. Mr. Kimbrell is Policy Director and Litigation Coordinator for the Greenhouse Crisis Foundation, and Legal Counsel for the Foundation on Economic Trends in Washington, D.C. He is both both general editor of, and contributing author to, this *Handbook*.

FRANCES MOORE LAPPÉ is co-founder of the Institute for Food and Development Policy, a San Francisco-based research and education center devoted to solving the problem of world hunger. Ms. Lappé has written several books, including *Diet for a Small Planet*, *Food First: Beyond the Myth of Scarcity*, *Betraying the National Interest*, and *World Hunger: Twelve Myths*. She is also a winner of the Right Livelihood Award (the alternative Nobel Prize).

CINDY MITLO is Associate Editor of *Building Economic Alternatives*, a publication of Co-op America. Mrs. Shartel also writes on socially responsible investing and other economic and environmental topics.

DAVID MORRIS is the co-director and co-founder of the Washington-based Institute for Local Self-Reliance. Mr. Morris, also a columnist for the St. Paul Pioneer Press Dispatch, has written and lectured internationally on energy and recycling issues. His books include *The New City States* and *Self-Reliant Cities*.

JOHN O'CONNOR is founder and Executive Director of the National Toxics Campaign, the fastest growing grassroots environmental organization in the United States. A victim of asbestos poisoning, Mr. O'Connor is also a skilled community organizer and co-author of *Fighting Toxics: A Guide to Local Environmental Actions to Solve Global Threats* (1990).

JEREMY RIFKIN is an author, activist, and philosopher, as well as president of the Foundation on Economic Trends in Washington, D.C. His critically acclaimed books, including *Entropy: Into the Greenhouse World*; *Time Wars*; *Algeny*; *Declaration of a Heretic*; *Who Should Play God?*; and T*he Emerging Order* are wide-ranging and interdisciplinary, covering topics from politics to philosophy and science. His books have been translated into twelve languages and are used in hundreds of college courses.

MARIA RODALE is Promotion Coordinator for *Prevention Magazine*, a publication of Rodale Press. A national committee member of Mothers and Others for Pesticide Limits, Ms. Rodale is also a free-lance writer and copywriter.

ROBERT RODALE is Chairman of the Board and Chief Executive Officer of Rodale Press in Emmaus, Pennsylvania. Rodale publications include *Prevention*, *Organic Gardening*, *Bicycling*, and *Runner's World*. Mr. Rodale also oversees the 305-acre Rodale Research Center in Maxatawny, Pennsylvania, where scientists are pursuing innovative horticultural and agricultural solutions to environmental and economic problems. Another project headed by Robert Rodale is the Rodale Institute, a non-profit research, education and service organization dedicated to promoting the use of existing resources to make agriculture more profitable and biologically sound.

EDWARD LEE ROGERS is an attorney in a private law practice in Washington D.C. His litigation efforts are focused on environmental and biotechnology issues affecting the public interest. From 1979-81 he served as Principal Deputy Assistant Secretary of the Army (Civil Works), exercising environmental policy oversight over the Army Corp of Engineers civil works and wetlands permit actions. He has also been Assistant Attorney General for Environmental Protection with the State of Maine, and General Counsel for the Environmental Defense Fund.

R. NEIL SAMPSON has served as Executive Vice President of the American Forestry Association since 1984. A former Executive Vice President of the National Association of Conservation Districts, Mr. Sampson is a 16 year veteran of the U.S. Department of Agriculture's Soil Conservation Service, where he last served as Acting Director of the Environmental Services Division in Washington. He has written extensively on land and water management policy, pollution control, and agricultural economics.

REPRESENTATIVE CLAUDINE SCHNEIDER (R-RI) is a five term Congresswoman from the second district of Rhode Island. She is the author and sponsor of the Global Warming Prevention Act (HR 1078), the most comprehensive legislation on global climate change in Congress, currently co-sponsored by one third of the House. Rep. Schneider is also co-author and lead sponsor of the Solid Waste Prevention Act. She has also championed legislation promoting the conservation of biological diversity.

KIRK B. SMITH, a licenced private investigator, serves as programs director of the Greenhouse Crisis Foundation in Washington, DC. He has been variously employed as a symphony musician, video tape technician, administrative director of a New York ad firm, and college professor prior to his professional involvement in environmental issues. He is both both general editor of, and contributing author to, this *Handbook*.

MARTIN TEITEL is Executive Director of the C.S. Fund, a private foundation that makes grants and conducts programs in promote survival, including biodiversity, reduction of toxics, protection of dissent, and peace.

JAY WALLJASPER has been Executive Editor of the *Utne Reader* since 1984. Previously he held editorial positions with *Better Homes & Gardens* and *In These Times*. Mr. Walljasper has written articles on environmental, cultural, and political topics for The *Nation, Harrowsmith, L.A. Weekly, Chicago Tribune Magazine, The Des Moines Register, Midwest Living*, and *Rock & Roll Confidential*.

THE GREENHOUSE CRISIS FOUNDATION (GCF), a non-profit corporation, is dedicated to creating a global awareness of the greenhouse crisis and related environmental problems. The GCF has devoted itself to changing the world view and lifestyle underlying our current ecological crisis. The GCF may be contacted at: 1130 Seventeenth Street, NW, Washington, DC 20036; (202) 466–2823.